Gadsden Family Tree

David Tasker

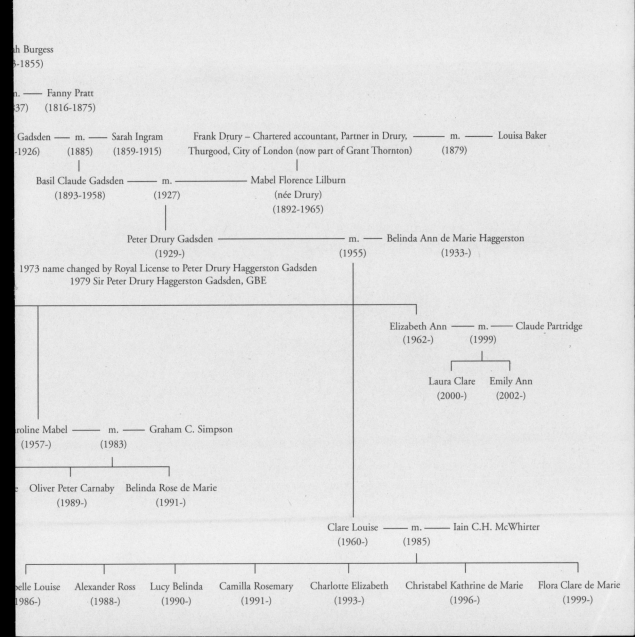

...h Burgess
(...3-1855)

n. ——— Fanny Pratt
(...37)   (1816-1875)

...Gadsden ——— m. ——— Sarah Ingram   Frank Drury – Chartered accountant, Partner in Drury, ——— m. ——— Louisa Baker
(...-1926)   (1885)   (1859-1915)   Thurgood, City of London (now part of Grant Thornton)   (1879)

Basil Claude Gadsden ——— m. ——————— Mabel Florence Lilburn
(1893-1958)   (1927)   (née Drury)
                                         (1892-1965)

Peter Drury Gadsden ————————————————— m. ——— Belinda Ann de Marie Haggerston
(1929-)   (1955)   (1933-)
1973 name changed by Royal License to Peter Drury Haggerston Gadsden
1979 Sir Peter Drury Haggerston Gadsden, GBE

Elizabeth Ann ——— m. ——— Claude Partridge
(1962-)   (1999)

Laura Clare   Emily Ann
(2000-)   (2002-)

...roline Mabel ——— m. ——— Graham C. Simpson
(1957-)   (1983)

...e   Oliver Peter Carnaby   Belinda Rose de Marie
      (1989-)   (1991-)

Clare Louise ——— m. ——— Iain C.H. McWhirter
(1960-)   (1985)

...belle Louise   Alexander Ross   Lucy Belinda   Camilla Rosemary   Charlotte Elizabeth   Christabel Kathrine de Marie   Flora Clare de Marie
...986-)   (1988-)   (1990-)   (1991-)   (1993-)   (1996-)   (1999-)

Thoroughly with Enthusiasm

Thoroughly with Enthusiasm

The Life of
Sir Peter Gadsden GBE AC FREng

Ina Taylor

With a Foreword by
The Rt Hon the Lord Carrington KG GCMG CH MC PC

Ellingham Press

Shrewsbury

First published 2004

British Library Cataloging-in-Publication Data

A catalogue record for this book is available from the British Library.

ISBN 0-9547560-0-2 (hardback)

Written by Ina Taylor www.inataylor.co.uk
Typeset by ISB Typesetting www.sheffieldtypesetting.co.uk
Design by Mark Lee www.marklee.me.uk
Produced by Heidi Robbins
Printed and bound by Antony Rowe Ltd, Chippenham, Wiltshire
Published by Ellingham Press, Spring Cottage, Spout Lane, Leighton, Shrewsbury, Shropshire SY5 6RY www.ellinghampress.co.uk

Contents

List of Illustrations

List of Plates

Acknowledgements

The author would like to thank the members of Sir Peter's family for their patient help and generous hospitality during the research for this book. In particular: David and Judy Gadsden, Daphne Minty, Juliet Cartwright, Caroline Simpson, Clare McWhirter and Elizabeth Partridge.

The ready assistance of Sir Peter's many friends and colleagues has been invaluable in piecing together his busy life and I am grateful to them all. I would especially like to record my thanks to John Allen, Sue Ash, Clive Ashby, Warwick Bartle, Jim Betteridge, Linda Binder, Dick Blaxland, Rosemary Viscountess Boyne, Pam Bradburn, Muriel Brittain, John Brooks, George Cauchi, Sir Neil Chalmers, Jonathan Charkham, Maurice Cocking (aka Whiffin), Barry Davey, Gwyn Davies, Deanna Delamotta, Ruth Denison, Cedric Charles Dickens, Peter Duckers, Glenys Espley, Geoffey Finn, Ron and Tina Fuller, Peter A Gadsdon, Ann Gale, Bryan Gibson, Christopher Giles (aka Augustus Snodgrass), Alan Gillett, Sir Peter Graham, Sir Anthony Grant, Clifford Grinstead, John Hart, Tony Harvey, Stanley Heather, Alan and Annabelle Henn, Arthur Hollis, Jim Holmes, Anthony Howes, Brian Howard, Michael Jenks, Darby Johns, Mervyn Joyner, Alexander Kidd, Sir Christopher Leaver, Hilary Machtus, Maureen Mackay, Douglas McClelland, Douglas McCully, Barry Millard, Tom Miller Jones, Lord Mowbray Segrave and Stourton, Jimmy Naguib, Brian O'Connor, Carl Openshaw, Heather Pentland, David Probert, Nigel Pullman, Gill Rides, Sir Michael Scott, Stuart Smith, Robin Stephenson, Suzanne Stubbins, Brigadier NR Sturt, David Tasker, Ella Taylor, Cecil Vyvyan-Robinson, Tony Wright, Jeremy York and above all the late Sir Peter Studd.

My greatest thanks and appreciation are reserved for Sir Peter and Lady Gadsden who have shown me such kindness throughout the research for this book that the whole project has been an immense pleasure. I have been welcomed into all the family homes and experienced the legendary Gadsden hospitality at first hand. Sir Peter is a biographer's dream, not only because he keeps a well-organised and full archive but because he has been such a delight to work with.

The author gratefully acknowledges the use of quotations taken from:

Gadsden—The First 100 Years, by Jules Feldmann, J Gadsden Australia Ltd, 1980

Exceedingly Lucky, by Anthony Makepiece-Warne, Sydney Jary, 1993

The Story of the Icebreakers in China, by Percy Timberlake, '48' Group, 1994

Brighton, by Osbert Sitwell and Margaret Barton, Faber and Faber, 1939

Christopher Gadsden: The Writings of Christopher Gadsden, edited by Richard Walsh, University of South Carolina Press, 1966

Foreword

'Thoroughly with enthusiasm' is Sir Peter Gadsden's motto and no one could live up to that better than the subject of this book. He has led a varied, peripatetic, successful and enthusiastic life, as those who read and enjoy this book will discover.

From the village of Little Gaddesden in Hertfordshire, the Gadsden family have settled all over the world. Peter's father, Basil, was ordained in Australia in 1918 and became a parson in the bush. Although Peter was born in Canada, his connections with Australia were one of the important influences in his life.

Peter became an expert on, amongst other things, mineral sands and had the skill and ability to present the most difficult of problems in the simplest language. He had a close connection with the Australian mining industry, an association crowned by his visit to that country as Lord Mayor of London in 1980. Perhaps his greatest contribution to Anglo-Australian relations was his success as Chairman of the Britain-Australia Bicentennial Committee. This was by no means an honorary position, but one which entailed a great deal of organisation. He was made a Companion, Order of Australia (AC), in recognition of his achievements.

Those of us who spend time in London will know of his hard work as Sheriff, Lord Mayor, and Alderman of the City where he is regarded with respect and affection.

In his speech in Guildhall, when he was elected Lord Mayor, Peter quoted the following which he had read on a sword in a museum in Poland:

My soul is for my God
My heart is for my lady
My arm is for my king
My honour is for myself

This perhaps sums up Sir Peter Gadsden's life, the account of which you will greatly enjoy.

The Rt Hon the Lord Carrington KG GCMG CH MC PC
April 2004

Chapter 1

Illustrious Ancestors from the Valley of the Goat

Some are born great,
Some achieve greatness,
And some have greatness thrust upon them.

William Shakespeare, *Twelfth Night*

1. Christopher Gadsden's (1724–1805) personal flag. The bright yellow flag which he designed was an appropriate symbol of the American Revolution. Christopher Gadsden has been described as an important colonial and revolutionary merchant and at the same time a builder of his state and the American nation. President John Adams remarked that Gadsden 'was a breed of man born for the public and not for themselves'.

L ike most children, Peter lived in the present with little knowledge of his forebears. Once Peter moved into public life, there were Gadsden family historians keen to demonstrate how he was related to them and to acquaint him with his famous ancestors.

The Gadsden surname seems to be associated with the village of Little Gaddesden in Hertfordshire and has undergone various modifications of spelling over the years. This village, some 30 miles from London, stands on a wooded spur overlooking the Gade valley in the direction of Whipsnade and Dunstable Downs. The place-name means 'the Valley of the Goat' derived from the Anglo-Saxon word 'gaete' meaning a goat and 'den' a valley.

There is archaeological evidence of occupation in the valley from as early as 500 BC although the name Gaetesdene does not appear on a manuscript until 944 AD. The Domesday Book refers to this area as Gatesdene and in 1196 a person is recorded as taking his name from the area. Adulf de Gatesden, Lord of Gatesdene in Hertfordshire, is mentioned in a document and Peter's lineage can be traced, a little erratically, from this point. The spelling of the surname varied a little but eventually settled down to Gadsden.

Over the years there have been many fascinating personalities amongst the Gadsdens. Today family members are so spread around the globe that a Gadsden Family History Society has come into being with a regular newsletter containing information about present day Gadsdens worldwide as well as many illustrious forebears. A brief backward glance reveals several of Peter's predecessors were also men of action just as prepared as he has been to step forward and hold public office.

In 1296 one notable ancestor, John of Gatesdene, is recorded as supplying Henry III with useful information and, as a result, being entrusted by His Majesty with an errand to travel to the court of Castile.

A later John of Gaddesden (1280–c.1361), whose life is better documented, also stepped into public life. He lived at Little Gaddesden but studied medicine at Merton College, Oxford, then went on to become a priest. In 1314 he wrote a treatise entitled *Rosa Medicinae* which was so well regarded that in 1492 it became the first printed medical book in England, thanks to William Caxton. John of Gaddesden was court physician to Edward II and entered the service of the Black Prince, where Chaucer also became a member of the household late in Gaddesden's life.

Tradition has it that Chaucer's 'doctour of Phisyck' in *The Canterbury Tales* was actually based on this John of Gaddesden. If so, then Chaucer clearly held him in high esteem as a medical man: 'He was a verrey parfit practisour' who 'knew the cause of everich maladye/ Were it of hoot, or cold, or moiste, or drye'. With a delightful touch of humour, Chaucer adds 'For Gold in Phisyk is a cordial, Therfore he lovede gold in special'. Chaucer's doctor kept up-to-date with medical writings and had evidently studied *Rosa Medicinae* because amongst the authoritative texts Chaucer cites are those by 'Bernard and Gatisden and Gilbertyn'.

It is recorded that this early Gadsden was a learned and well-respected man, who received a large fee from the Barbers' Guild for a prescription which contained three frogs as its main ingredient. Is it possible that descent from a physician, albeit one who used frogs liberally, later inspired Peter to become Chairman of the Private Medical Health Insurance Group, Private Patients' Plan and of the charity the PPP Medical Trust (which has changed its name several times and today is known as PPP health foundation)? Today the family medical tradition is continued by Peter's eldest daughter, Juliet, a nurse who trained at St Bartholomew's Hospital in the City of London.

It is tempting to follow the exploits of other notable Gadsden ancestors but space only permits mention of a few. Appropriately for Peter, who spent much of his business life travelling in Commonwealth countries, there are branches of the Gadsden family in Australia, New Zealand, South Africa, Canada and the USA.

Christopher Gadsden (1724–1805), one of the earliest advocates of American independence from Britain, was the first generation of that family to be born across the Atlantic after his parents emigrated to South Carolina. Like Peter, Christopher Gadsden was acknowledged as a shrewd businessman who established a thriving import/export business. Just as his descendant would do more than three hundred years later, Christopher took an interest in public affairs which led him to serve his community. In Christopher's case it was as a member of the Commons House of Assembly where he used his powerful rhetoric to rally the merchants and planters of Charleston to resist British rule. He was not one to shy away from the action either. When the American War of Independence began, it was as a brigadier-general that Gadsden fought against the British. His military career was brief because in 1780 he was captured by the British when Charleston fell. Christopher Gadsden's dedication to the cause was recognised after the war when he was elected governor of South Carolina. Although honoured to be offered such high office, he

2. James Gadsden was responsible for negotiating the Gadsden Purchase, which was 30 000 square miles of land in what is now New Mexico and Arizona, bought from Mexico for $10 million in 1853. The purchase enabled the building of the transcontinental railroad route, the Southern Pacific, to be completed.

declined in view of his ill health and advancing years, taking instead the post of lieutenant governor. Today this Gadsden ancestor is remembered as the designer of the rattlesnake flag, that symbol of the revolutionary struggle, with its motto 'Don't tread on me'.

Peter has often wondered whether his revolutionary forebear turned in his grave when in 1980 the National Anthem was played to welcome the Lord Mayor of London, Sir Peter Gadsden, to Gadsden, Alabama!

Christopher Gadsden's grandson, James (1788–1858) also made a name for himself in the USA, building Florida's first public highway, State Highway 65. This road is known as 'The Gadsden Highway'. His earlier work had involved taking responsibility for the construction of forts on the 'Gulf frontier' around 1818 and one fort near Apalachicola in Florida bears his name. James Gadsden was also the person connected with the celebrated 'Gadsden Purchase' of 1853 which was ratified the following year. A three cent US stamp was issued to commemorate this.

Brief mention has to be made of a British James Gadsden whose contribution to London civic life seems to presage Peter's own. Records show this

James Gadsden was admitted to the Freedom of the Worshipful Company of Drapers in 1757, became a liveryman in 1761 and went on to become Warden and member of the Court of Assistants in 1782, but refused the office of Master.

Jumping forward more than a hundred years, Basil Claude Gadsden, Peter's father, was born in Aylesbury on 17 April 1893. Although brought up in a settled domestic household as the son of an auctioneer and a Sunday school teacher, the Gadsden spirit of adventure and service was in his blood. He attended Aylesbury Grammar School as a scholarship pupil until the age of 15. Just over 70 years later, in March 1980, Peter was delighted to visit his father's former school and present a cup in memory of his father for the house with the best academic achievements. Standing on the platform in the school hall, Sir Peter Gadsden told the pupils that his father would have been thrilled to know that his son would one day be welcomed back to his old school as the Lord Mayor of London.

After leaving Aylesbury Grammar School, Basil Gadsden worked as a cashier at Marshall and Snelgrove in Oxford Street. Under the auspices of the Bible Class Union, his spare time was devoted to the Spitalfield's Mission in London. A contemporary describes how he 'acquired a rich experience in mission work in which personal Evangelism and social work were blended' and he 'was instrumental in relieving suffering in the East End both bodily and spiritually'.

When the Bible Class Union suggested the 20-year-old might consider going to Australia to help the overworked clergy, he rose to the challenge. On 21 August 1913 Basil set sail for the New World of Gippsland, Victoria, on the White Star liner *Runic*. In his pocket was a silver George IV five-shilling piece given him by his mother along with the advice 'Don't spend it unless you have to'. Fortunately Basil never had to resort to spending the crown and, even though things got tight on occasions, he was able to pass the coin on to his son, Peter, who still treasures it.

On arrival in Victoria, Basil lodged in the Divinity Hostel where he received a warm welcome from members of the Colonial and Continental Church Society and was immediately set to work in what even the Society described as 'some of our most isolated and difficult districts'. This was a world away from life in the Home Counties. In the three months after his arrival temperatures soared, bush fires were rampant and not a drop of rain fell. Though not a trained priest, Basil was soon riding off into remote parts of the bush to conduct services on his own and to visit the sick.

3. Peter's father, the Reverend Basil Gadsden, in Australia in 1918. He had been ordained the previous year and is seen here as curate of Buchan in Gippsland.

By October 1913, he had made up his mind to undertake the long period of study at Ridley College, Melbourne, which would lead to his ordination in December 1918. His first parish was vast, covering 2,500 square miles of bush and mountains. There was still a pioneering air in those days because, for lack of other accommodation, the Reverend Gadsden had to live in the vestry of his church. The 25-year-old was undeterred and saddled up his horse, Black Bess, every morning to set off on his ministry. He estimated that in an average week he covered a hundred miles on horseback. During the eight years following his ordination, the Reverend Basil Gadsden was priest in three parishes in the Gippsland diocese (1918–21 he was curate of Buchan; between 1921–2 he was vicar of Meeniyan and then he moved to become vicar of Mirboo North from 1922–6). An interesting insight into this man and clerical life in Australia exists in a letter written by his bishop, who said the Reverend Gadsden 'has never spared himself, but has faced his arduous task with courage and determination, keeping together the Church people in his District in spite of a forbidding winter climate and very bad roads'.

During his long service in Australia, Basil only returned to England to see his family once. However by December 1925 he was concerned about his father's ill health and tendered his resignation from his ministry in Mirboo North, Gippsland. His application to the Colonial and Continental Church Society to officiate in England was granted and the Society offered him six months' 'deputation work in the north of England' and six months' work as an acting vicar to cover any incumbent that might fall ill. According to family legend Basil was keen to leave Australia because he was nursing a broken heart but tantalisingly no details of this early romance survive. It is likely that his father's illness and the welfare of the family were the main reasons for his departure. Sadly Mr Gadsden senior died in January 1926, four months before his son arrived home.

Basil later wrote of his experiences as a parson in the bush. The manuscript was never published and sadly on his death it could not be found. It is thought that he may have lent it to a parishioner to read and it was not returned. This is a pity because it would certainly have been published in 1988 when Australia celebrated the bicentenary of the first European settlement and Basil's son, Peter, was chairman of the Britain-Australia Bicentennial Committee.

Basil's return to England in April 1926 coincided with the coal strike and the beginning of the General Strike. In an article he wrote for an Australian newspaper, the Reverend Gadsden commented on the changes that had happened during his 13-year absence.

> So this is London. The wonder city. London tubes and underground railways are really fine. I have already motored 400 miles and haven't noticed a bump. On Monday I again experienced the speed of our railways which is a little disconcerting to the uninitiated.

Although Basil Gadsden expected to work six months in one place then move to another placement six months later, events turned out differently. In May 1926 he went to Wembley to deputise for the vicar, the Reverend Sylvester (father of renowned dance-band leader Victor), who had suffered a break-down due to overwork. After six months Basil's official position changed from deputy to that of curate-in-charge of St John's Parish Church, Wembley. 'Parishioners are enthusiastic in their endeavours to retain his services permanently because he is a most capable organiser, very effective speaker and a hard worker. Energetic in action, and tactful in method he inspires his adherents with the desire to effort, and with confidence in the result,' the President of the Wembley Branch of the League of Nations Union wrote.

The Reverend Gadsden's ministry at St John's Wembley was like a breath of fresh air and church attendance soared. Sixty years later an elderly parishioner met the Lord Mayor of London, Sir Peter Gadsden, at a dinner and gave him a personal insight into those times. He recalled how the young ladies of the 1920s suddenly found a new interest in the church when the curate arrived. He was evidently quite a big draw in contrast to the rather conservative, autocratic and legendary Mr Sylvester, vicar of Wembley for 48 years.

Certainly there were some in the parish who found the ministry of the new cleric especially welcome. One of those was Mrs Mabel Florence Lilburn (née Drury), who lived in Wembley Hill Road, and had been recently widowed after less than three years of marriage.

May, as she was known, came from a well-to-do family in West Kensington who, according to Drury family tradition, in years gone by had once resided at Drury House, Drury Lane. May's father Frank was a partner in the respected firm of chartered accountants, Drury and Elliot, later to become Drury, Thurgood and Co and today part of Grant Thornton. (Frank was also a brilliant artist and Peter possesses some of his paintings.) The business provided the family with a comfortable living and gave May a private income all her life. Her marriage to the 40-year-old civil servant, George Lilburn, had not really been a love match but rather an arrangement the Drury family believed 'suitable' for their 30-year-old spinster daughter. Nevertheless she cared for her husband and was devastated by his unexpected death from appendicitis so soon after their marriage. (May later gave her first wedding ring to her son David, the first to marry, to give to his wife Judy on their wedding day.)

During the deputy vicar's visits to console the bereaved lady, the couple fell in love, but sensitive to the gossip this might cause, tried to keep their affection for each other private. As Basil's period at Wembley drew to a close, requests began arriving for his services from as far away as Sri Lanka, India and Mannville in Canada. His future was decided for him in August 1927 when a letter arrived saying 'the Bishop is keeping Mannville for you—the diocese has no funds to cover the cost of the journey there—but make arrangements and the Colonial and Continental Church Society will see what it can do to get a grant in aid of passage'. The parson in the bush was now set to become the parson in the prairies.

4. The marriage of Peter's parents, Reverend Basil Gadsden and Mabel Drury, on 24 November 1927 in Mannville, Alberta, Canada. Two local girls volunteered to be bridesmaids and Peter was amazed and delighted to meet them during his visit to Mannville as Lord Mayor in 1980 (see page 195).

Trusting in the Almighty, Basil and his fiancée made their plans. They decided he should go ahead and prepare a home for them in Mannville then May would follow. When she arrived they would marry in his new church. Local newspaper reports of the Reverend Basil Gadsden's departure for Canada universally expressed regret that this very popular clergyman was leaving Wembley, but no mention was made of his engagement to May or their plans for a life together in Canada. Evidently the couple's discretion had paid off.

Basil arrived in Alberta on 1 October 1927 followed by his fiancée a few weeks later. May showed enormous courage and faith in this enterprise because she had never been abroad. Until then she had lived a very genteel life with all the domestic chores carried out by paid helpers, so it was said that when she left England she could not even boil an egg. Boldly she sailed for Canada alone then took the Canadian Pacific Railway from

Montreal on a journey lasting three days and five hours. The final leg of her journey was finished off in an ox cart and May arrived at Mannville in deep snow at three o'clock in the morning.

Basil and May were married on 24 November 1927 at Christ Church in Mannville, Alberta, by special licence, with the Bishop of Edmonton officiating. Bride and groom were both 34, although May was in fact two days short of her 35th birthday and Basil six months her junior. The event was a cause of celebration for the parishioners who gladly attended both ceremony and reception. Since the couple had no family or friends to assist them, members of the congregation stepped forward to provide the necessary officers. The vicar's warden gave the bride away and his daughter agreed to be one of the bridesmaids. The second bridesmaid was daughter of the other church warden. It was a great pleasure to Peter, over 50 years later, to have the opportunity to meet both bridesmaids when he visited Mannville as Lord Mayor to participate in Alberta's 75th anniversary celebrations. Although the bride and groom were new arrivals in the area, the congregation clubbed together to give them a complete set of blue and white enamel kitchenware as a wedding present, the local paper recorded.

The snow that had greeted May's arrival in Mannville never shifted, indeed more fell. By the time the newly weds set off for their honeymoon in Edmonton, the drifts were so deep that their train was late. When it eventually arrived the parishioners had used up their supply of confetti and grabbed handfuls of snow to shower the happy couple as they boarded.

Life on the Canadian prairie was a big leap into the unknown for this English couple so it comes as no surprise that their first-born should inherit their sense of adventure in full measure. Many years later one of Peter's secretaries identified this trait when she wrote that 'he loves a challenge and will take on anything'.

Chapter 2

Early Life

There's a breathless hush in the Close tonight –
Ten to make and the match to win –
A bumping path and a blinding light,
An hour to play and the last man in.
And it's not for the sake of a ribboned coat,
Or the selfish hope of a season's fame,
But his Captain's hand on his shoulder smote –
'Play up! Play up! And play the game!

Sir Henry Newbolt

(These words were written on the wall of the cricket pavilion at The Elms School.)

Peter Drury Gadsden, later to become the 652nd Lord Mayor of London, was born in Mannville, Alberta, on 28 June 1929. There was never any doubt what name the Reverend and Mrs Gadsden would give a son, born the day before St Peter's Day. Doctor Joseph Heaslip, who attended the vicar's wife at her confinement, wrote to Peter 50 years later to congratulate him, adding: 'As for me, it is not everyone who gets a chance to hold the Lord Mayor upside down by the heels and to administer a couple of slaps on the bottom to see that he is crying and breathing properly.'

When he wrote back to Dr Heaslip, Peter asked him what Mannville was like and was so amused by the reply, that he read it out during a speech he gave to the Canada Club in London when he visited them as Lord Mayor in July 1980.

Spoken in the vernacular, it is known as a 'one horse town'. Alberta is rich in gas and oil, Mannville has none. It is a farming and stock raising community with not very rich soil. It grows fair crops when there is sufficient rain and no early frost. Population 500 to 550, 5 grain elevators, one bank, Post Office,

5. Peter was born in Mannville, Alberta in June 1929 and is proud to be a Canadian. The following year the family moved to Edmonton where this photograph was taken and where his brother David and sister Daphne were born.

two churches, in one of which your father, a clergyman, did his best for a wicked community, a crummy hotel with a beer parlour, two or three stores, a pool hall, and a bus service to Edmonton.

The area where Peter was born was referred to as 'the back o'beyond' by his father, which says a great deal when the Reverend Gadsden's previous parishes in the Australian outback are taken into consideration. Winters in Mannville were extremely harsh with temperatures falling below −40° for prolonged periods and with occasional displays of northern lights. The vicarage, which was home to the Gadsden family, was like most of the other homes in the small town—a wooden shack comprising four rooms and a cellar. The church too was made completely of wood, even its roof tiles.

The Reverend Gadsden's parish was 750 square miles, which meant some parishioners only had services every fortnight and others once a month. Because of the wide-flung nature of the parish, the vicar was assigned a car with this job, which was an advance on Black Bess, his official transport in Australia. Motoring on snow and ice in sub-zero temperatures required special driving skills especially as the water in the radiator froze regularly. On Sundays the Reverend Gadsden often travelled 50 miles to take services; a few were held in churches but the majority took place in the community's schoolroom. All too often the vicar had to spend time on his journey digging the car out of a snowdrift.

However, this was easy in comparison with the problems Basil encountered grave digging in the middle of winter. People still expected their loved ones to be laid to rest in a proper grave no matter how frozen the ground, so he had to perfect his own technique. This involved digging a bit, then lighting a fire in the grave to thaw the earth sufficiently to excavate a little further and so on. It was a long hard job!

Life was bleak for the villagers and vicar's family alike. These were difficult economic times and as the settlers' incomes dwindled so did the vicar's. The Reverend Gadsden received £5 a month funded jointly by the Colonial and Continental Church Society and the Canadian Church. The

6. There were extremely harsh winters in the Canadian prairies which meant Peter's father was often seen digging his car out of the snow before he could continue with parish business. His parish covered 750 square miles so a car was essential.

rest of his stipend was made up from the collection plate on Sundays. During his two years at Mannville, people's incomes dropped so low that he believed it was unreasonable to take a collection at all. Everyone struggled to make ends meet and a third of the community ultimately left the area in search of a better life. Mrs Gadsden gratefully received parcels of second-hand clothes from friends in England and distributed them amongst the parishioners.

Eventually the vicar was told he too must leave to minister to the more populous parish of St Mark's in Edmonton. Despite his protestations, the £5 a month grant for the Mannville parish was removed which forced the vicar to leave. Basil was deeply upset by this, but in no position to argue. With a heavy heart he left the dwindling community to fend for itself without a vicar. In 1930 Peter and his parents moved to Edmonton, where shortly before Peter's second birthday his brother David was born, followed in 1932 by their sister Daphne.

It is in St Mark's, Edmonton, that Peter has his earliest and only memory of childhood in Canada. He recalls a mischievous incident when as a four-year-old he got bored as his father's sermon droned on. To pass the time

7. Peter alongside his brother David born 1931 in Edmonton, Alberta. Their sister Daphne was born the following year.

8. Peter's father was present when the foundation stone for St Mark's vicarage was laid soon after his arrival in Edmonton in 1931.

9. In 1980 Peter, seen here with his brother David, was delighted to visit the same place as Lord Mayor.

he began surreptitiously changing seats, encouraging his little brother to copy him. What Peter had spotted was that one of the seats had no back. He knew that if he could manoeuvre his brother on to that bench, David was likely to fall off and scream the place down. Sure enough, he did! Mrs Gadsden was obliged to take both her sons out of the church in order that the congregation could hear the rest of the sermon in peace. Mission accomplished.

By the time Peter was five, the family were on the move again, this time to Ireland. His father had been appointed secretary to the Colonial and Continental Church Society in Ireland so the family went to live at Stillorgan Park, Blackrock, Dublin. There was no living attached to this post because the Reverend Gadsden was required to travel the length and breadth of Ireland preaching and lecturing about the work of the Church in the colonies, particularly Australia and Canada.

In Ireland it was time for Peter to start school and, first of all, he attended Mrs Murphy's nursery school. Then in the September following his eighth birthday, he was sent to board at Rockport Preparatory School in Craigavad, County Down, where he remained for two years. The school had a good reputation and was one of the very few preparatory schools in Ireland. What particularly appealed to Peter's parents was its strong Protestant ethos. Not only was Rockport an Anglican school, but the headmaster's wife, Mrs Geoffrey Bing, was a vicar's daughter. (Their son Geoffrey was to become Attorney-General in Ghana.)

Rockport took around 25 boys from the age of eight and taught them in small classes of six or seven. The heart of the school was a Regency building set in beautiful grounds that swept down to Belfast Loch where the boys could boat and bathe, weather permitting. Catching crabs in the bay with a piece of string and some bait was one of the boys' favourite Sunday evening pastimes. It all might sound like a little boy's dream but for Peter this was a period of terrible unhappiness and homesickness. Even his form teacher noticed that Peter 'found life confusing'. His weekly letters home are testimony to his misery. 'Daddy when are you coming to see me' and 'Please can you come to see me this week as I am wanting you' were the heartrending pleas that punctuated most letters during his first year. His remark 'I had a miserable birthday' must have caused his mother to weep.

Peter's spelling at the time makes for entertaining reading, for example, 'we are having our foter craff taken and going out for a picknec sulbrating two boys scollershisp'. Rockport did its best to give the boys a varied

10. Rockport Preparatory School in Craigavad, Co Down, Northern Ireland in 1938. Peter's unhappiness and loneliness at school can clearly be seen. He is the little boy sitting on his own on the extreme right of the front row. The headmaster, Mr Bing, is seated in the centre of the front row with Mrs Bing to the left of him. On her left are Mr and Mrs Tucker whom Peter met again when he visited the school as Lord Mayor in 1980. Miss Dickinson is seated fourth from the left. It was she who escorted Peter from Shropshire to school during his last year there. On the ground in front of the headmaster is a boy's tortoise.

education beyond the three Rs. They were encouraged to tend their own garden for which they gained marks. 'My garden is looking lovely now. I got 9/10 for my garden,' he wrote home proudly in 1938. Later he was pleased to report that he had won a fretsaw for one of the best-kept gardens that term, an achievement which would have pleased his father who was a keen gardener.

Being only too aware how much the boys missed home-life, Rockport did allow them to keep a pet. 'Boys at this school are buying animals,' Peter wrote home. 'This is the kind, a tortus costs 6d small, 1/6 big, gold fish cost 6d small and 1/6 big. Bowl to put fish in 1/8. Could I buy thoes things? Small or big?' The answer was evidently yes because a subsequent letter reported 'in carpting I am making a tortus hut'. There were other challenging tasks going on in 'carpting' too as Peter related: 'I am making stilts and a flute'. This was amended to 'I am not making stilts because there is no more time'.

Nevertheless these were miserable years when he was desperately home-sick. His letters home asked how the puppy was getting on and whether the chicks had hatched. These were delights his younger brother and sister were still enjoying under the supervision of a nanny. Life at Rockport introduced Peter to sport which initially prompted the comment 'I do hate football' but 'I like hockey a little better' and 'I love cricket very much'. But the sport Peter most wanted to have a go at was boxing and his weekly letters home contained persistent reminders that he *did* want to learn boxing. That didn't last long because at Wrekin College he hated boxing!

A year after Peter began at Rockport his father was appointed to his first living in England. The parson in the bush, who had moved on to become the parson in the prairies now settled into a new role as a country parson. Peter's father was becoming uneasy about the way events in Europe were developing and wanted to get his family back to England. Whilst in Dublin Basil had met someone with links to the Allied Schools and from him heard about a vacancy in rural Shropshire. The parish of Astley Abbotts, he was told, was in the gift of the governors of Wrekin College and if the Reverend Gadsden was interested he should go and take a look at it for himself. So it came as a great surprise to him when he arrived at the church to see his name had already been affixed to the church door.

Astley Abbotts was indeed a delightful country parish close to Bridgnorth; so in September 1938 the Gadsden family moved to Shropshire. This is the county Peter has always looked on as his home.

Although the Gadsden family were now resident in Shropshire, Peter remained boarding at Rockport for another year. Distance meant that half-term holidays were passed in the company of fellow pupil Christopher Smyly whose kindly parents (who had been medical missionaries in China) 'adopted' Peter for a few days. For a nine-year-old, the journey to and from school seemed endless. Fortunately the school matron, Miss Dickinson, lived in Wolverhampton and could usually accompany Peter as far as Wolverhampton station where his parents collected him from the ladies' waiting room. The return journey to school, which he dreaded, involved a train to Liverpool, a bus to the boat (where he was put to bed) and in the morning when the boat docked at Belfast, Peter was put in a taxi to take the train to get to Craigavad and the waiting arms of the headmaster's wife.

Despite his unhappiness as a schoolboy, when he was Lord Mayor Peter was more than delighted to return to Rockport to open their all-weather sports pitch. On that occasion he told the pupils, who included girls by then, 'When I was here, we wore etons, there was no electricity and the lights were lit by gas'—all of which must have made the children think they were listening to a Victorian!

During that visit Peter enjoyed meeting Mr Tucker who had taught him over 40 years before. His elderly form teacher said there were only two things that stuck in his memory about Peter as a pupil: the first was that he wore shorts that were far too long for him, and the second was that he had a fight with a boy called Eric Milligan which required a teacher to break up! Mr Tucker added, 'He was a nice little boy—but I could not foresee that he would become Lord Mayor of London.'

In the autumn of 1939, it came as a great relief to Peter that his father decided schooling closer to home would be sensible. Just after the outbreak of war, Peter became a boarder at The Elms at Colwall, near Malvern. This was a prep school with a history dating back to 1613 that had been recommended to the Reverend Gadsden by one of his parishioners. Now a more seasoned boarder, Peter was not quite as homesick as he had been at Rockport but he was still far from happy at school. Conditions at The Elms in the winter of 1939 sound as though they had progressed little since the seventeenth century: 'It is very cold here in our class-room, the ink is frozen stiff and the water in our dometry's bacons are frozen,' one of Peter's idiosyncratically spelt letters relates. His parents could only have taken comfort from the information given them when Peter enrolled where it stated 'Boys have three hot baths a week. They attend matins at the Parish Church on Sunday and evensong in the school chapel. Morning and evening prayers are held daily in the school chapel.' An amusing little footnote added: 'It is requested that parents will not take boys into cinemas or similar places where there is a risk of infections and illness.'

The headmaster, Mr Singleton, was known as 'Ping' by the boys and remembered for clicking his heels as he towered over some quivering miscreant. Then his voice boomed down from on high: 'You, the son of a gentleman, you have told me a cram—an untruth.' Peter can vividly recall Mrs Singleton, who was responsible for the general welfare of the boys. She would arrive in the dorm just before lights out every night with an armful of bottles that she put down on the bed. Every boy was visited each night and asked the same question: 'Have you been today?' Regular bowel movements were considered hugely significant in those days so if a pupil answered no he would receive the 'Casky White'. This was a sort of sweet liquorice that tasted delicious and meant there was a far greater incidence of constipation recorded at The Elms than really occurred.

Peter can remember the measles epidemic at the school soon after his arrival. All the boys were lined up for an injection in the bottom but he was delighted to be spared that uncomfortable indignity because he had already had measles at Rockport. Any visit to the school doctor was usually met with the question, 'Any aches, pains or diarrhoea?' Followed by the word, 'Strip!'

Some of Peter's termly reports from The Elms give an insight into the character of London's future Lord Mayor who 'is inclined to be rowdy and untidy in the house' but 'useful and hardworking on the football field'. It is also amusing to read that 'he is rather restless by nature and needs constant watching—but he has done some good work though I fear he will never be a classical scholar'. Peter may not have won acclaim for his classical knowledge, but he did manage to carry off prizes of books at the end of term: they were for 'folding his etons' (his clothes), as he proudly told his mother.

It is interesting that by the age of 11 Peter's restless energy was already evident. Although 'Ping' probably considered it a fault, it has been this prodigious energy which has propelled Peter through a successful business and civic career and is certainly an aspect of his personality that has drawn wide admiration. Hilary Machtus (now Clerk of the Worshipful Company of Plaisterers of which Peter is an honorary liveryman), Peter's secretary at one time, remarked many years later that 'he moved round the City so fast I was convinced he must be on roller-skates!' Another said he is 'a man of action rather than inaction. He works at great speed and, quite frankly, it is not always easy to keep pace with him. He crams into a week what another would cram into two or three, yet he is always relaxed.'

In the autumn of 1940 there were nightly bombing raids in the Malvern area which lasted into the following spring. 'The jerries come over every night now and the siren goes, we take no notice of them, but lie in bed listening to them,' Peter wrote home during the winter of 1940. But things were not always so low-key at the school. In March 1941 he noted that:

> it was half past seven when the nasty jerries went over and there was a lot of bombs and gun fire, the siren went, we were all doing prep, just about to go for prayers in the chapel. We had to take up our places in the passage by the chapel, and get our rugs. We enjoyed ourselves very much by eating biscuits, we sang and talked, the biscuits were plain cholicote [sic] and a very few cream-centred ones, between the hole [sic] school we ate one of those big tins we have at home, we went back to bed at half past eight, after one hour in that cold passage. When we were in bed bombs dropped all around. The all-clear woke me up at half past three in the morning. I was the only one to wake up.

It is now thought the reason this area came in for such heavy pounding was probably connected with a radar research station in Malvern.

A certain amount of bullying and teasing went on at The Elms as it did in most schools. One taunt Peter hated that dogged him for years was: 'Have you ever been had by the Reverend Gad.' Not all were malicious: 'The boys call me Felix (which means happy in English) the cat as a nick-name. Oh they do tease me, but I don't mind I laugh at them,' he reassured his mother. When it was known that he had a sister, he came in for more ribbing because girls were 'the pits'. So on the few occasions the Gadsden family came to visit Peter at school, Daphne had to be persuaded to hide under a blanket on the back seat of the car in order to spare her brother further embarrassment.

Whilst his schooldays were far from happy, Peter took part in the usual boyish pranks. Along with the other boys he placed ha'pennies on the railway line at Colwall hoping the passing trains would flatten them into pennies. Whilst he was busy down on the line, some of his schoolmates were extracting cigarettes from the vending machine in Colwall railway station by deft use of a penknife. Those who couldn't master the art had to content themselves with smoking their own 'Woodbines' which they made from dry hollow stems of Old Man's Beard.

Church attendance was naturally compulsory on a Sunday but the service could be enlivened by a spot of caterpillar racing. The boys paraded to church in a crocodile wearing their boaters. These were extremely useful for storing the caterpillars they collected on the way down. (The hats served as good discus implements as well!) Once seated in their pews, the boys reverentially took their hymn books off the ledge and placed them on their laps. Then they lined their chargers up on the ledge and caterpillar racing commenced.

Another way of passing the time in church was to eye up the neighbouring girls' school who sat in pews across the aisle. The boys chose the girl they 'fancied' then tried catching her eye. More daring lads attempted to catapult messages directly into the girls' pews using an elastic band. Peter spent some of his time ogling 'Goldie teeth' as the boys nicknamed her. Years later, to his amazement and pleasure, he met 'Goldie teeth' at a Lord Mayor's reception and had his first conversation with this love from his boyhood.

As far as Peter was concerned the 'Caty Club' was the highlight of his schooldays at The Elms. Along with other members, he collected as many varieties of caterpillars as possible and tried to keep them alive on leaves. The real prize exhibits, he recalls, were the Puss Moth caterpillars which they hunted for on the leaves of nearby poplar trees. The boys hoped to keep their pets alive so they could watch them pass through the chrysalis stage and hatch into butterflies or moths. If the unfortunate insect did succeed in emerging, it was promptly gassed and pinned out. One of Peter's letter's home shortly before his twelfth birthday contained the request: 'I would like best of all 2 butterfly setting boards and a proper gassing bottle, please get me this. We have got 119 caterpillars in all.' Some boys collected birds' eggs but things got out of hand and they were caught hacking into apple trees on the nearby racecourse to retrieve woodpecker's eggs.

Other daring schoolboy exploits involved dodging the gardener and raiding the school kitchen garden. Peter has clear recollections of the rumpus caused one morning when the gardener looked out to see his prize row of carrots had flopped over. On investigation he discovered the whole row had been eaten and replaced by a line of wilting green tops by Peter's brother, David. On another occasion the gardener saw Peter in his garden looking for peas to eat and said, 'I knows yer name, Gadsden.' Peter implored him not to tell Mr Singleton that he had been caught raiding the kitchen garden because that signalled big trouble. Garden raids lost their appeal after this.

Lessons don't feature at all in Peter's memories when he looks back on his prep school days. What made a far greater impression on him was the enormous effort they all channelled into trying to outwit the headmaster. There were the raids on the school stationery supplies. These were kept in Ping's cupboard and only unlocked once a week to dole out the required materials. Unbeknown to the headmaster, his cupboard was being secretly drained of its contents after one boy discovered the left-hand door could easily be prised open. There were also daring raids into Ping's study to retrieve confiscated water pistols from a cupboard.

It goes without saying that little boys are always hungry, so raiding parties into the staff dining-room come as no surprise. After the staff had finished their supper and departed, some of the boys would creep in and eat up the left-over food. Usually that was bits of cheese.

'Big dorm feasts' were another memorable event at the end of term. Food was purchased with pocket money, scavenged from the staff dining-room, or in rare cases saved from tuck boxes. Then some time after lights-out the feast began. Peter remembers how they stuffed the surplus scraps into the knots and cracks in the floorboards, which must have fattened up the vermin wonderfully!

Luminous paint was much in demand at that time because the paint could be put on a wooden stick and energized by light. Later the boys used their light sticks to read under the bedclothes after lights-out. Today it is known that this paint was dangerous and gave rise to cancer on account of its high radioactivity.

Discipline at The Elms was similar to that in other prep schools at the time although by today's standards it sounds cruel. Corporal punishment was the norm. Being caught out of bed after lights-out was an extremely serious offence. A miscreant would be told 'Come to my study in the morning' which he knew meant a beating but there was such a strong sense of honour amongst the pupils that a boy was expected to own up. Failure to do so would bring retribution on him from his fellows. 'Big dorm beatings' were another part of prep school life. Younger boys caught doing something a senior boy considered wrong could be slippered by senior boys. Peter can remember the older boys, usually aged between 12 and 13, would delight in taking a run at the offender to wack him across the behind with a slipper.

Peter also has memories of being troubled by strange lights in the 'Big dorm' and that led him to believe the dormitory was haunted.

His greatest achievement at The Elms has been recorded for posterity in the school's annals. It happened in the summer of 1942 when The Elms played cricket against The Downs school. The Elms' Second Eleven bowled The Downs' Second Eleven out without a run ever being scored and the stars of that match were Gadsden (Major) and Lee (Major) who each took five wickets for nought. 'A record which can never be broken,' the headmaster noted in the log book. So proud was he of the school's achievement that Mr Singleton wrote to Wisden in the hope the school might receive a mention in the prestigious tome. To his disappointment, he received a letter back saying it was nothing unusual: 'it happens all the time in prep schools'.

Peter never managed to shine academically at The Elms but his mother remained encouraging, telling her elder son that it didn't matter if he failed to get the highest marks, she would be quite happy if he excelled at games. Buoyed by this Peter managed to finish school as Captain of Games and win the school's fives competition. For the latter he competed alongside Rougier (later the High Court judge, Mr Justice Rougier) who enjoyed celebrity at school as the son of the popular historical novelist Georgette Heyer.

Although Peter's time at The Elms was not particularly happy, he has always been grateful for the quality of education he received there. Years later he was delighted to accept their invitation to launch the school's appeal for a new swimming-pool. In March 1980, he returned to open the new heated pool. To the amusement of the pupils the Lord Mayor, in his full regalia, arrived in a police car because his official car had broken down on the way to the school. He then went on to entertain them with stories of his skinny-dipping in the old school swimming-pool early on a Sunday morning. It also transpired that he had once belonged to a group the headmaster referred to as the Stream Gang. Inspired by something they had learned about King Canute perhaps, the boys devoted much of their spare time to trying to dam a nearby stream.

Peter's links with the school have never been restricted to the odd cere-monial visit, far from it. When he takes an interest in an organisation he is extremely generous with his time and energy and in the case of The Elms, Peter has played a very active role as chairman of the governors since 1993.

Chapter 3

Growing Up

There is a tide in the affairs of men,
which, taken at the flood, leads on to fortune.

William Shakespeare, *Julius Caesar*

(The armorial bearings of Wrekin College)

The term following Peter's 14th birthday, after passing his Common Entrance exam, was the time for him to leave prep school. Wrekin College in Wellington, Shropshire, was the natural destination for him because the family now lived some 15 miles from Wellington at the Astley Abbotts' Rectory, close to Bridgnorth.

Another equally compelling reason for the family to choose Wrekin was its connection to the Reverend Gadsden's parish. The living of Astley Abbotts was in the gift of the Wrekin College governors, so it was sensible for the rector to send his sons there, especially in view of his meagre stipend. When the headmaster, Mr Walter Maxwell Gordon, wrote confirming Peter's place he indicated there had been a little 'divine intervention' of another kind: 'I saw Canon Bate [of the Church Missionary Society] at my Governors' Meeting in town, and he was interested. It would be a good thing, I think, for you to drop him a line and thank him for his efforts on your behalf.'

Developing the clerical association further, the head decided to put Peter in Tudor House because it was under the personal supervision of the school chaplain, the Reverend Drake, 'with whom Peter will be very happy, I know,' Mrs Gadsden was reassured.

Lest Master Gadsden gain too high an opinion of himself the head added, 'I have had Peter's marks for the Common Entrance, and they are adequate. His work should not be trouble to him, or to us, which is a good thing. I look forward to seeing you and Mrs Gadsden with the Boy on the first day of term.' Assembling the proper school uniform during wartime rationing was not easy but the headmaster was realistic, adding: 'I send a clothes list, and you must just do the best you can.'

In 1943 the regime at Wrekin was grim. 'Life is quite miserable for me. I have never felt so lonely and far away from home in my life, not even at Rockport or The Elms. Whenever I think of home, a tear comes into my eyes, and I have to look the other way, which is quite often,' Peter confided in his weekly letter home. A year later things had not improved. On one occasion he wrote: 'I feel very lonely somehow as though I have been stuck here all by myself with no one to help me to fight my way through the world. I feel lonely; I miss all the homely life and freedom.'

In an effort to fill his spare time, Peter became an avid reader. It wasn't just boys' stories and the Meccano magazine either. He followed the daily news. As he told his parents in one letter: 'I read the *Daily Mail* cover to cover every day and I listen to the news three times a day.' For a young boy this was a valuable pastime which gave him an exceptionally good grounding in current affairs that would prove useful in the future.

Under Walter Maxwell Gordon, nicknamed 'Maxie' by the pupils, there was scant sympathy for any new boy who might be homesick. In his opinion Wrekin College was there 'to make a man of you'. Trouser-pockets were sewn up on arrival so no boy would be tempted to walk around with his hands in his pockets, and the strong emphasis on sport Peter frankly found terrifying. 'At least one person goes off the field every game with a broken or fractured wrist or something,' he told his mother.

Telephones: WELLINGTON, SHROPSHIRE
HEADMASTER · · · 263
BURSAR · · · 5
SANATORIUM · · · 250

WREKIN COLLEGE
WELLINGTON
SHROPSHIRE

19th March, 1943.

Dear Mr. Gadsden,

    Many thanks for your letter and entry form. I am delighted that Peter is to come to us next term, and I am putting him down for Tudor House (the Rev. F.M. Drake) with whom he will be very happy, I know.

    I send a clothes list, and you must just do the best you can. Please write to Mr. Drake if there is anything you want to know, but do not worry overmuch, you cannot do more than you can.

    I have had Peter's marks for the Common Entrance, and they are adequate. His work should not be a trouble to him, or to us, which is a good thing.

    I saw Canon Bate at my Governors' Meeting in town, and he was interested. It would be a good thing, I think, for you to drop him a line and thank him for his efforts on your behalf. His address is:-

        The Rev. Canon F. Bate,
        c/o C.M.S. House,
        6, Salisbury Square, London, E.C.4.

    With kind regards and looking forward to seeing you and Mrs. Gadsden with the boy on the first day of term, Wednesday, May 5th.

        Yours sincerely,

WM Gordon

11. Remarks about buying the school uniform in this letter informing Reverend and Mrs Gadsden that Peter had a place at Wrekin College indicate the difficulties wartime rationing caused.

As if that weren't enough, one of the masters took a perverse delight in taunting him. '"Proper little prep school boy isn't he," he said because I did some work wrong,' Peter wrote miserably. ' "Oh I see you did not go to the village school. Not good enough for you I suppose." All these things he says before the whole class and it makes me feel uncomfortable.'

Now Peter looks back to Maxie's rule with gratitude despite the misery he endured at the time. Peter is convinced that his progress through life owes much to the standards instilled in him at that time. 'But,' Peter says, 'Maxie didn't tolerate fools; his great thing was "Be a man!" If you did that, and stood up to him, he was alright. That was his philosophy, and I think it turned out boys who made their way in life because of this discipline he imposed.'

Old Wrekinians meeting up today can still recall Maxie's maxims, given out in confirmation classes, such as: 'Write it down!'; 'When in doubt stand up'; 'Never jump to conclusions'; 'Beware of starting in the wrong place and finishing there'; 'The most valuable lesson you learn at

12. Wrekin College 1st XV Rugby team in 1947. Peter was secretary of rugger that year and is seated second on the left in the middle row.

school is criticism' and, strangely perhaps, 'Take care of your eyes!' This, Maxie maintained, was because nothing could ever make up for losing your eyesight, an affliction he believed was worse than deafness.

Peter always considers that Maxie's most valuable piece of advice to him was 'Take advantage of your chances and opportunities' and Peter's subsequent career shows just how much could be achieved when that advice was acted upon. Reflecting on his life and the part his school played in shaping it, Peter told pupils at a recent school speech day that he was convinced Maxie's words were as valid today as they were 60 years ago. Based on his own experience, Peter urged the students, no matter what their examination subjects, to

> learn languages, learn to appreciate great art, literature and fine music. You may think there is not enough time, but when you leave school there will be *many* demands on your time. At school you are making the person you will become and although it is never too late to take up *new* interests—the habits and interests you establish at school will be with you for life.

In the summer of 1944, things took a turn for the better at Wrekin, as far as Peter was concerned. A breath of fresh air arrived. Maxie retired and his successor, the Reverend Guy Pentreath, could not have been more different. For one thing he was rumoured to be a socialist, which was certainly not expected of a person in his position in those days! It is evidence of the pupils' regard for Pentreath that throughout his career he was always respectfully called 'HM' (Headmaster) behind his back, whereas other teachers received nicknames like 'Tiger' (Mr Lillie), 'Willie Bones' (Mr Wilson-Jones), 'BCWJ' or 'Sam' (Mr Johnson) and 'Dumpy' (Mr Rogers).

In his opening address to the school Pentreath spoke of the 'broadening of horizons by films, lectures, societies, expeditions of many kinds; the increase of creative and satisfying skills and of the appreciation of the beautiful by the liberal provision of facilities for art, music, handicrafts and hobbies'. Out went the old guard, taking corporal punishment with it, and in came the new. Trouser pockets were no longer stitched up. Hockey was introduced as a sport for the Easter term and prefects were permitted bicycles. Pentreath brought with him a liberal regime that emphasised personal responsibility. Peter flourished. His school reports, which had previously spoken blandly of 'a sound sensible lad', now reported 'a fine boy—but not yet a clear-headed one. In school life as a whole he is becoming a force and a very good one.'

From this distance in time it is hard to grasp what a difference Guy Pentreath made to the boys' lives, although Peter tried to express this many years later when he gave a tribute at Pentreath's memorial service.

> Guy could not have been a greater contrast to his predecessors and, at first, some masters did not understand him. But gradually he won acceptance for his ideas, and we began to enjoy new freedoms: we were allowed into the countryside on bicycles to discover for ourselves interesting places— Housman's Shropshire, the Ironbridge Gorge and the Welsh borders. A host of new activities developed—films, plays, current affairs discussion groups, overseas trips. Inside the classroom normal school work flourished, and more boys went on to university.

> Guy sought to create a working environment for the school where nothing was ugly or inefficient but all was beautiful, colourful, simple and in good taste. I remember how walls came down, trees were planted, pictures hung on classroom walls and new paint lightened our studies.

> Besides opening up new views and vistas Guy had a very clear aim for the kind of school he wanted to emerge: a real community, in which diverse characters would learn to live and grow together in harmony. From submission to 'discipline without' should come 'self-discipline'.

Peter seized the new opportunities on offer with both hands. When inter-house debating began he put himself forward—'I felt a bit shaky at first addressing 30 to 40 people,' he told his mother, 'but soon got over it and made my speeches; I quite enjoyed it in the end.' Peter was barely 15 at the time but this was excellent preparation for a future civic career which would require him to address far larger and more prestigious audiences. Guy Pentreath not only gave Peter opportunities but he also offered him responsibility and guidance in handling them wisely.

A vital part of life at Wrekin College during the war years was member-ship of the Junior Training Corps, the JTC. One of Peter's letters home in his first year gives an amusing insight into some of their activities: 'we were shown all about hangrinades [sic] and fired half a dozen off last week. Next week we have to learn all about signalling, crawling and attacking with baronets [sic]'—an activity that might have caused his future father-in-law some concern had he learned about it! Peter finished as a Company Sergeant Major in the JTC and 'a first class shot'.

Peter went to army camp with the JTC one summer. Initially the suggestion that he might attend the JTC camp met with displeasure back at the Rectory. Peter's father said that he was 'becoming a product of school' and so this should not impinge on his holiday time at home.

13. Wrekin College JTC annual inspection 1947. Brigadier CD Fairbanks CBE is seen talking to Sergeant Gadsden. Standing behind the Brigadier is the headmaster, the Reverend Guy Pentreath.

However, school won the day and Peter went. With hindsight he might have preferred to have lost that round with his father because one excursion involved an assault landing that was terrifyingly rough. Peter still remembers drawing strength from the knowledge that the Reverend Pentreath was in the same boat with them. Peter felt sure all would be well and it was.

There was another camp of a different sort during the holidays. Peter remembers going on a farming camp in Herefordshire where the boys worked on the land as their version of 'dig for victory'. It was when he was at 'Harvest Camp', as it was known, that Peter decided to pedal over to The Elms and say hello to 'Ping', his former headmaster. The visit is etched in Peter's memory because on the way he split his trousers which had been getting a bit thin in the seat. Resourceful even at that early age, Peter got out a spiral-bound notepad from his jacket pocket and unravelled the wire. Once he had straightened it sufficiently, he began threading it through the split to effect a repair, then continued on his way. Peter considers this to be his first engineering experience!

As another part of Wrekin College's war effort, Peter remembers working at the big ordnance depot at Donnington in Shropshire. On various afternoons in term-time boys were taken over to the depot to assist in packing materials (never armaments) into wooden boxes for transport overseas.

The school's ethos might have changed with the advent of the Reverend Pentreath but some lessons remained the same. In history Peter was taught the four reasons for the downfall of the Roman Empire: they ceased to believe in God; there was a mass influx of foreigners into Rome; they were cynical towards central government; homosexuality was widespread.

Whilst Maxie's rule had been characterised by a sprinkling of adages, Pentreath's required only that 'everything should be of good report'. This harmonized well with Peter's upbringing which demanded integrity and the highest moral standards. The postscript to a letter from home Peter received while at Wrekin offers further insight into the moral tone of the Gadsden household. 'Do your best at your lessons; speak the truth at whatever cost; be kind to smaller boys and not cheeky to older ones and they will all soon be very friendly,' the Reverend Gadsden advised his son.

As he progressed up the school Peter was given more responsibilities such as the most coveted of jobs, chapel keeper. This job was sought after because pupils believed it was a stepping-stone to prefectship. The keeper's duties involved putting the seats in the chapel in a straight line ready for each service and, when the boys entered the chapel, standing at the door to inspect their shoes for any signs of mud. The penalty for mud (indeed for being caught walking on the grass at Wrekin) was a 2/6 [twelve and a half pence] fine. This was a considerable sum of money to the boys in those days so most behaved themselves.

Peter found the academic work much harder at Wrekin than he had at his prep schools but he did apply himself, spurred on by his father's insistence that 'if you work hard at school, you won't have to work so hard later'.

Although school life was hard work, it had its light-hearted moments. Peter recalls the evening he was running a bath and could not get a decent flow of hot water. Applying a little initiative to the situation he decided to undo the tap to find out what the problem was. That was a mistake. So much water gushed out that he could not get the tap on again. In desperation Peter turned on all the hot water taps on all the baths to reduce the pressure and enable him to screw the first tap back in place. Right on cue, in walked the housemaster.

Another amusing exploit hinged on the rivalry between Tudor House and York House. The prefects in Tudor House, of which Peter was one, got wind that York prefects were planning a raid on the kitchen orchard that night. So, with great cunning, a few Tudor prefects kept watch during the raid and noted where the booty was secreted afterwards. Once the thieves were safely back in their dorm, the Tudor prefects crept out. They removed the apples but carefully replaced the empty suitcases. This created an interesting situation the next morning because the York prefects were unable to report the loss of the stolen apples. They were also convinced their apples had been pinched by the cleaners in the early hours. Never did fruit taste so sweet to the victors!

Peter grew in stature both physically and metaphorically. 'He takes his responsibilities as a prefect seriously and is maturing well,' Pentreath wrote of the 17-year-old Peter Gadsden, 'though I would like to see a little more bite in his demeanour.' When Peter sought to employ some 'bite' with his young brother, it landed Peter with more than he had bargained for.

David followed Peter into Tudor House at Wrekin two years later and because he was 'family', David thought he could get away with cheeking his older brother. After a few weeks of this, Peter decided Gadsden minor needed a private dressing-down, not the humiliation of a public one. Taking his brother aside into the prefects' bathroom, the elder boy perched himself on the side of the toilet seat and began explaining where the boundaries of sensible behaviour lay. Bored by the lecture, David suddenly spotted a way of getting even. Mischievously he reached up and pulled the chain. Retribution really caught up with David then!

Reading through Peter's school reports it is easy to see him developing skills that would stand him in good stead in a later public life. The headmaster concluded one report: 'His influence is always for the sound and decent and active things... He shapes well and in time he should be a very successful leader. His appointment as a School prefect is a tribute to his reliability, his soundness and strength of character, and his most wholesome influence on all his fellows.' Being a school prefect meant that Peter could now carry a furled umbrella as a mark of his status and wear a 'silver' badge in his lapel buttonhole so lesser mortals were aware of his rank. Peter has kept that silver badge to this day.

However, not everyone was impressed by Gadsden major's abilities. The English master awarded Peter 40% stating in his end-of-year report: 'What work he has been able to do in English shows him still to find self

WREKIN COLLEGE. _Lent_ Term, 1948

Name GADSDEN P.D. Index No. House I Forms VI. & Up. V.

Age 18 yrs. 9 mths. Average Age of Form 17 yrs. 2 mths. No. of Boys in Form 23

Weight at end of last Term 10:11½

Weight at end of present Term 11:4¼ Next Term begins Thursday April 29

	PLACE	
Latin	a/b	His industry has been admirable, and I hope that he has attained the required standard for the Cambridge Previous Examination. J.J.D.
ENGLISH	3/3	40%. He still finds difficulty in expressing himself with clarity and simplicity, his style containing too many errors of syntax to be good. B.C.W.
CHEMISTRY		He has done some useful work this term in the laboratory and shewn considerable ability in practical work of a new kind to him. D.R.F.
ENGLISH ESSAY.		Short work he has been able to do shows him, unfortunately, still to find self-expression in writing a very difficult book. J.P.W.
LATIN.		A commendable effort: may it prove a successful one! J.P.W.
PHYSICS	-	Most of his time has been given over to latin, but even so he has done some useful work. J.P.
Physical Training		

Form Master's Report :— Consistently good work. Congratulations on his success in the Previous examination. J.P.

House Master's Report :— He leaves with the inward satisfaction of knowing that he has carried out the manifold tasks and duties of a long school career with fidelity, devotion and courage. His success in the Previous Examination is only a final tribute to the determination to overcome difficulties which has brought him to the summit of a schoolboy's career. He has proved an outstanding Head of the House, and will leave his mark for a very long time. My good wishes go with him.

Headmaster's Report :— By giving, he has gained & grown — the success has been fully earned, without any element of luck. I have the highest hopes of this sterling personality in the days ahead — a grand boy, and a good friend. I shall always want to help. Headmaster J.P.

14. Peter's school report in 1948. He left Wrekin College at Easter that year.

expression a very difficult task and he also finds difficulty in expressing himself with clarity and simplicity, his style containing too many errors of syntax to be good.' Given these impediments it is surprising that Peter has been able to write so many speeches!

Peter had absorbed Maxie's advice to take the opportunities that presented themselves. When the Reverend Pentreath introduced drama at Wrekin, in the form of house plays which culminated in a two-day drama festival just before Christmas, Peter was ready to take part. So successful was he at amateur dramatics that he eventually produced the house play and went on to win the dramatics prize when he was in the sixth form. This was for his leading role as John Brown in the school play, *Gallows Glorious*. Although Peter never developed his drama skills after Wrekin, he was destined to put them to good use later playing a leading role on a larger stage and wearing the most impressive costumes.

15.   Peter was fortunate to have the lead part as John Brown in the school production of *Gallows Glorious* in 1947 and can be seen fully bearded. Others were less fortunate in their costumes! Back row L to R: RM Scott, RH Passmore, JN Holmes, J Cook, MC Maude. Centre L to R: JG Waterworth, PD Gadsden, PHV Hart, BJ Higgs. Front row: MVG Ealdes, RA Cross, MR Cross, BL Peace, HME Grogan.

Responsibility and success in drama, in sport (Peter ended up as secretary of rugger, fulfilling his mother's earlier hope that he might at least achieve something in games), in house activities and other spheres stacked up as Peter progressed through the school. 'He brings to his task a quiet and unassuming manner, great powers of leadership and an exceptionally mature and balanced judgement,' Pentreath wrote in 1947.

At the same time there also existed a quiet kind boy. A totally unsolicited letter sent to Peter in 2001 gives a glimpse of the warm humanity he possessed even as a sixth former. The correspondent wrote:

> I stood by the noticeboard in the quad on my first day in September 1947. My parents had left early, at my insistence, I had no idea where to go or what to do. I can't remember what you said, but you were kind and gentle...when I read about you recently, the memory of that very first encounter came up very clearly... I've always been grateful for the kind words of welcome you offered me.

Although Peter had gained a place at Cambridge, he had to stay on at Wrekin an extra term to get the necessary credit in Latin, essential in those days for entry to Cambridge. Thankfully he passed the 'Little-go' exam (as it was known) after one term's study under 'Bonzo' (aka Mr Kerr). Now he was able to move on to more enjoyable things.

During his time at Wrekin Peter had worked his way up the school's hierarchy, from school prefect to Head of House and finally to the pinnacle, Head of School. (His brother David was Head of School in 1950.) Pentreath summed up Peter's time at Wrekin College saying: 'By giving he has gained and grown—His success has been fully earned, without any element of luck. I have the highest hopes of this sterling personality in the days ahead, a grand boy, and a very good friend I shall always want to help', which indeed he did. In 1970, Canon Guy Pentreath was delighted to accept Peter's invitation to be chaplain to 'Mr Sheriff', Peter Gadsden.

Pentreath always followed Peter's career with enormous interest and wrote to him during the mayoralty saying, 'You have made London a human warm and friendly place in the minds of many I'm sure.'

A wonderful friendship existed between the two men, each regarding the other with the greatest respect, admiration and affection. Many years later, Peter was asked by the family to give the tribute at the thanksgiving service for Canon Pentreath's life in Westminster Abbey. In a speech at Wrekin College in 2001, Peter spoke of his great debt to this former headmaster who established views and vistas, colour and beauty, harmony and a sense of community epitomised in his school prayer:

16. Tudor House, Wrekin College 1948. This was taken in Peter's final term when he was head of Tudor House and Head of School. He can be seen sitting on the 3rd row, 4th from the left next to Mr Thornburn (housemaster of Tudor House), whom Peter entertained during his year as master of the Clothworkers' Company (see page 271). On the 4th row, 3rd from the left stands Brian Shaw who can be seen with Peter many years later on page 278. Peter's brother David is sitting 2nd from the right on the 3rd row.

May its foundations ever stand firm in truth and righteousness,
That beauty, order and reverence may be the message of its walls and fields,
And that so long as one stone remains upon another,
It may ever stand for all things that are strong and lovely and of good report.

Peter has never been in any doubt about the value of the education he received at Wrekin College and the friendships he made there. As a result he has always supported the Old Wrekinians, attending dinners of the London branch from the time he first began working in the City. In recent years he has been able to attend school functions in Shropshire as well and is also a member of the Old Wrekinian Lodge.

It has given Peter great pleasure to be in a position to give the present school the benefit of his City connections to widen pupils' experiences as well as support the school in other ways. His influence was seen most notably during the school's centenary year which fortunately coincided with Peter's mayoralty and enabled the school to hold its Centenary Dinner in Guildhall. At other times Peter has been a popular guest speaker at several Wrekin College speech days and served as a school governor from 1997 to 1999.

Chapter 4

Life at the Rectory

From quiet homes and first beginnings,
Out to the undiscovered ends,
There's nothing worth the wear of winning,
But laughter and the love of friends.

Hilaire Belloc

Given the strict regime that was enforced in boarding schools in the 1940s, it is not surprising holidays were greatly prized by all the Gadsden children. The Rectory, however, must have wondered what had hit it when the three spirited youngsters returned. Fortunately there was plenty of space for them to charge around both in the garden and the adjacent fields. The Rectory at Astley Abbotts was a six-bedroomed, one bathroom, Georgian farmhouse, a little way out of the village, next-door to the Parish Hall. It was surrounded by half an acre of cultivated garden with trees to climb and hedgerows for bird-nesting. Not far away was a pond where the brothers enjoyed fishing for eels.

The Rectory had its own grass tennis-court, which is fondly remembered for having more plantains than blades of grass. It was also a bit short so it was accepted practice that a player would have to run up the rockery behind the court in order to get a lob. Both Peter's parents were keen tennis players and ensured their children, especially Daphne, grew up with that accomplishment. It was the children's responsibility to prepare the tennis court before they played and that involved rolling it out and marking it up. As Peter's sister, Daphne, recalls, once they had finished it was invariably the cue for rain!

Whilst their mother encouraged the children to play tennis, the rector held strong opinions about when it was, and wasn't, permissible to play tennis. Sunday was not a day when it was permitted, although there are

17. Astley Abbots' Rectory had been a Georgian farmhouse on the very edge of the village. The tiny figures standing outside are Peter with his father, Daphne and David.

stories of Daphne quietly making her way down the Rectory drive with a strange shape protruding from under her skirt!

Although cards and other games were forbidden on a Sunday, reading was an acceptable pastime and the children recall being extremely keen on reading the *Sunday Despatch* at one stage. The big attraction was the serialisation of the risqué novel *Forever Amber*, which the rector considered highly unsuitable for his offspring. Daphne remembers her father scooping up the newspaper on a Sunday morning and vanishing to the outside privy with it. The newspaper then seemed to 'disappear' so the children spent much of the day hunting for it with the cry 'Wherever's Amber?'

An ability to play tennis, combined with the rector's additional pastoral responsibility for the parish of Willey (since that vicar had gone to war), led to a widening of the children's social circle. Willey Church was on Lord Forester's estate and the rector's children found themselves invited up to the Hall for tennis parties. Some of these childhood friendships made on the tennis-courts were resumed later in Peter's life.

It was on the tennis-courts at Willey Park where Peter first met Michael, who became Viscount Boyne in 1942. Their paths did not cross again until Peter was Lord Mayor when the two met up in the City. Thereafter he and his wife, Rosemary, became close friends with Peter and Belinda and they shared holidays abroad. Michael became a non-executive director of PPP during Peter's chairmanship in the 1990s. They were such close friends in later years that Peter was asked to give the tribute at the thanksgiving service in Ludlow parish church following his untimely death in 1995.

The tennis parties led on to invitations to attend pony club dances. Although the pony club was not part of the Gadsden children's social scene, they did have a pony called Twinkle. She lived in a field adjacent to the Rectory but attempts to ride her usually ended up with one of the children falling off backwards. Dancing may not have held any great appeal to the Gadsden boys at that time either, but their mother believed it was a useful social skill they should learn. Out came her wind-up gramophone along with some 'seventy-eights' of Victor Sylvester's dance-band and the rector's children practised their steps in the dining-room, executing some neat manoeuvres round the large table—slow, slow, quick, quick, slow.

Not surprisingly, when the children were reunited after a term apart there were plenty of high jinks. Peter and David remember the occasion when they mischievously lay in wait behind a hedge, water pistols at the ready. Their plan was to 'ambush' the Mothers' Union as they walked back from their meeting in the Parish Hall one sunny afternoon. To their delight the boys could hear the venerable ladies expressing amazement that it should rain on them out of a clear sky. Behind the Rectory hedge there were stifled giggles.

Another amusing prank also stuck in the brothers' memory. It was the day some workmen were digging a trench for the new water main in the road outside Major Phillimore's house. Later after dark, they noticed that nobody had bothered to light the lamps round the trench. They vied with each other to think of all the most outrageous things that might befall unwary passers-by. Then it suddenly occurred to one of the boys that they could take matters into their own hands. Off they ran in the direction of the village phone box. The first the Major knew of it was a slightly muffled call that evening: 'Sergeant 'Awkins 'ere from Bridgnorth Police. If them lights are not lit you'll be reported.' Peeping out higher up the lane, the two boys watched the Major meekly hobble along to light the lamps along his trench. Fortunately he was too sheepish to contact the local constabulary and check on the phone call he had received.

School holidays never meant anyone went away, quite the opposite. When the children arrived home from school, father had their jobs waiting. Believing the devil finds work for idle hands, the Reverend Gadsden certainly intended taking no chances. As Peter recalls, most of his jobs involved gardening.

Evidently the years of living in the outback had left their mark on Basil Gadsden. By dint of his own labour, the family were virtually self-sufficient, which made a big difference to their standard of living during the austerity of wartime. An enthusiastic gardener himself, the Reverend Gadsden worked hard to ensure his family had a steady supply of fresh vegetables and fruit as well as catering for his own smoking needs. Alongside the lines of raspberry canes and carrots grew rows of tobacco plants. When the leaves were harvested, he pegged them to dry on strings in the kitchen where they exuded the most frightful smell.

There wasn't just produce from the kitchen garden either. The family had honey from their own hives, eggs and meat from their chickens and geese, as well as rabbits, pigeon and game from the rector's gun, not to mention his successes at fishing.

Peter was taught to fish by his father but the late Sir Peter Studd maintained that Peter could not really cast properly and recommended he spend a long weekend learning how to put a fly on the water a good yard upstream of the fish. This done, the expert fisherman judged 'Peter can cast quite well now' and the two of them went on to enjoy many a happy hour on the Test.

The Gadsden children's holiday chores included digging and weeding the garden as well as weeding the drive, which David recalls had little or no gravel on it anyway! The children also had to do their stint of pumping water up to the house because the Rectory was not on mains water. Another job that came the children's way towards the end of the school holidays was fruit picking—damsons, apples and soft fruits. They quite enjoyed this chore because it gave them the chance to earn some pocket money for next term. Father paid one penny for every twelve pounds of fruit picked.

School holiday jobs were seasonal and one of the more memorable springtime chores involved cleaning lambs' tails. Based on the old adage 'waste not want not' father collected the tails that had been docked from the new lambs up at the farm. A full bucket was left on the cellar floor to 'mature' a little, then the children had to set to work plucking the wool off. What sustained them through this gruesome task was the knowledge that their mother would cook the most exquisite dish with the meat.

Another equally unsavoury task, again not one for the squeamish, involved preparing pigs' chitterlings. Their father would arrive home with a bucket from the neighbouring farm where a pig had been slaughtered. Inside the bucket porcine intestines swished around. First the boys had to wash them off under the garden water butt, then set to work with hazel sticks to push the gunge out of the tubes. Once these were thoroughly cleaned, their mother plaited and cooked them. The result, it is said, was delicious.

In Peter's opinion, life at the Rectory was 'disciplined and happy, with an emphasis on service, integrity, hard work and saving for the future'. His perspective on this is interesting because to many this would sum up very accurately his own approach to life.

The tone of family life at the Rectory was set by Father and, without question, he has been the single most powerful influence on Peter. Relations between father and son could never be described as relaxed. Peter acknowledges that he didn't have an easy relationship with his father because he was inclined to rebel against discipline. His brother and sister also felt their father was not only domineering but remote and came down harder on Peter than he did on them. As the eldest Peter was expected to set a good example. Basically he got the blame for everything, his sister Daphne said.

Basil Gadsden was a devoted father and demanded extremely high standards from his children who respected him. Peter describes his father as having 'very fixed views and only seeing things in black and white'. Some of his views seem quite puritanical for the time, like his strong disapproval of make-up on women, even of earrings. He also had an abhorrence of drunkenness, swearing and gambling. Though not teetotal himself—indeed he brewed some excellent elderflower and damson wines—he left his sons in no doubt that he strongly disapproved of them visiting pubs. Drunkenness was evil and in later years when he possessed a television, he would switch it off immediately should any programme come on which depicted drunken or sensual behaviour. No swear words were ever heard in the Rectory; the strongest word to pass anyone's lips if things got 'serious' was the occasional 'bother'.

18. Peter, Daphne and David with the Reverend Basil Gadsden. He was essentially a Victorian father and none of the children enjoyed an easy relationship with him.

Peter describes his father as a hard-working and conscientious priest who visited every parishioner once a month. He had no time for socialism as in his opinion it was an attempt to do the right thing without the help of God. His Christianity was uncompromisingly Protestant to the extent that he regarded Roman Catholics as papists who were misguided. Such entrenched views were to cause the family great unhappiness in the future when Peter became engaged and married to Belinda, the daughter of one of the oldest Catholic families in the country. It was an alliance, Peter said, which broke his father's heart.

Basil Gadsden had his faults like most mortals but he was a great inspiration to Peter. A love of travel and a strong sense of service were undoubtedly passed to his elder son. Peter thinks of his father as being very practical, 'a person who would get on with life', and would never ask anyone to do something he was not prepared to do himself. Basil told his children: 'If there's no one there to do it, then you don't make a fuss, you do it yourself.' Perhaps that was what John Hart, sheriff when Peter was Lord Mayor, observed in Peter when he commented: 'Peter doesn't recoil at anything.' One can't help thinking that the motto Peter chose when his coat of arms was designed—'Thoroughly with Enthusiasm'— would have been as appropriate for Basil as it was for his son.

Peter has always had enormous respect for his father and done his best to aspire to the high standards he demanded. It remains one of Peter's great sadnesses that neither parent was alive to see him become Lord Mayor of London. That would have given them such pleasure.

Peter's mother was a completely different personality and all the family adored her including her daughters-in-law. She was kind to everyone, family and parishioners alike. May's respectable middle-class upbringing in West Kensington, followed by a boarding-school education in Folkestone, made her a stickler for etiquette. She taught her children the importance of good manners and insisted that thank-you letters be written promptly. Peter and David were also taught to stand up when 'seniors' entered the room, especially if one was a lady, and to open doors for ladies and allow them to go first. It would surely have pleased her to know how many people have appreciated her elder son's good manners. One business

19.   Peter and David with their mother, May. The three children adored her.

colleague remarked that 'Peter is the politest man I know', whilst another described him as 'a very caring person'—a personality trait he surely owes to his mother.

In contrast to what the children saw as their father's discipline, their mother was lenient towards them. She loved her children and had no difficulty in showing it, telling them that children were all she had ever wanted. The home she made for them reflected her gentle personality. She loved her garden and, whilst her husband took charge of vegetable production, she created beauty by growing flowers—a division of labour that Peter and Belinda have continued. Mrs Gadsden was fond of animals so in addition to Twinkle the pony, there was a dog, who was taken shooting on occasions, a couple of cats and baby rabbits. The rabbits were actually wild ones of which she made pets.

'I had a very easy relationship with my mother,' Peter says fondly, 'she was almost a saint. She was such a gentle person.' Nevertheless she too demanded a high moral standard and was insistent that if a job was worth doing, it was worth doing well—her philosophy is also behind Peter's motto 'Thoroughly with enthusiasm'. May impressed upon her children that if they said they would do something, then they must do it. Personal integrity was everything and she did not compromise it even to reuse an unfranked stamp. Mrs Gadsden would never borrow anything and neither would she buy something unless she could afford it. Peter has striven to live up to the standards his mother set, and people have admired him for this.

Although before her marriage May had lived in a household with sufficient servants to undertake all the domestic chores, she had to learn to cook in Canada. She undoubtedly made a success of it because many of the teatime treats her children liked best, like coconut macaroons and mouth-watering coffee and walnut cake, were made from old Canadian recipes. Four o'clock tea in the Rectory drawing-room was the highlight of the children's day because their mother always produced a delicious selection of cakes and sandwiches. In their opinion few other mothers came up to her standard. Peter's brother David still recoils in horror at the memory of Daphne embarrassing him when they were invited to have tea with a well-to-do neighbour. Looking down at the limited offerings on the cake plate, the little girl piped up, 'Is that all the cakes there are?'

Even when the children were away at school their mother did her best to send them a little taste of home. Writing to thank her for 'the eatables' in 1944 Peter said, 'You can't imagine how much I liked them. I have eaten

the cake, the 2 eggs and about three-quarters of the cheese. I don't seem
to be able to find suitable words to thank you, but you can imagine how
happy I was when I opened the parcel. I hate to ask you but could you do
the same kind of thing next week?'

The 1940s in rural Shropshire were still a time when social boundaries
were clearly defined and were not to be overstepped and Mrs Gadsden
knew exactly on which side of the boundary her family stood. She expected
the children to tread the narrow path between playing their part in parish
life but not fraternising with the village children. Peter also remembers
how they had to dress in their school uniform for church services, even in
the school holidays. He found it acutely embarrassing because, in the eyes
of the villagers, it marked them out as 'posh'.

Mrs Gadsden enjoyed being the rector's wife and was most supportive
of her husband's work, visiting the sick in the parish and running the
Mothers' Union. She knew what was expected of a parson's wife because
her sister Elsie, twelve years her senior, had also married a clergyman.

Whilst Elsie's visits to Shropshire were few and far between, May's
brother Horace spent most of the war years in Astley Abbotts. He was
always known as 'Unk' by his niece and nephews because he disliked his
Christian name. Unk was Peter's godfather, though by proxy, since the
christening had taken place in Alberta. Although he was known to be a
solicitor by profession, no one could remember Unk ever practising. This
might have been on account of ill health because he did suffer from a skin
complaint as a result of blood poisoning. When war broke out Unk was
living in a hotel in Brighton where he witnessed some terrifying bombing
raids so he evacuated himself to the relative safety of Shropshire. He was
a great favourite with the children in holiday time because he was full of
fun, blessed with a keen sense of humour and an expert at crosswords.

Peter has a clear memory of the moment war broke out because he
was sitting in church. Evidently there had been a general expectation
of the announcement because the Reverend Gadsden had taken the unusual step of having a radio in the church. Peter remembers listening to
Chamberlain's broadcast. A little later the rector said pessimistically to his
eldest son 'I may not see the end of this', though mercifully his prediction
was wrong.

The Second World War did not impinge on daily life in Astley Abbotts
very much. Peter's father was an air raid warden and the children
remember him sitting in a deckchair at night time in the cellar with his tin

hat, rattle, stirrup pump and an axe. Fortunately he was never required to use these implements. Most of his duties involved going round the village after dark to make sure no light was showing through people's curtains. There were occasions when the family had to sleep in the Rectory cellar for fear of bombing raids but generally this part of Shropshire was left in peace. Only on the night when Germany bombed Coventry did Astley Abbotts see much action; German planes jettisoned bombs on the return and some fell in a field near the Rectory.

Like other families in the area, the Gadsdens had an evacuee billeted on them. A mother and young child came to live at the Rectory for a period during the war. At the end of her stay the woman caused some consternation in the household by asking Peter's mother to keep little Thelma—an offer which was politely declined.

Father loved his children and encouraged them to have healthy outdoor hobbies they could pursue in the school holidays. Knowing Peter was an avid member of the 'Caty Club' at The Elms, it comes as no surprise to learn that his hobby was collecting caterpillars, moths and butterflies. David watched birds and collected their eggs, whilst for Daphne the more lady-like pursuit of collecting and pressing wild flowers was suggested. All these hobbies reflect a different attitude towards the preservation of wildlife from that of today; indeed most would not be permitted now. Nevertheless, even then it was well understood that you never took more than one egg from a nest.

It was whilst helping David with his bird-nesting one day that Peter fell out of a tree and landed on a barbed-wire fence. He ended up with a large tear not just in his trousers but in his bottom and, it is said, he bears that scar to the present day. This 'distinctive mark and minor defect' was duly noted in his Soldier's Service Pay Book during National Service as 'scar left buttock', enabling Peter to be identified should he be killed in action.

Village life in Astley Abbotts was taken at a leisurely pace and plenty of rural 'characters' still existed like the roadman. Of a Sunday he could be found walking in the village in his Sunday best, smoking a cigarette and inspecting his handiwork from the previous week.

During holiday times the rector's children were expected to go round the parish with their father delivering the monthly magazine. They also had to undertake other little jobs within the parish, but under no circumstances could they accept tips. Mrs Gadsden made a clear distinction between paid employment and public service and she expected her children to do the same. The fact that Peter has divided his public life into three— business, charitable work and civic duties—is testament to his mother's influence.

One parish visit that still remains vivid in Peter's mind was to old Tom Vickery, who lived in a cottage in Astley Abbotts. Although Peter was unaware of it at the time, Thomas Vickery was a clockmaker of international renown who had exhibited at the London Arts and Crafts Exhibition of 1935. His pride and joy was his 'wonder clock' with a mass of dials that showed not only the time, day of the week and date, but also a considerable amount of astronomical information. He had taken 25 years to design and build this clock which had an extremely complex chiming and striking mechanism that could produce either Westminster or Whittington quarter chimes. The clock also played a tune every three hours, changing at midnight to a new tune for the next day. Many of the tunes were hymns, which naturally found favour with the rector.

Equally fascinating to Peter was Mr Vickery's planetarium, again made to his own design. It showed six principal planets revolving round the sun and was so accurate that Vickery calculated if he had made an error it would not be apparent for three hundred years.

Peter has vivid memories of the instrument maker himself.

I was a schoolboy and to me he looked the typical genius or professor, with his dark hair and bushy moustache and rather absent-minded appearance and behaviour. I was always fascinated with his numerous clocks when I accompanied my father to his cottage. The whole room was alive with ticking.

I remember when he agreed to repair the church clock at Willey which had not been going for years, and I was asked to assist him in cleaning the parts with paraffin, for which I got 10/- [fifty pence]—I considered it a generous reward!

Mrs Vickery was a regular attender at church and I used to help her up to the Communion rail. When she died she left me her emerald engagement ring which Belinda now wears. But Mr Vickery did not go to Church very much and this displeased my father. I remember that Mr Vickery was of the opinion that it was not necessary to go to church to be near his Maker. I frequently saw him sitting in a deckchair in his greenhouse reading a book, and I think he found great peace in the quiet of his greenhouse amongst his flowers, not to mention warmer than sitting in the garden.

An interesting postscript to Tom Vickery's story is that when he died in 1945, Peter's father not only took the clockmaker's funeral service but also dug his grave. The local newspaper considered this such an unusual occurrence that it reported on 'the Salop rector turned grave-digger' who had neither sexton nor verger to help him due to the war. The Reverend B Gadsden 'rolled up his sleeves and himself dug the grave of his old friend Mr Thomas Vickery, the well-known Shropshire clock maker'. Recalling Basil's grave-digging feats in the frozen Canadian prairies, excavations into the sandy soil of St Calixtus' churchyard must have seemed easy. The journalist reported that, 'For the site the rector chose one of the loveliest spots in this beautiful churchyard—a green patch under the spreading branches of a 500-year-old yew tree, and after the funeral service yesterday afternoon the rector remained behind to fill in the grave.'

The newspaper also reported that 'by the terms of his will Mr Vickery leaves his world-famous clock, planetariums, astronomical dial, 28 old movements in a gold case, watches in silver cases, sun dial, pocket chronometer and a double centre seconds watch in silver case to the Worshipful Company of Clockmakers'. This was 1945 and the first time

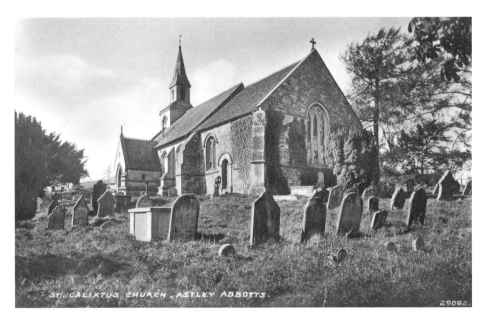

20. St Calixtus Church at Astley Abbots where Peter's father was rector from 1940 to 1955. The church was dedicated to St Calixtus who became Bishop of Rome in 291 AD. A memorial to Francis Billingsley and his son Colonel Billingsley who was killed defending Bridgnorth against Cromwell's army is on the chancel wall.

that Peter had ever heard mention of the City livery companies, yet some years later his name would be inextricably linked with them. After Tom Vickery's death, Peter's father was given a bookcase that had been made by the clockmaker. That has since been handed down to Peter who has the beautifully crafted piece of furniture in Northumberland.

Church attendance at matins and evensong was naturally expected of the rector's children but Peter never felt that his father rammed religion down their throats. Being the rector's son attracted jibes at school and respect in the parish, but it could still be embarrassing. When the children were home from school there was the ritual of morning prayers before nine o'clock breakfast. The family knelt down in front of their chairs whilst the rector recited the prayers. It was something which made the children embarrassed if they had school friends staying.

In church the rector expected his sons to take their turn reading the lesson. Fortunately this was not so much of an ordeal for them as it might have been because they were used to reading in the chapel at Wrekin College. Standing at the lectern to read the lesson proved excellent grounding for London's future Lord Mayor who would be called upon to attend 48 church services during his year of office and read the passage for the day on many of those occasions.

Another necessary Sunday duty Peter undertook as a school boy was pumping the organ and the instrument had its own way of taking revenge on the operative who didn't concentrate. It made dreadful swooping sounds when the air was running out in the bellows so everybody in the congregation knew 'the pumper' was shirking.

Singing in St Calixus' 30-strong church choir was something Peter never participated in. He freely admits he is hopeless musically although his mother possessed a beautiful singing voice and took her place in the church choir. Even his tutors at Wrekin College had to admit their failure to make a musician of him despite trying him in the choir, then attempting to teach him the piano and the bugle. Tone-deaf was their judgement of Peter's musical abilities.

One thing the rector demanded of his children above all else was that they should behave impeccably in church. All three Gadsdens retain a vivid memory of the time they transgressed and received a public reprimand from the pulpit. As usual the three children were sitting in the family pew immediately below the carved Jacobean pulpit whilst their mother took her place in the choir. As the 20 minute sermon droned on, the rector's offspring got restless and began messing around with their prayer books. To their horror, public retribution swiftly followed. There was a pause in the sermon whilst the rector leaned over the pulpit and chastised his own children, telling them to behave themselves and put the books down.

The joyful freedom of school holidays always passed too quickly and once again brothers and sister were packed off to their various schools.

Chapter 5

Army and Cambridge

If you can talk with crowds and keep your virtue
Or walk with kings—nor lose the common touch,
If neither foes nor loving friends can hurt you,
If all men count with you, but none too much;
If you can fill the unforgiving minute
With sixty seconds' worth of distance run
Yours is the earth, and everything that's in it
And—which is more—you'll be a Man, my son!

Rudyard Kipling, 'If'

When Peter left Wrekin College in 1948, he was obliged to do National Service before he could take up his place at Cambridge. The army was the obvious choice because he had enjoyed the Junior Training Corps (JTC) at school. It was Easter when he left Wrekin College after the extra term to pass his Latin exam. By the beginning of June he was being transported down to Bordon in Hampshire in a 'cattle truck' along with a mixed bunch of raw recruits. When they got there, all were immediately given a haircut ('I was nearly shaved all over my head') and that was followed with a bath and a shower—'some chaps really needed it!!!' he wrote home. They were also lined up for inoculations.

Despite being the only public schoolboy in a hut of twelve, Peter had no difficulty in getting on with everybody. The ease with which he can mix with people from all walks of life has remained a feature of his personality and has been a great asset all his life. Recently Darby Johns, Peter's business colleague of many years' standing remarked, 'Peter's great personal quality was that he was able to merge with the locals in every country and business situation without being ostentatious. Although he mixed with a wide variety of business characters Peter never abandoned his own standards and ethics.'

Life at Bordon was in complete contrast to anything he had experienced before. To his amazement he encountered lads who could neither read nor write because, they said, they had never been to school. Another revelation was that for some recruits every other word was a swear word and most of those started with an F. What shocked the parson's son more was that nobody batted an eyelid at such language. Another thing Peter was 'taught' was that whilst it was alright to steal from the army, it was not acceptable to steal from a colleague.

Peter also discovered that 'only officers play tennis'. Having seen tennis-courts at Bordon, he got ready for a game, only to be put in his place. Nevertheless 'the fact is I am rather enjoying it here,' he wrote to the family back in Shropshire. 'The only thing I fear is the dentist [a fear which has stayed with him to the present day]. There is a wonderful spirit between men and recruits and officers which you don't get in civvy life—if anyone is behind with duties, cleaning etc one of us always does the job for him and helps him.'

Peter also discovered that life for a private was 'one huge rush and parade, parade. I am very fit, but very tired as from 6am to 11pm is a long day—I drop off to sleep as soon as I get into bed at night.' But remembering his mother's motto, 'if a job is worth doing it is worth doing properly', Peter gave it his all. This resulted in him being selected for the Officers and NCO's platoon which meant he was considered potential officer material.

After ten weeks he went before the War Office Selection Board—the WOSBY—from which a few would be chosen as officer material. The odds against him were 100 to 1, he was told, because the army already had too many officers. At one stage he feared he had blown his chances of selection completely. Wanting to go home on leave, and urged on by another chap to 'thumb it', Peter and a friend successfully hitched their way up from Bordon to Farnham, in Surrey. 'Thumbing it' once again they were delighted when a smart car stopped to pick them up. But their delight soon changed to horror when they recognised the driver was their commanding officer. Instead of telling them off, he said 'Jump in!' and drove them on to Aldershot!

No matter how many officers the army already had, even the WOSBY were not prepared to pass over a gifted young man and, to Peter's delight, in August 1948 he was selected to go to Eaton Hall, near Chester, as an officer cadet. The difference from life at Bordon was unmistakeable. Peter was posted to 'B' Company which meant he resided in the Hall rather than one of the huts provided for those in 'C' and 'D' Companies. 'It is lovely here—carpet on the floor, three to a room and sheets on the bed,' he wrote home excitedly.

Once again the pressure was on. He had sixteen weeks in which to pass out as a second lieutenant and, if Peter's letters home are any guide, this largely involved freezing cold exercises in November standing around in fields for four hours at a stretch. Many who were at Eaton Hall in those days retain a vivid memory of Regimental Sergeant-Major Copp who trained them. He disliked all potential officers except those in the Brigade of Guards and was downright rude to the cadets, but he got away with it by always finishing his sentence with 'sir'. As he was keen to point out, 'You calls me sir, and I calls you sir. But you means it.'

His piercing yell could be heard across the parade-ground: 'You in the Chaplain Corps, the Education Corps or what the hell you're in. Stand to attention!' Just in case there was still an ounce of arrogance in the trainee officers the RSM added, 'It's a b... good thing the British Army has got some good sergeants with chaps like you as officers.' Another yell regularly fired at a trainee was, 'Wake up, sir! You're the wettest, sloppiest most dozy individual I've ever come across.'

21.   1 Platoon B Company at Eaton Hall near Chester in December 1948. Capt Bailey, CSM Dobson, Major Edgar, Sgt Tedds and Capt Matthews sit at the front. Officer Cadet PD Gadsden is fifth from the left on the back row.

One of Peter's colleagues Cecil Vyvyan-Robinson remembers being renamed by RSM Copp after having the misfortune to draw attention to himself through some misdemeanour.

'Sergeant-Major Dobson, take the name of the fifth man in the front rank!' Copp's voice rang out across the parade-ground.

'What's your name, sir?'

'Vyvyan-Robinson.'

'His name is Vyvyan-Robinson.'

'I don't want 'is b— Christian name,' came the retort. 'Ask 'im what 'is surname is.'

'He says his surname is Vyvyan-Robinson.'

'Tell him 'is surname is Robinson.'

Another of Copp's memorable exchanges would begin, 'Am I 'urting yer?' To which the reply was always, 'No, sir.'

'Well I'm treading on yer b— 'air. Get yer 'air cut.'

Life at Eaton Hall was no picnic. If a chap fainted on the parade-ground the yell would go out, 'Get 'im up! March him to the Guard Room! Left, right, left, right...' In many ways Peter thought the notice that said 'No Escape' on a mess door summed things up admirably.

Nevertheless Peter tried really hard during his time at Eaton Hall because he was keen to get a commission and there was one occasion when he felt that he had probably made his mark. When his turn came round to command the platoon. Peter was sent on a night exercise. Whilst out on patrol, he managed to feel the trip wires set by the 'enemy', without setting off the flares. The next morning, when he was feeling rather proud of the successful operation that he had led and was sure that he must be in line for a commission, he was told that the enemy had forgotten to prime the trip wires!

One of Peter's more bizarre memories of Eaton Hall involves hypnotism. Amongst the officer cadets was a young man who was an extraordinarily competent hypnotist. He regularly entertained colleagues with his exploits and was never short of volunteers. Some he persuaded to relive childhood experiences and behave accordingly to the amusement of onlookers, and others allowed him to push needles through parts of their hands without any signs of pain. Peter never volunteered for any of his exploits!

Despite RSM Copp's poor opinion of the officer cadets, Peter ended up being CO's stick orderly for an unprecedented four times when on guard parade. Clearly his prep school training of 'folding his etons' had stood him in good stead! Normally the smartest person on parade was excused further guard duty and could go back to bed while the rest did duty all night. If a person was CO's stick orderly three times then they were excused any further guard duties, however they were so short of officer cadets that one night Peter landed up doing a fourth parade. If you scan the official records for evidence, you won't find it because three is the maximum number of times permitted. On Peter's fourth duty another person's name was entered on the list.

At the end of his training Peter was commissioned into the King's Shropshire Light Infantry (KSLI) which he was delighted about because the JTC at Wrekin had been linked with them. The only problem was that the KSLI were on guard duty at St James's Palace—regarded by some as a boring posting. The Colonel who interviewed Peter thought he would like something a little more exciting and recommended him for posting to the 1st Battalion of the Oxfordshire and Buckinghamshire Light Infantry at Göttingen in Germany. However, that battalion was soon to leave for Greece and, because Peter only had a short time in which to complete his National Service on account of his university place, before they moved he was posted to the Durham Light Infantry at Dortmund.

It was January 1949 when Peter arrived in Germany only to find himself face to face with someone he did *not* have fond memories of from Bordon. After saluting, the soldier asked 'Do you remember me?' 'Oh I remember you, Corporal Ball,' Peter replied with some feeling. 'I shall never forget you!' That particular corporal had been etched in Peter's memory.

It was not long before he found himself commanding border patrols of 8 non-commissioned officers and 23 other ranks in thick snow at Braunlage. On occasions they had to don skis in order to get around, which was the first time Peter had ever put skis on—and it certainly wasn't the last! He enjoyed his skiing experiences so much so, that in later years there were several Gadsden family skiing holidays.

The groups Peter commanded were sent out on a 72-hour patrol to show the flag and bolster German morale in villages next to the Russian zone. They travelled round in three lorries and met up with local German police who accompanied them. Along the border were Russian propaganda signs in English referring to the western zone as 'The zone of monarchists, capitalists, plutocrats and Ruhrists.'

Peter's report on one of these exercises is not only testimony to the 19-year-old's ability to grasp a situation and give a concise account of it, but

22. Second Lieutenant PD Gadsden.

also provides a fascinating insight into life in this part of Germany in the aftermath of the Second World War. Reporting on the information he had learned, much of which Peter admitted was based on hearsay, he wrote:

> Russian trained German police bring all who try to cross into the British zone to Weisenborn, where they are questioned by Russian intelligence officers. There they are kept in a dark cellar for three days without food. It is said the girls are handed to Russian officers. The police are paid according to the number of border crossers they arrest. On a number of occasions the police have shot persons trying to enter the British zone.
>
> Russian officers in twos and threes have on many occasions been shooting buck in the woods (in the British zone) around Nuxei, particularly of late.
>
> Russian trained German police were seen inside the British zone on a track near Bartofelde. On seeing the British troops approach they returned to their own zone. The police frequently enter the British zone in search of food.
>
> The German civilian population are pleased to see British troops in their villages and would feel happier if British troops were stationed nearer the border or were to visit their villages more often.

23.   In February 1949 Peter was posted to Germany where he can be seen on exercise along the Russian border.

From experience of military life close to the Russian zone where the officers were billeted in German farmhouses and other ranks slept in the barns, Peter enjoyed a totally different existence when he went on leave to a local leave centre. 'This is a wonderful place with hotels all around the lake. The British have taken over all the German hotels and turned them into officers and other ranks local leave centres,' he wrote to the family back in Shropshire. 'The Officers' Club where we stayed was on the water's edge. We had dinner on the verandah and the water was below us.'

Life in Germany did have its lighter moments. On occasions there were opportunities to play cricket, much to the fascination of the local German population who had no idea of the rules. Peter believed they had the misguided notion that fielders stood on the pitch in order to get a better view of the batsmen. As a result Germans regularly wandered onto the pitch to watch the action and the British were forever pointing out to them that they must watch from the boundary.

By the summer of 1949, Peter had moved on to Dortmund to be second-in-command of mortars platoon because the officer commanding mortars was on leave. 'There were people who thought this job was a bit of a skive,' he says with a twinkle in his eye, 'because whilst everyone else was obliged to march on exercise, those of us involved in mortars drove around in Bren gun carriers!'

At weekends he would visit Mohne See, scene of one of the famous 'Dam Busters' raids in May 1943. These were only brief respites for Peter and his next main task involved locating sites for further ammunition shelters and 'we are certainly building up a stock of war materials out here!', Peter wrote cheerfully.

There was another bonus to the new job. The Motor Transport Officer at Dortmund issued Peter with a permit to drive that included 'vehicles steered by their own tracks'. This specific clause enabled him to drive a Bren gun carrier but has also meant that, even though Peter has an excellent driving record, he has never passed a driving test—quite the opposite. Peter actually failed his driving test shortly before he was called up!

It was whilst on exercise that Peter made his mark when the colonel was giving instructions for battle.

'Gadsden! We'll have mortars firing at 0600 hours with smoke!' the colonel ordered.

'No, sir,' came the reply. Everyone froze in horror at such insubordination.

'Why not?' enquired the colonel.

'Because it's out of range, sir.'

'Very good,' was the reply and Peter breathed a sigh of relief. He was handed a map and instructed to move the mortars to a new map reference.

'Yes, sir,' replied the young officer.

Life in the army was so varied and enjoyable that Peter admits to being tempted by the idea of a military career but he had been looking forward to going to Cambridge, so he put the idea behind him. Years later as an alderman he became a member of the Court of the Honorable Artillery Company and was appointed Honorary Colonel of the 5th Battalion (Shropshire and Herefordshire) Light Infantry (volunteers), abbreviated 5LI, Peter couldn't have been more happy to accept it.

Despite his National Service being only a matter of months, it left its mark on him. A tradition grew up in the City when Peter worked there that he traversed the square mile so quickly because he had been with the Light Infantry who are famed for marching at 140 paces to the minute. Their fast marching could present problems at times. Peter remembers one regimental parade in Germany when the infantry's quick march landed their band immediately behind another regiment. This resulted in total chaos because the poor soldiers in front couldn't hear their own band and completely lost their marching rhythm. It was probably Peter's memories of that incident which ensured the LI received special treatment in the Lord Mayor's procession during Peter's mayoralty. On that occasion the parade was halted for a while to allow the KSLI to march past the Mansion House at their traditional fast pace. Once they caught up with the rest of the procession, they settled into the standard marching pace.

Peter also believes that his army days taught him the importance of good time-keeping. The corporal who yelled 'Move! When I say move, I mean move!' left his mark. Peter has been a stickler for punctuality ever since—a trait that has done him no harm.

His army career might have been brief but Peter managed to serve with an unusually large number of Light Infantry regiments. He was trained by the Somerset Light Infantry, commissioned into the King's Shropshire Light Infantry and served in Germany in the Oxfordshire and Buckinghamshire Light Infantry (January–April 1949) and the Durham Light Infantry (April–September 1949)

In the autumn of 1949 Peter went up to Cambridge. He had chosen to read Natural Sciences because science had interested him most at Wrekin.

When it came to choosing which subject to study the rector had given his son a free choice, but when it came to which college to apply to Peter had less freedom. The cost of a university education meant Peter was attracted to two colleges that gave grants to sons of the clergy. He applied to Jesus College and sat the scholarship for sons of the clergy but failed to win it. He was, however, awarded a grant of £40 per annum from the Rustat fund for clergy sons, which assisted the Reverend Gadsden whose stipend was under £500 a year. Peter has always been extremely proud that he went to Jesus College. 'It is the best college in Cambridge,' he maintains. He was amused to receive a letter from his old headmaster at The Elms congratulating him on getting in to Jesus College, Cambridge. 'It's the best college at Cambridge,' wrote 'Ping', 'after my own college Pembroke.'

Initially Peter read Physics, Chemistry and Geology, but physics involved a lot of maths and that was a struggle so he changed to Mineralogy. This move shaped his future career. Natural Sciences involved a lot of practical work in the afternoons and with a good social life filling his evenings, Peter's studies got squeezed into the vacations.

He found Geology great fun because it involved excursions in 'the field'. There was also an unexpected perk to being a Geology student. You were allowed to have a motorbike (with a university licence) so you could go on the field trips. His pride and joy was a blue and silver BSA 250 overhead valve motorbike which he bought off Shropshire friend and neighbour, Alan Henn. The bike already had quite high mileage because Alan had just ridden it back from Malta, where he had completed his National Service. Peter managed to scrape together £75 for the bike, which he adored and even today he says nostalgically that he wished he still owned it. The motorcycle served him well. Not only did he zoom around the Shropshire countryside on it but the bike took him on field trips as far afield as the Isle of Skye in 1951. The beauty of this remote spot made such a great impression on him that he chose to take his bride there on their honeymoon four years later—not, it must be said, on the back of his motorbike!

Peter's enjoyment of motorbikes has never been forgotten. When he was Lord Mayor, he caused quite a stir when he abandoned the official Rolls-Royce for one engagement. To the surprise of many onlookers the Lord Mayor roared into Guildhall Yard astride a motorcycle to present the award to the Despatch Rider of the Year!

Although Peter found his studies hard work, the social and sporting opportunities at Cambridge more than compensated. Rugger, which had been his first love at Wrekin, was swopped for rowing. Inspired by the fact that Jesus College had a good reputation for this sport, Peter set out to 'get an oar'. Undeterred by the fact that he had never rowed before, he set about it with the same determination he has always used when tackling challenges in his life. Practice also made perfect.

In the Lents and Mays Bumping Races, the aim is to catch the boat in front and bump it before getting bumped yourself. If you succeed in bumping the boat in front, the following day you move up a place. Rowing in the fourth Lent boat, Peter was delighted to make four bumps and win his oar in 1951. The oar he was presented with now hangs in his study in Northumberland along with a copy of the photograph commemorating his achievement. Many years later another copy of that photograph prompted one of the oarsmen to write to Peter saying: 'It was a great pleasure to suddenly see a familiar face looking out from a 4th Lent Boat photograph now waving from a golden coach.'

24.   Peter's pride and joy was the motorbike he bought for £75 from Alan Henn.

In his last term in the Mays, Peter rowed in the Jesus Second Eight which rowed over each day, without bumping or being bumped, starting and finishing eighth boat on the river. It was the highest second boat on the river and ahead of many college first boats. Peter's rowing experience has not been totally forgotten. Recently it was reported that he entertained diners in London with a demonstration of the Fairbairn style of rowing, as the Jesus College style is called. It involves hitting the water hard with the oar giving rise to a 'bell note' in contrast to the traditional method of pulling the oar through the water and leaning back, which is a more lengthy movement.

When Peter was at Henley Royal Regatta on one occasion, as a member of the Stewards' Enclosure, with Colonel Miller-Jones (of Thomas Hill-Jones and Co, of which Peter was later to become a non-executive director), Peter was invited to dine at the Savoy. This generous invitation took Peter by surprise and presented a slight problem because he only had his white flannels with him. The colonel brushed his concerns aside saying that

25. The Jesus College fourth Lent boat rowing eight in 1951 when they made four bumps and won their oars. Peter is seated on the far right.

would not cause a problem. However, when they reached the ballroom at the Savoy, the head waiter was very reluctant to admit the incorrectly dressed young man. Colonel Miller-Jones managed to persuade the waiter to let Peter in provided he undertook neither to dance nor draw attention to himself.

A posse of young men surrounded the white-trousered Peter and led him to his seat in the ballroom. For the whole evening he remained sitting, happily listening to Petula Clarke, watching the couples dance, but never getting to his feet until the coast was clear at the end of the evening.

One of Peter's favourite pastimes at Jesus College, which provided valuable training for his future civic career, was debating. He joined the Orators' Debating Society and served on their committee, but never joined the infamous Roosters (that light-hearted club with rituals based on the college's cockerel emblem) as an undergraduate. However he remedied that 30 years later when he returned to Jesus College as Lord Mayor and was 'egged on'. What is normally required is that a student 'rolls to the incubator' but this was thought inappropriate for such an august personage. Sir Peter was allowed to 'turn again' (a highly appropriate expression for one of Dick Whittington's successors!) and it was reported that 'he turned on his vertical axis beautifully'.

Having been brought up to consider the needs of others before himself, it is hardly surprising that Peter should choose to play his part in the College's charitable work. He served as secretary of the Jesus Club for Boys in Camberwell, which was the College's mission. This seems an echo of his father Basil Gadsden's voluntary work in the East End of London when he was a similar age.

As well as the official life of the 'in statu pupillari', as the Cambridge undergraduate is known, there was also the unofficial life. Peter lived with a group of students at 71, Jesus Lane, under the watchful eyes of the landlord and his wife, Mr and Mrs Aves. Each new batch of lodgers was left in no doubt as to how the land lay at number 71: 'I votes Labour because I am Labour,' Mr Aves was in the habit of telling the young gentlemen.

The Aves believed that after years of experience looking after undergraduates, they didn't miss a trick, but that was not always the case. There was one lark when David Tolson, an inmate of number 71, was debagged in college and his trousers were spirited away. The unfortunate young man was left to get back to his digs, minus his trousers, after curfew. The college porter, another person who missed nothing, spotted a trouserless undergraduate dashing out of college, and guessed correctly who it was. Determined to crack down on such unseemly behaviour, the porter set off to telephone the landlady at number 71 in order to verify that the miscreant had returned to his digs minus his trousers. To the porter's surprise Mrs Aves confirmed that David was in his digs, why he had even poked his head round the door to wish her goodnight.

The Aves were not noted for their sense of humour, but to the amusement of the lodgers a notice appeared in the toilet at 71, Jesus Lane, which said 'Don't dribble on the floor'. A few days later this had been amended to 'or the walls' followed the next day by 'or the ceiling'. Levity about such a serious matter was not permitted and Mr Aves complained to the college. Next day all the inmates of number 71 were summoned to appear before the tutor. He stressed the seriousness of this matter and wanted to know who had defaced the notice. As one resident was keen to point out, the amendments were actually in several different hands. Maybe some of their guests were responsible for the graffiti, he added helpfully. Mr Percival was not easily deflected from his enquiry. 'If one of you has got a problem, I can put you in touch with a doctor,' he said grimly as the undergraduates stared down at the floor struggling to contain their giggles. Peter's suggestion they call the perpetrator 'the mystery pee-er' caused everyone to erupt into laughter, including Mr Percival thankfully, and the tension was eased.

Jesus College expected good standards of behaviour from its undergraduates and they were issued with a notice which read:

Unprecedented displays of hysterical hooliganism on the part of undergraduates are treated seriously. Gentlemen are reminded that letting off fireworks in streets and public places is a criminal offence punishable in the Police Courts, besides being an extremely dangerous kind of folly.

It should be understood that it is not the practice of Tutors of this College to go bail for pupils taken by the police; if any gentleman is unfortunate enough to find himself in that position he should not attempt to telephone his Tutor but should make himself as comfortable as possible in the police cells for the night.

Fotunately Peter did not get himself into any such predicaments. Indeed, he would have to wait until he was a sheriff at the Old Bailey before he glimpsed the inside of a police cell.

Even during university days, holidays in Shropshire were cherished because they reunited the Gadsden family. Like most students, university vacations were dominated by the need to earn some money and Peter had various jobs. Whilst at Wrekin he had been a farm labourer for Mr Usherwood in the summer when extra hands were always needed at harvest. Peter soon became a dab hand at scything as well as walking behind the horse-drawn binder and grabbing a corn stook under each arm. The technique was to walk towards another labourer so that when the two of you met, the stooks could be leant in towards each other to form the traditional pyramid shape. Farmer Usherwood never made any concessions for the public schoolboy labourer, quite the opposite! Peter noticed he always got landed with the dirty jobs like creosoting the hen houses.

When he was at university, farm labouring gave way to some slightly better paid jobs. Christmas holidays always meant working at the Bridgnorth Post Office sorting Christmas mail. One summer he worked at the Radiogramophone Development Company (known as RGD) in Bridgnorth. Then in the summer of 1951 he took an altogether more exciting and dangerous job working for the Aviation Department of Pest Control (UK) Ltd who were based in Cambridge. Peter and a colleague had to don white overalls and gas masks to stand in the potato fields of Lincolnshire or the hop fields of Kent. Far from being scarecrows, they were actually human markers for the crop-spraying helicopter which strafed the lines of plants with noxious sprays. The pilot lined his machine up on the men at each end of the row then flew down spraying. As soon as the helicopter began its run the marker quickly got out of the way before it reached him. Whilst the helicopter was turning the markers moved to stand at the end of the next row ready for the return run. Scary stuff!

The job did have its hazards at least for the pilot if not for the human markers. One time when Peter was standing in position in the hop field, he watched the helicopter take off then nosedive straight into the adjacent sports field. Fortunately no one was hurt but the helicopter blades were broken and the day's work lost.

Three years at Cambridge passed all too quickly and it was decision time. Peter graduated as a Bachelor of Arts in June 1952 and four years later he received a Master of Arts degree. In 1988 Jesus College, Cambridge, was pleased to make their distinguished graduate an Honorary Fellow.

Initially Peter had considered a career in teaching, then lured by the prospect of foreign travel he wondered about a post in the Colonial Service. However the prospect of another year's study soon quashed both ideas. But what else? When he went to the University Appointments Board he

26. Peter and a colleague, both here heavily disguised, worked for a crop spraying company during college vacation. They acted as human markers in the field whilst a helicopter strafed the crops with toxic sprays.

told them he was keen on something in 'administration'. 'It was the great word then; we all said that but nobody really knew what it meant,' he recalls. The Appointments Board fixed up six interviews for him.

In May 1952 Peter went for an interview with Mr Mungo Campbell, a director of Fergusson Wild and Co. The firm, a subsidiary of William Baird and part of the Northern Mercantile and Investment Corporation, was proudly Scottish and Peter was warned by the University Appointments Board that the firm had 'a natural leaning towards Scotsmen', so he should not be disheartened if they did not offer him a job. However Mr Campbell was so impressed by the 22-year-old that he offered him a post at a salary of £500 per annum. Interestingly in his letter of appointment, Mr Campbell mentioned that his nephew would also have liked to employ Peter for his company, the Sierra Leone Development Company, whose mines produced the iron ore Fergusson Wild sold.

27.   Peter graduated with a Bachelor of Arts degree in June 1952 and received his Master of Arts four years later. Initially he went up to Cambridge to read Physics, Chemistry and Geology, but soon changed from Physics to Mineralogy.

Chapter 6

Starting Out in Business

Lawful gain may and ought to be made of the business which you engage in; for without this, few men would be able to support themselves and their families, or do much good to others. But greediness after gain is a mischievous thing.

(Rule XXIX from *Rules for the Conduct of Life*, a book written by a former Lord Mayor and given to every freeman of the City of London.)

Fergusson Wild and Co Ltd was founded in the nineteenth century as an iron ore and ship chartering business based in the City of London. In September 1952 when Peter Gadsden joined them straight from university as a trainee in the marketing of minerals, it was felt he needed some basic office training. The firm arranged for him to spend his first three months on a Pitman business course in Bloomsbury, where he would attend lectures on accountancy, company law, economics and general secretarial practice as well as visit other offices to get an idea of how these things worked on a daily basis.

Freshly armed with his knowledge of modern office practice, Peter reappeared at Fergusson Wild's office at 15, St Helen's Place, Bishopsgate, at the beginning of 1953 for the next stage of his induction. This was the hands-on part of the work he had been looking forward to. A week's visit to a French iron ore mine was arranged and then Peter was required to submit a report on all aspects of the company's work beginning with the extraction of the ore through all the processes to the transportation of the finished product.

Writing reports has never presented Peter with any problems. It may not be something he relishes but his clear logical mind can extract the pertinent points and present them in an organised form which is a delight to read. Wrekin had prepared him well.

Quite early on Peter learned an important lesson. His boss, Guy Falla, encountered the trainee manager arranging to cross the channel by boat

28.   This was one of Peter's first overseas business trips in 1953 when he visited Sierra Leone. It seems hard to believe that he was at first apprehensive about flying when he later travelled many thousands of air miles during his business career.

because he wasn't keen on flying. 'If you are not prepared to fly, you might as well get out of business now,' was the blunt advice. It seems amazing that Peter, who has flown thousands of miles and lost count of the number of times he has flown round the world, should ever have had qualms about flying to Paris, but this was his first trip on a BEA Elizabethan. He had no opportunity to build up his flying experience gradually because his next overseas assignment was in Africa. In October 1953 he was sent on a three-week visit to the group's mines at Marampa in Sierra Leone to report on all aspects of their production of iron ore.

And so began his flying experiences. During an extensive business career, Peter would undertake vast amounts of air travel that would take him through the age of piston engine aircraft (De Havilland Rapide, Ambassador (Elizabethan), Argonaut, Stratocruiser, Super Constellation, Dakota (DC3, DC4 and DC6), into the turbo-prop age (Viscount, Vanguard, Electra and Britannia), then into the jet age (Caravelle, Comet, VC 10,

BAC One-Eleven, Boeing 737, 707, 767, 777, 747, Tri-star, Trident) and finally into the supersonic age with Concorde, which sadly is no longer with us. Of these planes his favourites were the Viscount, VC 10, Comet 4, 747 and Concorde.

When Peter was 24, long-distance flights involved stopping overnight with the crew at one of BOAC's Speedbird houses, before carrying on the next morning. A journey to Sierra Leone involved flying with the West African Airways from Dakar to Bathurst then on to Lungi. In contrast to London airport, Peter descended onto a landing strip at Lungi with a tiny hut to one side. He was warned that it was quite likely on the return flight the pilot might need to run down the landing strip himself to shoo the cattle away before the plane could take off.

The mines were 50 or 60 miles from the airport along a bumpy unmade track. The whole thing was a baptism of fire for Peter—almost literally. That night the hot oppressive air changed dramatically into a thunderstorm of biblical proportions. 'The bungalow in which I was staying was struck and damage was caused to the roof, the bath, electric light fittings and fuse boxes,' Peter's official report noted in a matter-of-fact way. Privately he conceded he was terrified.

During his visit to Marampa there was no opportunity for sightseeing, far from it. Apart from socialising with the mine operators in order to understand how the production process worked, he followed the passage of ore from where it was mined, through its chemical analysis and onto the lorries. Administration and maintenance at the mines also had to be observed and reported on. Then it was off to Pepel Port to watch the ore being loaded onto ships, and see the customs procedures for himself. At all stages of production Peter was required to find out what wages were paid to the Africans and to the Europeans employed at this plant. He had a wide-ranging brief which required him to look at the housing, health, leisure and welfare facilities the employees received as well as their general morale. All of these things helped Peter to build up a picture of the reliability of supplies from this mine and how the costs were arrived at. As he went around, Peter kept detailed notes, drew maps of the area, of the site and took his own photographs. Within a day of returning home the finished report landed on Guy Falla's desk. Peter had demonstrated he could grasp a situation and report on it succinctly. This has been a skill which has stood him in good stead throughout his business career and been often admired when he has chaired committee meetings.

Peter has always felt a deep debt of gratitude to Guy Falla. He was a larger-than-life figure who lived life to the full and urged his protégé to do the same. 'The worst thing in life is to do nothing,' Falla told Peter. 'Make a decision. You won't be right all the time but hopefully you'll be right more times than you are wrong.' Peter found this valuable advice and a logical extension of his headmaster 'Maxie' Gordon's insistence that you should 'make the most of your opportunities'.

Although Peter was fresh out of university, he was trusted to travel round the world on Fergusson Wild's business. There were the exotic locations like Morocco and other parts of Africa, Australia, New Zealand and China, as well as European countries such as France, Germany, Holland and Eastern Europe where he bought and sold minerals.

If Peter was travelling long distances that required stop-overs on the way he tried to incorporate business into these breaks as well. Careful planning to maximize the use of his time has remained a feature of his travel, both business and private. Things didn't always run smoothly. Peter recalls how some of his best-laid plans came to nought. On his way home from the Far East one time, he dozed on the plane and when he awoke was suddenly aware that the sun was coming in from the other side of the cabin; engine trouble had forced the plane to turn back to Bahrain. In those days before mobile phones, it was nigh impossible to get messages to your next appointment to warn them of unexpected delays.

Travelling so much, Peter got wise to some of the airlines little ploys. When he was flying Qantas from Cairo, a member of the ground staff came up to him asking for his boarding card to be handed back. 'There has been some mistake,' she began, putting her hand out to receive his card. Peter was not going to fall for that one and refused to surrender the document. He later learned that Qantas had overbooked the flight and were planning to bump him off the plane.

Considering the large number of flights Peter has made, he has been very lucky and only has a few horror stories to tell. His most frightening flight was on a Pan American Boeing 707 bound for San Francisco across the Pacific. So turbulent was the passage that the crew remained strapped in their seats the whole time. Peter had visions of his family reading a newspaper over breakfast that carried headlines about a plane having gone down in the Pacific.

Life was not all foreign travel. Peter drove around the United Kingdom in the Standard car provided, to places like Sheffield, Liverpool, Bilston,

Stoke-on-Trent and Cardiff selling minerals to the chemical and ceramic industries. He soon learned that turning up on firms without an appointment rarely produced any business. As a keen trainee he tried phoning round first to enquire whether a firm might be interested in Fergusson Wild's minerals but that never worked. The Sheffield firms were loyal to their suppliers so it was extremely difficult to even get an appointment to see the buyers. They were always 'too busy'. However, Peter thought he was on to something the time he phoned one steel producer. A bright young voice asked him which department he wanted and Peter said,

'Minerals.'

'Certainly, Sir, I'll put you through.'

There was a click, and a pause, and a voice the other end said, 'Canteen manager.'

Not put off by this, Peter developed another strategy to get potential British customers to see him. He would first phone the firm and after sweet-talking the telephonist would manage to get the buyer's name from her. This enabled him to write directly to the buyer and make an appointment. Once again experience taught him that any request for an appointment was invariably ignored, so he would write saying he was in the area on a certain date and would call at a certain time unless he heard to the contrary. This was a reasonably foolproof method of getting an appointment because Peter knew full well the buyer would not bother to acknowledge the letter or to cancel the appointment. When Peter turned up at the arranged time he was able to show the receptionist he did have an appointment and usually gained the access he sought.

After getting the necessary appointment with one Sheffield buyer, Peter and a colleague, Edgar Ridgeway, decided to follow up their business meeting by inviting the buyer out to lunch. Peter recalls with amusement that the buyer spent ages perusing the menu before looking up at the waitress and saying, 'I'll have the Con Some to start with.' With a twinkle in his eye, Peter's colleague added: 'Yes, and I'll have the Mine Strone, please.'

Fergusson Wild were keen to develop their employees' business skills and they encouraged further training. Two years after he joined the company, Peter was funded to spend August at the university in Barcelona to learn Spanish and gain some insight into Spanish business practice. The knowledge proved useful when he visited Morocco because in 1956 the country was divided into two zones: French Morocco and Spanish

29. 'Miner Gadsden'.

Morocco. As usual Peter's brief was to visit the mines, meet the people involved in all aspects of production and assess whether Fergusson Wild should take a financial interest in one of the mines. In his report Peter remarked on the contrasts he had observed in the French zone which, he explained, he had gained first-hand knowledge of 'by eating with a group of poor Moroccans squatting on the ground and by spending an evening with the wealthy Tazi family and attending a cocktail party at the Governor's Palace'. Here is interesting evidence of the way Peter has been able to join in with people of all nationalities and walks of life. This oft-admired skill he puts down to his upbringing because the rector's son was expected to get on with everybody. Others put it down to the charm of this talented man.

Having a working knowledge of Spanish was certainly a help in the Spanish zone but travelling through it was still potentially hazardous. To reach the mine there was a 10 km mule ride through mountains patrolled by armed bandits. 'One person, Mr Mikesell (on a Ford Foundation scholarship for 18 months studying geomorphology),' reported Peter, 'was taken prisoner by the army of liberation for four days and eventually taken before their CO who spoke English. When he heard Mikesell's subject he gave him a letter in Arabic. Now whenever Mikesell shows this letter he gets a tremendous welcome although few Moroccans can read its contents but they all recognise the seal.'

Peter's experiences were less hair-raising but still testing. 'We experienced many difficulties during our visit, including the breakdown of a jeep at midnight, and time wasted due entirely to lack of organisation. On one occasion we set out for a mineral deposit and were told that it was not far and we would be back about noon for lunch. The deposit turned out to be very far away and we finally arrived back about 5 o'clock having had nothing to eat since breakfast. We also had many difficulties over visas, all of which could have been avoided had the necessary action been taken before we left Casablanca,' he reported to the London office.

Doing business in some parts of Africa had its own quirks especially if you wanted to make a phone call to the UK, Peter recalls. Whenever possible he sent a cable to London using his own special shorthand code to keep costs down. However on one occasion whilst visiting Salisbury in Rhodesia, a problem arose that had to be discussed with the London office. Only a phone call would do. These had to be booked with the operator and literally took days to arrange. This was unproductive time spent hanging around as Peter explained to his host. 'Don't worry, I can sort that out for you,' the man said. 'I've got influence.' And with that he rang the telephone exchange and explained that he needed to make an urgent phone call to London because it was a matter of life or death. Within an hour the call to London came through.

Just as Peter and his friend were congratulating themselves on the fact that it's not what you know, but who you know, the phone rang again. This time it was the operator. 'I've just been listening to that call you made,' she said. 'And that wasn't a matter of life or death. I'm reporting you to the postmaster general.' Thinking quickly, Peter's colleague said, 'I assure you that conversation you listened into was a matter of life or death. It was all in code, that was why you didn't understand it.'

You learn as you go: Peter certainly did. One friend told him that to boost the price of a certain share it was necessary to start a rumour. So a rumour was started in Africa but nobody showed the slightest interest. Eventually the man decided that it was no good starting rumours in Africa, they had to originate in London, so he flew back to London and started the

30.   The Marampa mines were owned by the Sierra Leone Development Company, part of the same group as Fergusson Wild, Peter's employers. The mines produced iron ore.

rumour there. Sure enough when it reached Africa, investors sat up and took notice!

One conversation Peter had with a doctor in Sierra Leone made a profound impression on him. The doctor was trying to help Peter understand the differences between African problems and European ones. 'If you have a cold,' he said, 'it is a nuisance. But if you have a stomach problem that is serious. Now if the Africans have a stomach problem it is okay, but a cold is very serious.'

It was the health of the locals that worried Peter when he first travelled to India on business. So many people he encountered appeared to be bleeding from the mouth that he was sure the country must have a rampant TB problem. Conversations with regular business travellers put him right. Many of the people he had seen had been chewing betel nuts in much the same way as Americans chew gum, the only difference was that betel nuts dye everything blood red. 'One time when I stayed in a hotel in Quilon, I shared a bathroom with a large cockroach and the sheets and pillow here were stained red by betel nut,' Peter said. All very unnerving for the novice traveller!

On one occasion Peter's kindness caused him rather more difficulties than he anticipated. An Indian customer asked if Peter would bring a package out to Calcutta when he next came. Peter was surprised when he received the message that he must collect some tropical fish from a shop near Victoria Station. Fortunately they were all packed up in polythene bags and put in a cardboard carrying box. With them came instructions for transit: each bag must be opened every four hours to let the fish breathe and food must be given.

On the plane the fish box was stored behind his seat in first class and he duly attended to them on the flight. At Cairo, where he was stopping over, customs refused to let the fish in on the grounds they might harbour disease. Arguing that officials would have to feed them, Peter was eventually permitted to 'import' them on condition he never did it again.

In his hotel room some plastic bags were put in the washbasin while the rest remained in the box. In the night Peter was woken by strange sploshing sounds to find that the soggy box had tipped over and released fish all over the floor. They were eventually caught and Peter returned to bed.

Next morning he and the fish were permitted on board the flight to Calcutta, but on arrival he had the same problem importing his fish. Employing all his negotiating skills, Peter argued his case once more. It was probably the look on his face, when he vowed he would *never ever* do it again, that persuaded the Indian customs officials to let the fish through.

And then, after all Peter's loving attention, the fish's new owner later admitted that he had lost one down the sink when he unpacked them!

Visits to Africa in the 1950s were memorable for all sorts of reasons. The first time Peter flew into Johannesburg from Australia, the officials decided he needed a visa travelling on a Canadian passport. But Peter had already checked this before he left London and was assured no visa was needed. However when he arrived on an evening flight from Perth, the immigration officer took a different view. 'Without a visa you spend a night in the cells and we issue a visa in the morning,' he said with every intention of enforcing it. Peter was horrified. His protestations about what the travel agent in London had told him were ignored and it was far too late in the evening to get hold of anyone to help him.

Then he remembered. 'I have a letter of welcome from your ambassador in London who has put his office at my disposal. I don't think he will be too impressed to hear about the way you have treated me,' Peter said, watching the official's expression change as he looked down at the letter. The immigration officer was straight on the phone. Instantly a visa was issued. Whilst attempting to maintain an apparent lack of concern, Peter could not help but breathe a huge sigh of relief.

Visits to Africa were never tedious and Peter encountered great friendship. One of the things he always liked was the standard greeting he received when visiting Sierra Leone. 'Thank you for your journey,' they would say graciously. Many years later as Lord Mayor, Peter surprised the President of Sierra Leone at a Mansion House dinner by opening his speech with this lovely greeting.

In the 1950s what struck Peter most about South Africa was that here was 'a continent of great scenic beauty and animal life that was being torn

31.   Peter photographed a group of residents during his visit to the Marampa mines of the Sierra Leone Development Company in 1953. As well as learning about iron ore production, he was required to find out about the different wages and welfare facilities employees received.

asunder by deteriorating race relations'. He wrote an account of a visit in 1958 explaining that as the plane came in to land in Johannesburg, he saw the gold dumps that surrounded the city. Once on the ground though it was the cruelty of apartheid which made a profound impression on him.

> We see the apparent desolation, the hopelessness, the hate, the bitterness and the fear from a people in their homeland without a vote. We will probably never again see such contrast as between European palaces with their servants, cars, tennis courts and swimming pools and the bewildered Africans with their corrugated huts. As the paper is pushed under the door of our hotel room each morning, we catch a glimpse of headlines such as 'Non-whites Barred from Pretoria Athletics'.

During this business trip Peter took the opportunity to join Sunday worshippers in the township of Sophiatown. This was only a few years after the Reverend Trevor Huddleston had done his best to prevent the forceful eviction of black Africans from the township.

> Picture it—a big church with cheerful Africans, their eyes sparkling as they hold their lighted candles—a choir singing beautifully and then the procession with sacred ministers, servers and African congregation. A simple and beautiful sermon by Father Jack Guinness C.R. which is translated, sentence by sentence into the two main languages—Xhosa and Secunana—by two interpreters standing on his right and left. One felt honoured to be one of two or three Europeans amongst hundreds of Africans. Here is a spark of love amidst hate and bitterness.

> Outside empty shells remain as temporary memorials to those who have been evicted. Anyone found in Sophiatown without a pass is arrested and probably handcuffed. The Minister of Native Affairs has power to segregate the races completely and Europeans may not be allowed to work in new African areas.

This wonderfully evocative extract is from an article Peter wrote for the parish magazine of St Stephen's, Gloucester Road, South Kensington, a High Anglican church which he attended and where he served at Mass. At that time Father Eric Cheetham was the priest-in-charge and a most inspirational leader. 'It may truly be said of Eric Cheetham that he was a Pastor and a Shepherd of souls in the fullest sense,' his obituary writer stated. TS Eliot, the poet, was a member of the congregation at the same time as Peter and his tribute to Father Cheetham in the parish magazine said the pastor had made St Stephen's 'a centre of Evangelical Catholicism: truly Catholic and truly wholly Anglican'.

Looking back over this period in his life, Peter has nothing but the greatest admiration for Guy Falla. He, more than anyone else, influenced the way in which Peter went on to conduct business. Guy Falla has to rank alongside Peter's father and his headmaster, Guy Pentreath, as one of the major influences in Peter's life. It is a fitting legacy to Guy Falla that his protégé should have gained worldwide recognition as a successful businessman.

All too quickly Falla was removed from the scene, brutally cut down by a massive heart attack at the age of 50. Peter felt things were never the same at Fergusson Wild after that. Falla's successor, David Dale, worked in a completely different way and his approach to business did not sit comfortably alongside Peter's. With customary charitableness, Peter believes he did learn some useful lessons from his new boss. One of them was that every piece of correspondence must stand alone and be accurate. Dale insisted, for instance, that if Fergusson Wild required a reply to their letter, then a date must be specified and the matter not be left open-ended. Peter incorporated these points into his own business practice and many colleagues since have had cause to be grateful that they could pick up any one of Peter's letters and at a glance know the current position of a transaction.

Having learned a great deal from his first job, Peter felt it was time to move on. His regular visits to Australia on behalf of Fergusson Wild had given him excellent contacts in the mineral sands industry down under and he was now prepared to listen to the sirens' voices from that quarter.

One of the things Peter is proud of from his Fergusson Wild days is that he corrected a long-running error. 'We bought "Manganese Peroxide" regularly,' he recalls, 'But from my chemistry I knew that was an incorrect name. So I changed the name to Manganese Dioxide—and so it is called today. You change the name for everyone thereafter.'

Chapter 7

A Family Man

All the world's a stage,
And all the men and women merely players:
They have their exits and their entrances;
And one man in his time plays many parts.

William Shakespeare, *As You Like It*

In the early 1950s Peter rented a room in digs near Sloane Square where the landlady, Miss Clark, carefully angled her mirror in the hall to observe the comings and goings of the lodgers. At that time Peter's work was based in St Helen's Place, Bishopsgate. It was a long running joke that someone would ring up and ask, 'What makes Fergusson wild?' The answer given was always 'St Helen's place'. In his first 18 months with Fergusson Wild, he had already travelled throughout Europe and Africa.

Although Peter did not earn a great deal of money, it did not prevent him enjoying a good social life. Since arriving in London he had a few girlfriends, but none it must be said to rival his childhood sweethearts. One of his earliest flames had been 'Goldie teeth', the girl he had gazed adoringly across the pews at when he was a pupil at The Elms school. By the age of sixteen his affections had transferred to Juliet, the daughter of a local landowner. When the rector's children were invited to tennis parties, Peter, the eldest of the group, always partnered Juliet, the youngest in the group. She was, however, only ten years old so this was unlikely to be a re-enactment of Shakespeare's famous love story; indeed the young girl was probably totally unaware of the feelings she engendered.

When it came to 'real' girlfriends, Mary from a village near Bridgnorth can probably claim to be the first. However, one major impediment to the progress of this romance was that Mary's mother strongly disapproved of her daughter zooming round the lanes on the back of Peter's motorbike.

During their romance, which took place during Peter's time at Cambridge, he took her to London to see *South Pacific*. He remembers being so moved by the song 'Some Enchanted Evening' that he told Mary whenever he heard that song he would think of her and to this day he still does.

Other romantic attachments followed when he was working in London and it was as Peter was parting company with Jennifer, a model, that he met his next girlfriend Sheila, and then later Dominie at the English Speaking Union. None of these were destined to be long-lasting but as Peter and Dominie's relationship ended, she mentioned that she had a school friend whom she thought Peter would get on well with. He mentioned this to a Cambridge colleague he was now sharing a room with off the Kings Road, and the two decided to invite Dominie and her friend, Belinda, round for coffee one evening to 'check her out'.

When Peter asked Dominie more about the girl he was going to meet, he was surprised to learn that Belinda worked at 15 St Helen's Place where he did; whereupon he commented that he hadn't seen anyone there he thought he'd like to see again! In the lift the next day he asked the lift attendant in his office block if she knew a Belinda. 'Who? Belinda blue-eyes? Yes she works on the top floor,' came the reply. He asked her to point the girl out if they shared a lift. True to her word she did.

On the day they were due to meet Peter was standing in a crowded lift with his bowler and rolled umbrella, when he noticed a pretty girl who was obviously late, dash into the lift. 'Oh that's the girl you wanted to meet,' announced the lift attendant loudly. A rather embarrassed Peter said to Belinda, 'I believe we are meeting this evening.' After that romantic little encounter in the lift, the rest is history, as they say.

The two became unofficially engaged in the July and officially engaged on 23 September 1954. The official date offered the chance of a double celebration as it was also Belinda's 21st birthday. Seventy people joined the couple for a cocktail party at Ellingham Hall in Northumberland, Belinda's ancestral home. This was to be the beginning of a very happy relationship and a wonderful partnership.

As Darby Johns, a friend and business colleague, put it: 'Any biography of Sir Peter would be incomplete without mention of Lady Gadsden. She, like Sir Peter, blends into local situation so well that people just think of her as their friend.'

Their engagement was widely reported in all the newspapers and magazines from the *Berwick Advertiser* through to *The Times*. A beautiful portrait of Belinda graced the opening page of *Country Life* on 24th March and announced her forthcoming marriage to Mr Peter Drury Gadsden on 16 April 1955. For Peter this was the beginning of a life where many of his activities would be reported in the newspapers.

As the eldest daughter and heiress of Sir Hugh Carnaby de Marie Haggerston the eleventh Baronet (Carnaby Street in London was once part of the family's property), Belinda belongs to one of the oldest Roman Catholic families in the country, descended from the Plantagenets through Henry II. In 1297 John de Hagardeston swore fealty to Edward I. The first Haggerston (as the spelling eventually became) to be created a baronet was Sir Thomas, a colonel of one of the Royalist regiments during the Civil War. In return for his allegiance in October 1642, Charles I created him first Baronet of Haggerston Castle.

An amusing anecdote has been handed down the family from the late seventeenth century when Mass was celebrated at Haggerston Castle. It is said that on one occasion when the priest announced, 'Next Sunday Mass will be celebrated at nine o'clock', Lady Haggerston interrupted, 'Nine-thirty.' The priest smiled and continued, 'Next Sunday I shall be celebrating Mass at nine. Lady Haggerston will say Mass at nine-thirty.'

The second Baronet became governor of Berwick Castle and by the time of the fifth Baronet, the family were well-established in royal circles. The baronet's sister-in-law was Mrs Fitzherbert, unofficial wife of the Prince Regent, later George IV.

A humorous story about the fifth Lady Haggerston appears in a book about the social fortunes of Brighton written by Osbert Sitwell and Margaret Barton. During the Regency period her ladyship rented a house for the season in fashionable Brighton and invited the Prince to a 'fête champêtre', as she termed her pastoral tableaux. She had her garden transformed into a genteel farmyard for the occasion, complete with Alderney cattle. When the Prince arrived with his entourage, her ladyship came tripping out of a side gate dressed as a milkmaid ready to make His Royal Highness's favourite syllabub. One of those present reported what happened.

> She had a silver pail in one hand and an ornamental stool in the other. Lady Haggerston tripped along, with ribbons flying from her dainty little milking-hat that hung on one side of her graceful head, and the smallest little apron tied below her laced stomacher, till she came opposite his Royal Highness, to whom she dropped a rurally graceful curtsey. Then passing lightly over

32.   Engagement portrait of Belinda in *Country Life* in 1954.

the beautifully plaited straw, her tucked-up gown showing her neat ankle as well as her coloured stockings, she placed her stool and pail conveniently for use. Leaning against the flank of one of the crossest of the Alderneys, she was attempting to commence her rustic labours; but not having selected the right sex, the offended animal did not seem to fancy such masquerade, for he first kicked out and then trotted away, nearly upsetting stool, pail and Lady Haggerston, who then covered with confusion, made a hasty retreat back into her little dairy.

Belinda's mother, Mary, Lady Haggerston, bore absolutely no resemblance to her frivolous predecessor. She was a member of the Macy family from New York who could trace their ancestry back to a whaling family on Nantucket Island. Years later the family moved to New York where they founded Macy's department store. Belinda's parents met in Bermuda where her mother was on holiday and Captain Sir Hugh Carnaby de Marie Haggerston was serving with the 1st Battalion Royal Northumberland Fusiliers. The couple married in New York but their first child, Belinda Ann de Marie was born in Hamilton, Bermuda, in 1933. She remembers little of her time on the beautiful island because the family left for Egypt in 1936 where they remained for a couple of years. It was there that Lady Haggerston contracted typhoid and Belinda's little brother Peter was born prematurely. Tragically he died of meningitis at the age of three months and is buried in Cairo. Belinda was taken to America by her mother who wanted to return to her own family for a while to recover from her illness. Sir Carnaby never got over this tragedy which left him without a son and heir and meant the end of the Haggerston lineage.

At the beginning of the war by a strange twist of fate, Belinda and Peter both resided in the Blackrock district of Dublin for a few months. Belinda had come over with her American grandmother, her Aunt Pamela, her mother (then expecting her third daughter Helias) and little sister Jennifer. Since Aunt Pamela was only ten years older than Belinda, they both attended the Convent of the Sacred Heart, Mount Anville, for several terms. (In November 1980, during Peter's mayoralty, it gave Belinda great pleasure to revisit her old school at Mount Anville, Blackrock, and to be reunited with one of the nuns who had taught her.) Later the family moved to the United States and thence to Bermuda, eventually returning to England aboard a troop ship in a convoy. Belinda has clear memories of struggling to carry her cork life jacket whilst her mother coped with the two younger girls. Their father, Sir Carnaby, was away on active service at the time.

Most of Belinda's schooling took place at the Sacred Heart Convent, Woldingham, in Surrey and holidays were spent in Northumberland. The Haggerstons no longer lived at Haggerston Castle which had parted company with the family in the 1850s and fallen into such a ruinous state that it was largely demolished in 1931 and is now a caravan site. Belinda's family officially resided at Ellingham Hall on their 4,000 acre estate near Chathill in Northumberland. The original Queen Anne building had also been demolished because it had become dilapidated and the present hall, complete with its own chapel, dates from 1900. However, during the Second World War Ellingham Hall was commandeered by the army, then as soon as they left the Ministry of Food took it over. Flour and sugar were stored on the ground floor and the family were only permitted to move back into the upper floors. So when Lady Haggerston returned from Bermuda with her three daughters towards the end of the war, she had to stay with her mother-in-law, Florence, Lady Haggerston, in the Dower House.

33. Ellingham Hall, the Haggerston family seat in Northumberland. The original hall was demolished at the end of the nineteenth century and replaced by a new hall in 1900.

This lovely stone house, called Harelaw, became Peter and Belinda's official Northumberland residence when Lady Haggerston died in 1981. The Gadsden family enjoyed escaping the pressures of city and business for the peace of the Northumberland moors. Today the house is still a place for family gatherings like weddings and Christmas festivities although some of the four children and seventeen grandchildren have to be billeted around the neighbourhood a little nowadays.

Peter has a clear recollection of how nervous he was the first time he was taken to meet Belinda's father, though he needed to have no concern. His future father-in-law was more than happy to welcome him as Belinda's prospective husband. Peter believes this was because Sir Carnaby was a gentleman of the old school, admired by many, who missed having a son to share the masculine country pursuits of hunting, shooting and fishing on the estate. Lady Haggerston, however, took a little more convincing that Peter was the right person for her eldest daughter. She would have preferred a Roman Catholic husband for Belinda. Years later though, Lady Haggerston was proud to attend the Lord Mayor's banquet when her son-in-law held high office. Sadly Sir Carnaby did not live to see that, but he had taken great delight in attending Sir Peter Studd's Lord Mayor's banquet when his son-in-law was a sheriff of London. On that occasion the well-read gentleman intrigued his fellow diners by describing the family history of those being presented to the Lord Mayor.

Behind the happiness of the newly engaged couple loomed one dark cloud in the form of Peter's father. As a fervent Evangelical Anglican, the Reverend Basil Gadsden was vehemently anti-Catholic and dismayed at the prospect of his son's marriage to a Roman Catholic girl. Whilst Peter understood that his parents might not wish to attend the marriage ceremony he did hope they might be present for the reception. Sadly that was not to be. There could be no compromise for the clergyman who regarded his son's marriage to a Catholic as an insurmountable problem. Peter's mother was upset by Basil's view but out of loyalty to her husband could not attend her elder son's wedding though she dearly wished to.

Although the wedding was not attended by Peter's parents, his godmother Avenel Drew represented the family. The marriage took place in the private oratory chapel at Ellingham Hall. Because this is a family chapel it is tiny and the ceremony could only be witnessed by the closest family and friends. By contrast the reception at the Hall was attended by 160 guests described by the local paper as 'some of the most prominent Northumbrian families'.

34. Peter and Belinda emerge from the private oratory chapel at Ellingham Hall after their wedding ceremony on 16 April 1955.

At the time of their marriage in April 1955, Peter was made aware that he would have to take the Haggerston surname and arms at some point. After Sir Carnaby's death his solicitors requested Peter sign the deed of covenant undertaking to take the Haggerston surname as well as quarter the family coat of arms with his own. By that time Peter was well-established in business nationally and internationally. He was concerned that a complete change of surname could cause problems. Fortunately the Haggerston solicitors were sympathetic to Peter's wish to observe the spirit of the agreement and permitted him to incorporate the Haggerston surname into his name. In 1973 he became officially recognised as Mr Peter Drury Haggerston Gadsden by Royal Licence.

Back in London in 1955, the newly wedded Gadsdens needed larger living quarters than Peter's single room in Sloane Square, so they moved to a bigger bedsit in Campden Hill, off High Street Kensington. Several months later, and with a baby on the way, they moved to a one-bedroomed flat in Earls Court Square which they rented for the princely sum of two

35.   Peter and Belinda, the proud parents of Juliet, their first daughter born in 1956.

pounds and ten shillings a week. Fortunately in the days after the war, rent was controlled. Belinda had anticipated resuming her secretarial work once she had set up a home for them both but the arrival of two babies in quick succession put a different perspective on things. Both Juliet and Caroline were born when the family lived in the one-bedroomed flat, so space was tight. Fortunately Peter's employers, Fergusson Wild, offered them a family house in Surrey for rent. This was gratefully accepted. The house in Woodmansterne Road in Carshalton Beeches proved an excellent family home and was convenient for Peter to get to business in the City. Later, on leaving Fergusson Wild, he was offered the chance of buying the property from his employer and that enabled the Gadsdens to remain there until 1969 when they moved into the Barbican, City of London.

The Surrey house was conveniently situated for a growing family because school and shops were all within walking distance. This was especially important to Belinda who could not drive then. Peter was abroad for weeks on end sometimes, so she was able to put the youngest girls in the pushchair and walk round, via the shops, to collect the elder two from school.

The Reverend Basil Gadsden died in June 1958. After 15 years as rector at Astley Abbotts he had moved to the parish of Whitney with Winforton in the diocese of Hereford in 1955. He and May were staying with Peter's brother David near Horsham at the time. It was the day before they were due to go on holiday to Spain. Basil retired to bed early because he felt unwell and died from a heart attack. This came as a great shock to the family since he was only 65, in good health, and had not yet retired from the ministry.

Following Basil's death, May went to live in Kidlington near her daughter Daphne. Peter admits that relations with his father had been difficult at times but after his death Peter grew close to his mother, as did Belinda. Indeed Belinda nursed her mother-in-law during her battle with cancer. Sadly May died in 1964 before she was able to see her son hold the highest civic office. However, she was able to take pleasure from Peter's impressive start in business and the knowledge that he had become a member of the Worshipful Company of Clothworkers. Another great joy to her were the four granddaughters Peter and Belinda gave her.

In the early days of their marriage, Peter promised Belinda he would buy a gold charm for her bracelet for every country he spent a night in on his travels. Today she has 65 charms on the 'infidelity bracelet', as Peter nicknamed it—so many in fact that they have to be accommodated on two bracelets! The couple also have a huge stack of postcards because Peter sent Belinda a postcard every day he was away. Sometimes there was a bit of a backlog, he admits, and he had to write three in one go!

The years the family lived in Surrey remain as fond memories in the minds of them all. The girls recall sunny Sundays spent sitting on the grass watching their father play cricket for Purley Cricket Club. ('But he was usually out for a duck' one of his daughters added!) Peter so enjoyed those sunny afternoons that he was happy to return to Purley Cricket Club, where he had once served on the committee, to open their new clubroom when he was Lord Mayor. He presented them with the Sir Peter Gadsden cup to be awarded to the winner of the annual squash tournament they held.

It was in the early 1960s, when they were still living at Carshalton Beeches, that Peter met Derek East, a friend of Christopher Rawson's, who offered the Gadsden family use of his little house called The Refuge at East Wittering for a seaside holiday one year. Peter, Belinda and the girls spent the most wonderful time there because the garden of The Refuge opens directly onto the beach. When they returned to Surrey, Peter mentioned to Derek that if he should ever consider selling his holiday home please would he give them first refusal. He smiled but said, 'Sorry, we'd never sell it.'

Three months later he seems to have had second thoughts. Totally out of the blue, Peter received a phone call from Derek asking if they would like it as he was moving to the Channel Islands. There was never any doubt. This was the seaside home for them and Peter said 'Yes please'. Since then the Gadsden family have spent every August at East Wittering and many other weekends there too. It was customary for Belinda and the girls to go down to Wittering as soon as school broke up in July and to stay until term resumed in the autumn. Peter joined them every weekend and took his summer holiday there. When they did return to Woodmansterne Road in September the lawn was usually sky high and drawing frowns from their keen gardening neighbours!

36. The Refuge at East Wittering as it looked when Peter and Belinda first bought it in the early 1960s. Then as now, this was the scene of many happy family holidays although today the house has been demolished and totally rebuilt.

37. The new Refuge in the process of construction in 2002.

Owning a property in Wittering for so long has enabled Peter and Belinda to become involved in activities in the area. Most notably Peter has been a loyal supporter of the Chichester Festival Theatre whose performances take place during the summer weeks they are at The Refuge. He has been a trustee of Chichester Festival Theatre since 1977 and is now a Friend and patron of the Theatre. In a speech he gave as Lord Mayor at a civic luncheon in Chichester Peter said, 'We have been supporters of the Chichester Festival Theatre almost since its foundation and I don't think we have missed a play since 1964.' This has pretty well remained true because the only play they missed was in 2001 when Peter was ill.

'At Wittering, weather permitting, every main meal is a barbeque and I am quite good at barbequed pheasant! You would not find me dressed up like this either,' the Lord Mayor added, ' I am usually in shorts. There is nothing I like better than having breakfast outside in the garden in the summer.'

Many friends and colleagues have fond memories of The Refuge because Peter and Belinda's hospitality is legendary and people have been invited to share in the family's summer break there. Indeed as numbers grew, Peter had to arrange for a caravan to be berthed in the garden to accommodate the overflow guests. Then another room was built on but The Refuge continued to be very tight for space. As Juliet, Peter's eldest daughter, recalls, 'Everyone was welcome at Wittering and appearances were not the most important thing. Rather it was a case of "take us as you find us". There was always an open door and space would always be found for people no matter how many others were already there.'

Peter's daughter Clare remembers a distinguished and rather portly couple who turned up at a busy time and were accommodated in the bunk-room where the freezer cut in and out all night. It caused great mirth amongst the younger generation who wondered how these eminent people would cope in the child-sized bunk beds. Who would take the upper storey? And was there a chance one of them might come crashing down in the night? Fortunately history does not record anything untoward happening.

Another great joy of The Refuge was its proximity to Chichester city and marina. During the late 1960s and the early 1970s the Gadsdens enjoyed the company of Christopher Rawson and his wife Rosemary. Their two daughters were of similar age to the Gadsden girls so there was lots of fun. Christopher had a boat berthed at the Marina and the Gadsdens were regular guests on board. The girls can recall Christopher regaling their father with the familiar cry 'Come on Gad, let's go and get some ice from Cyril to put on the boat.' This was the accepted code for Peter and Christopher to go for a drink at the pub where Cyril was the publican.

Peter and Belinda's family have grown in size as the girls have married— as one friend commented, 'in the correct order of seniority'. Juliet married Nigel Cartwright in 1978, Caroline married Graham Simpson in 1983, Clare married Iain McWhirter in 1985 and Elizabeth married Claude Partridge in 1999—and 17 grandchildren have come along. The Refuge, which has often been bursting at the seams, could not accommodate them all. In 2001 Peter and Belinda decided to raze the dear old bungalow to the ground and rebuild. This was completed by November 2002 and a marvellous six-bed, six-bathroomed version of The Refuge emerged like a phoenix. The much-extended family still adore going down to Wittering for seaside holidays and weekends. Peter continues to entertain their many guests with his legendary 'Barbies'—honed after many trips down under. Nobody who has tasted his delicious barbequed bananas forgets them in a hurry!

In the past there were also family holidays skiing in Austria as guests of John and Elspeth Little. Peter had met John Little in China in the late 1960s and been invited to become a non-executive director of JH Little and Co specialising in Chinese trade. As Clare recalled, this began as another instance of one of her father's business colleagues being taken into the bosom of the Gadsden family. The Littles were so appreciative of being welcomed into Gadsden family life that they loaned the family their ski chalet in Alpbach for a holiday.

One amusing incident from that period concerned Peter dealing with the host of admirers that his lovely daughters had attracted. To the girls' delight a load of motorbikes roared up to the chalet and a group of Austrian boys got off saying in heavily accented English, 'We 'ave come for ze girls.' That really was more than Peter would tolerate. As Elizabeth related, 'Daddy was pacing up and down outside the chalet shooing them away with his arms and shouting in French "Allez! Allez!" to the complete bafflement of the boys!' Meanwhile four girls were peeping out of the

38.   Peter's barbeques at The Refuge are legendary. Sporting the appropriate attire he gives Sir Hugh Wontner, his fellow sheriff in 1970 (and Lord Mayor in 1973), an insight into the delights of barbequed pheasant.

window with a mixture of horror and embarrassment on their faces at their father's antics.

There were a few skiing holidays when Peter went on his own, or as Peter termed it 'on a pink ticket'. This was because Belinda had to stay behind to look after the children. In time the skiing holidays ended and Harelaw became the favoured venue for the Christmas and Easter break which gave Belinda a chance to renew her former acquaintances in Northumberland.

From 1988 until 2002, Peter and Belinda also owned an apartment on the Costa del Sol in Spain, which had the most stunning views over the bay from its balcony. The apartment provided them with some wonderful warm breaks especially in the winter months. And with customary hospitality, the Gadsdens shared it with friends. The late Sir Peter Studd recalled an enjoyable holiday he spent with Peter and Belinda in Spain. Many other friends have fond memories of the apartment. Rosemary, Viscountess Boyne, recalls Peter's kindness in inviting her and her late husband to stay there: 'It was a time of perfect sunshine and warmth, such bliss'.

Peter is essentially a family man who is very fond of his four daughters. He has always been proud to introduce them to his friends. Sunday lunches were cherished family occasions and the girls remember how much their father enjoyed taking the whole family out for Sunday lunch. 'It was always Daddy's thing,' Juliet said.

All too often business took Peter away from the family for long periods especially when the elder two girls, Juliet and Caroline, were growing up. Even when he was not abroad, he was frequently in demand as a dinner guest and therefore out in the evening. Many of Juliet's childhood memories are of taking her father to the airport or of collecting him: 'I can still see his suitcase now.' The girls kept a map of the world on their bedroom wall and used to plot where their father was at any given time. To help the family keep in touch Belinda periodically booked a trunk call (as long-distance telephone calls used to be called) so they got the chance to talk to Peter when he was away. By the time the family were living in the Barbican in the 1970s Peter's travels were less protracted and his younger two daughters, Clare and Elizabeth, have different childhood memories. They recall their parents being out every night attending functions in the City, but when they came in from school in the late afternoon, Peter was usually there to greet them warmly from his study across the hallway.

39.   The family pictured on the balcony of their home at 606 Gilbert House, the Barbican, where they moved in 1969. Peter and Belinda lived at the Barbican for 30 years. From left to right: Juliet, Clare, Belinda, Elizabeth, Peter and Caroline.

Like Belinda, Peter's daughters have all played a part in supporting him and not just as beautiful young maids of honour during the mayoralty. One of his daughters even secured a job for him once. Darby Johns, from Associated Minerals Consolidated (AMA), who had arrived in London from Australia, phoned to speak to Peter and the phone was answered by nine-year-old Clare. He was so impressed by the efficient and polite way in which she handled his call that Darby offered Peter a job!

The relationship between Peter and his daughters has been, and still is, extremely close. 'We all hero-worshipped him,' one of Peter's daughters explained. They all have fond memories of Peter as a father who was very much a presence in the home even if he was away. Clare recalls, 'We had a lot of freedom as girls but much was expected of us in terms of behaviour. We knew what we had to do, so we didn't go wild. If we did do wrong, Daddy never shouted or ranted at us, but he was "disappointed" and went very quiet. That worked.' There are numerous stories of Peter entertaining them as little girls with various antics. One favourite involved poking his head round the door then bringing his own hand above it to grab his hair and seemingly pull the head back. That trick guaranteed shrieks of laughter. It is a game he now plays on the grandchildren with just as much success.

Chapter 8

Trading in the People's Republic of China in the 1960s and 1970s

'GADSDEN'

The Chinese people wish to have friendly co-operation with the people of all countries to resume and expand international trade in order to develop production and promote economic prosperity.

Chairman Mao Tse-Tung

A year after Peter wrote about his impressions of Africa during apartheid, he travelled to another country in the throes of an interesting period in its history. His visit to the People's Republic of China in 1959 was the first of 15 made over a 20-year period. Initially Peter went there representing Fergusson Wild but later he traded on behalf of Murphyores, JH Little (which became part of Inchcape) and Associated Minerals Consolidated (part of Consolidated Goldfields). Peter looked forward to his visits to China and admired the dedication and loyalty of the Chinese people. He was convinced the country would become a leading industrialised nation.

After Chairman Mao Tse-Tung had 'liberated' China, it was in 1953 that some British businessmen had seen what a huge potential the People's Republic offered for business. Forty-eight British companies united to form the '48 Group' pledged to develop trade links with China and persuade the

British government to scale down its trade boycott. Thanks to the group steadily building up trust, businessmen from Britain were able to trade with China, despite the lack of encouragement from official quarters.

In 1957 a twice-yearly 'Chinese Export Commodities Fair' opened in Canton (now called Guangzhou) and foreigner traders were warmly invited. Peter encouraged Fergusson Wild not to let the opportunity pass them by particularly as the fair had a dedicated 'Hall of Metals and Minerals'. As usual Peter had done his homework and knew what ores and minerals the Chinese had to sell as well as what metals they required to develop their own industries. Once a visa was granted he was able to visit China in April 1959 and spend a month in the country.

The usual route into China for Westerners was via Hong Kong. Travellers had to catch a train to the Hong Kong border then walk across. After a meal they boarded the train to Canton where they were welcomed. Peter and his colleagues developed their own ritual on the way that involved having a last gin and tonic on the Hong Kong train and correspondingly a first gin and tonic on their return. Once in China they knew the drink would be vodka, beer, wine or tea. Moutai was also available but, being virtually pure alcohol, it could be lethal for the unwary traveller! Five Goats (Wu Yang) beer and Tsingtao beer (now imported into the UK) were Chinese brews popular amongst British businessmen.

Although the beer was good, Peter found that it was tea that was usually offered at business meetings. A flask of china tea, drunk without milk, was to be found in every room he went.

'Visas were required for each city in China in those days. You would probably get one if they needed you for business,' Peter said. 'Once inside China you needed another visa to stay there and an exit visa to leave the country. So if you were a frequent visitor your passport soon needed renewing!'

The Chinese government travel agency, China Travel Service, was a great help to foreign visitors. Within a few minutes of arriving at a hotel visitors were checked by a guide who made certain that everything was 'comfortable' and that all travel documents were in order. Any traveller who forgot their vaccination certificate was vaccinated on arrival. Everyone was assigned their own interpreter (known privately amongst visitors as 'my interrupter') and they facilitated appointments (known amongst British visitors as 'disappointments') for the visitor to have a meeting with the interested organisation.

Because of the shortage of hotel accommodation, visas would not be granted for visiting Peking (now Beijing) unless you had received an invitation to visit a particular organisation. One businessman who worked for a Dutch company was delighted when he secured the required invitation by phoning the firm in Peking. Peter, who knew the procedure from earlier visits, offered to accompany him to the China Travel Service to arrange the visa.

When they got there the official said: 'We can't issue you with a visa because you don't have an invitation.'

'Yes I do,' the man replied. 'I telephoned my customers this morning and they have invited me to visit them.'

'We have no information about this,' the official maintained.

'Of course you do. You listen in to all our telephone calls,' he answered cheekily.

'No, only international calls,' came the correction.

The Chinese made a big effort to look after their foreign visitors. 'In order to make life as enjoyable as possible for our guests during their stay in Canton,' one tourist information leaflet read, 'they will be entertained, off business hours, with dancing performances, operas, cinemas or athletics demonstrations.' Not all the visitors welcomed this entertainment. One businessman declined his hosts' invitation to watch yet another Chinese film because, as he pointed out, they were always about war and he was a man of peace. He was soon put right: 'You should understand that our wars are quite different from the wars you fight in the west—all our wars are wars for peace.'

Peter preferred to keep his own counsel and dutifully attended the required 'entertainments'. A flavour of these can be gained from a programme he kept for 'The Great Wall on the South Sea—a five-act play performed by The Fighters' Drama Troupe of the Political Department of the Canton Unit of the Chinese People's Liberation Army'. The English language programme given to the businessmen to help set the scene has a quotation from Chairman Mao on the cover. 'The Imperialists are bullying us in such a way that we will have to deal with them seriously. Not only must we have a powerful regular army, we must also organize contingents of the people's militia on a big scale. This will make it difficult for the Imperialists to move a single inch in our country in the event of invasion.'

Foreign visitors were regularly assailed with propaganda leaflets and booklets during their stay and, to the immense pleasure of the Chinese, Peter

40. A light-hearted interlude during one of Peter's business trips to China. He visited the country 15 times between 1959 and 1980.

often requested extra copies. This was because booklets like 'Mao Tse-Tung on the question of the National Bourgeoisie and the enlightened Gentry' or 'Smash the big US-Soviet conspiracy' made interesting reading for his friends back home because of the occasional misprints. In one piece of propaganda much was made of the sterling character of the Chinese working classes, however this appeared as the 'woking classes'. Another of Peter's favourites involved a reference to the blood-friendship between China and the Soviet Union which once appeared as their 'bloody friendship'.

Sometimes the misprints were brought to the attention of the Chinese authorities as one erratum indicated. Referring to a cookery recipe they had published earlier, the editor apologised for the error saying it should have read 'cooking soda' not 'caustic soda'.

Banners displaying the words of Chairman Mao hung everywhere in China because (as they announced): 'His words are a spiritual atom bomb'.

Peter kept a note of the banners he saw and these now offer a valuable insight into this interesting period of Chinese history.

Holding high the great Red banner of Mao Tse-Tung's thought march forward bravely.

What Imperialism fears most is the awaking of the Asian, African and Latin American peoples, the awaking of the peoples of all countries. We should unite and drive the US Imperialism from Asia, Africa and Latin America back to where it came from.

Study Chairman Mao's works, follow his teachings, act in accordance with his instructions.

Chairman Mao is the red sun that shines in our hearts. The aim of the great proletarian cultural revolution is to revolutionize people's ideology and as a consequence to achieve greater, faster, better and more economical results in all fields of work.

Long live the general line!
Long live the great leap forward!
Long live the people's commune!

Long live the great and invincible thought of Mao Tse-Tung.

Always follow Chairman Mao's advance in teeth of the great storms and waves.

We are advocates of the abolition of war. We do not want war, and in order to get rid of the gun, it is necessary to take up the gun.

Chairman Mao lives with the people of the world heart by heart forever.

We must give active support to the material independence and liberation movement in countries in Asia, Africa and Latin America as well as to the peace movement and to the just struggles in all the countries of the world.

Comrade Mao Tse-Tung is the greatest Marxist-Leninist of our era.

Comrade Mao Tse-Tung has inherited, defended and developed Marxism-Leninism with genius, creatively and in an all round way he has raised Marxism-Leninism to a completely new stage.

The brilliance of Mao Tse-Tung's thought illuminates the whole world.

The masses are the makers of history. Once they master Mao Tse-Tung's thought they will become the wisest and the most courageous people capable of exerting inexhaustible strength.

> *Pakistani friends have boundless love for Chairman Mao's works.*

> *Long live the great proletarian cultural revolution.*

> *The seizure of power by armed force, the settlement of the issue by war, is the central task and the highest form of revolution, this Marxist-Leninist principle of revolution holds good universally, for China and for all other countries.*

> *We can learn what we did not know. We are not only good at destroying the old world. We are also good at building the new.*

> *Long live the great, glorious and correct Communist Party of China.*

> *Guided missile nuclear test. A great victory for Chairman Mao Tse-Tung's thought and brilliant result of the great Cultural Proletarian Revolution.*

> *Long live Chairman Mao our great teacher, great leader, great supreme Commander and great Helmsman!*

> *The days of Imperialism are numbered. The Imperialists have committed all manner of evils and all the oppressed peoples of the whole world will never forgive them.*

> *Imperialism and all reactionaries are paper tigers.*

Despite all the rhetoric, Peter found the Chinese people extremely courteous and hospitable. He enjoyed excellent receptions with delicious food including dishes such as shark's fin soup, bird's nest soup, 100-year-old eggs, Pearl River fish, Peking Duck, whole rice birds, civet cat, frog's legs, sea cucumber and snake. In return he tried hard to understand their customs and avoid causing offence. Fortunately there were seasoned British travellers on hand to advise him about protocol. A useful piece of advice Peter was given was that the time written on a dinner invitation was the exact time people were expected to arrive. This presented Peter with no problem because he is habitually punctual. However, knowing when he should leave did catch him out.

At the first dinner he attended, he was interested to observe that the speeches came between the courses, all twelve of them. At the end of the meal, tea and hot towels were brought round. Aware how rude it was to jump up and dash off as soon as a meal was over, Peter continued chatting

41. Marches by members of the Red Guards were a regular part of daily life in China at this time. 'Holding high the great Red banner of Mao Tse-Tung's thought, march forward bravely,' one of the banners proclaimed.

amicably to his hosts. After a while he noticed their questions were becoming very solicitous about his personal state. 'You are very tired?' 'No,' he assured them, 'I'm fine.' 'You have lot of work to do tomorrow?' 'Not too much,' he replied, 'I think I have got things paced out nicely thank you.' 'You have an early start in the morning?' 'Not too early,' he was able to reassure them. 'It has been a long day for you?' his host persisted.

After a while Peter had the feeling there might be a message in these remarks, so he got to his feet. Everyone immediately sprang up and began bidding him farewell. Talking about this back at the hotel, Peter was informed by an old hand that foreign guests were expected to depart immediately after the tea and towels—it was the signal to go.

Drinking the toast to cement a business deal also needed careful handling as Peter discovered. A colleague briefed him that when drinks were poured it was customary for many toasts to be proposed. The toast might be to peace and to friendship amongst other things. ' "Gangbei!" is the favourite word,' he was told. 'It is like "bottoms up" and means you are expected to empty your glass.' Armed with this knowledge, Peter believed all would be well. However, part way through the social ritual he suddenly realised each host was proposing their own toast which he was expected to respond to. With ten hosts at the meeting it was ten to one and he knew that he stood little chance of surviving that bout! In order to slow the pace a little, Peter jovially insisted 'Everyone gangbei'—which meant all his hosts had to drink each time a toast was proposed. Since the Chinese were certainly not hardened drinkers, the toasts began to fall away or became 'Sweibian' which meant 'as you please' and only required the politest of sips.

When flying from Canton to Peking, Peter was seen by the air hostess looking for his seat belt. 'We don't need seat belts in Chinese planes,' he was informed. Maybe this was true because Peter noticed their airlines took great care if they had a foreigner on board, not daring to take off if it was raining.

Such solicitous care of foreigners could be frustrating as an episode related in Percy Timberlake's account of the 48 Group *The Story of the Icebreakers in China* demonstrates. He writes:

> Finally the full group moved to Shanghai for another tight programme of meetings to round off the Working Party's schedule. Then the weather closed in. Not just the persistent rain, but anxiety about getting back to keep appointments in London caused mounting nervousness as the scheduled departure date approached with frequent reports of flight cancellations. Finally Peter Gadsden and another member of the party could spare no more time and the Chinese International Travel Service were asked to come to the hotel some hours before the evening flight and confirm that the two men would be on it. The representatives arrived with happy faces. 'We have good news for you,' they said, 'also some bad news. The good news is that both gentlemen are on the flight. The bad news is that the flight isn't going tonight.'

Maybe that was just as well because one of Peter's 'horror' flights actually took place when he was on his way to a Canton Trade Fair. In Calcutta he had boarded an Air India Super Constellation bound for Hong Kong. The plane taxied to the end of the runway and took off but just as it became airborne there was a stomach-wrenching bang. To the consternation of all the passengers the plane circled then came back to the airport to be greeted by a full contingent of fire engines and emergency services. A rather breathless captain's voice came over the tannoy system repeating 'Very lucky. Very lucky. Very lucky.' Later when Peter asked one of the cabin crew what had happened they too repeated the mantra 'Very lucky. Very lucky not full.' Then someone explained to him that an engine had 'feathered' and if the plane had been full they would certainly have crashed.

Back at the terminal rather shaken by his experience, Peter phoned a business colleague who had dropped him off earlier. David Workman arrived armed with a full bottle of brandy. 'Thought you'd need this,' he said considerately. Grateful to have landed in one piece, Peter decided not to chance his luck on another Super Constellation flight to Hong Kong the next day. Instead he opted for a flight on a BOAC Comet.

In China even the most innocuous remark about the weather might be misinterpreted. One British businessman caused great offence when he said, 'There is a cold wind coming from the east,' as he gestured in the direction of Peking (Beijing).

Equally an innocent gesture in a restaurant threatened to erupt into a serious incident. Peter was dining with some business colleagues when one of the men laughingly put his hand round the waitress's waist. The next day a policeman arrived at the man's hotel room and held him responsible for striking a waitress. 'It required all our diplomatic skills to convince the policeman that in Britain putting an arm round the waitress was the normal way to express thanks for good service in a restaurant,' Peter said.

After hearing about the heavy-handed reaction to this innocent gesture, there was great consternation amongst the diners on another occasion when their champagne cork flew up and hit Chairman Mao's portrait full in the face as it hung above them on the wall. They tried carrying on as normal but everyone was extremely tense. Fortunately nothing happened because the incident had not been spotted by the staff.

The Chinese language did not present any great barrier to business dealings because everyone had their 'interrupter'. But it could be difficult for the interpreter, though, because they were constantly swopping between buying and selling situations. Peter remembers his confusion on one occasion when he was negotiating the sale of aluminium. After he had named his price, the interpreter stopped translating for a moment and turning to him said, 'Your price is too low.' It must have been the look of sheer amazement on his face that suddenly alerted her to the fact she had made a mistake. After spending all morning working for a selling organization, she said she had forgotten that she was now working for the buying organisation.

The interpreters were not usually present out of office hours so when Peter and his colleagues were dining on their own the language sometimes did present problems. There was the time when Peter ordered two eggs boiled for four minutes and received four eggs boiled for two minutes. On another occasion, the English group decided that sign language would be more reliable. One of their number asked for a glass of orange juice but it was quite evident from the waitress's face that she hadn't got a clue what they meant. Spotting the orange badge proudly displayed on her bosom, he pointed to it. Her eyes lit up; she knew exactly what they wanted and returned bearing a glass of milk.

Business travellers to China during this period were always on full alert. No British delegate was ever sure whether his conversation was being bugged, so when any of them wanted to meet for a chat it was usually in one of their hotel bedrooms. They talked there with the bathroom taps running or music playing which made it difficult for anyone to listen in. Not only did they assume their international phone calls were listened to but they noticed complicated cables (in the days before emails and faxes) from the office were usually delayed. Peter has clear memories of the time he visited the Chinese Corporation to tell them that the deal had been confirmed by his office in the UK. Their response was: 'Yes, and we have the contract waiting for signature.'

The Chinese also had a rule at the time that all visitors' films must be developed in the country before they returned home. However, Peter knew that they were unable to process Kodak film, which he preferred, so he made sure he always used it and consequently was one of the few travellers who brought undeveloped film out of China. In fact there was nothing compromising on his film in any case.

Peter earned himself a title in China which he would not have wanted his Chinese hosts to hear about. Dick Blaxland tells the story of a group of them returning from a social event to their hotel in Peking. Before they were anywhere near the hotel, Peter was already hopping around on one leg, absolutely desperate for the loo. Since none of them had any idea where there might be public facilities, the group closed ranks round him in the manner of a rugby scrum. The only difference was that this scrum took place over a conveniently situated drain. Thereafter he was referred to as 'the Pee-king of Peking'!

Friendly and hospitable as the Chinese were, politics was never far away. One of Peter's visits to China took place when the U2 was shot down over the USSR. As a result all foreigners were mustered to watch a large anti-American demonstration in Tiananmen Square. In Peter's opinion there was nothing to be done but go along with it. One member of the trade delegation thought differently. He protested to his 'interrupter' that he had come to China to sell chemicals, not to watch demonstrations against the USA. For such 'discourtesy' it was immediately arranged for him to leave China.

During the Cultural Revolution there was red paint everywhere and frequent Red Guard parades. Searchlights lit up the night skies and police on bikes were very much in evidence. The Roman Catholic Cathedral in Peking had been turned into a cement store and martial music could be heard at all times of the day and night. Peter still has the record of 'The East is Red', one of the popular songs at the time. Notices in the towns impressed upon the Chinese that 'foreigners are present as our guests, be nice to them'. The Chinese believed that Chairman Mao's little red book offered protection and always carried it on their person. To this day Peter retains his English copy of the little red book which was freely available at that time.

Peter always found the quality and range of the food in China superb, but he felt uncomfortable at the huge gulf between the lavish banquets laid on for foreign visitors and the meagre fare of the Chinese peasants. When he tentatively raised this he was assured by his interpreter that it was 'the will of the peasants that foreigners be entertained in this way'. Seemingly it was also 'the will of the peasants' that foreigners received preferential treatment on the ferries and were given seats in the shade at sporting events whilst the peasants stood in the hot sun.

Care of guests was a very serious matter in China. When the husband of a French trade delegate died in China during a trade mission, the Chinese were embarrassed. They felt that as hosts they had not taken proper care of their guest, so in a gesture designed to make amends for this she received preferential business.

Over the years Peter visited China, he remained impressed by people's complete honesty. He said that he felt safer walking down a street in Peking than he did in any other country, including the UK. There was no begging to be seen and both tipping and gambling were forbidden. In China the emphasis was on work. Men and women in equal numbers could be seen going about their duties in the Chairman Mao blue uniform dress. They worked long and hard with no weekend breaks. The workforce only received two days a month off. Many foreign visitors, like Peter, felt uneasy about using the shops specially designated for foreign currency users because they were packed full of goodies the locals could only dream of.

Doing business with such a different culture was challenging but after a few visits Peter developed his own ploys. He could often be seen puffing away on a cigarette when negotiating a deal, even though he was a non-smoker. He knew the Chinese expected this of him under pressure, so he was happy to oblige.

During some complex negotiations on another occasion, Peter was asked, why he had not got a reply from London. He replied that he was doing his best. To which Mr Chang replied, 'Please try harder.'

Experience taught him that when the Chinese wanted to buy something from the West, they could open negotiations by asking for a huge amount of the product and still expect the same terms for a very small quantity. Another thing Peter learned about the way the Chinese bought was that they liked to spread their favours around. If they required 20,000 tons of metal, the order would never go to one supplier, but was more likely to be shared between four. That way the Chinese were never beholden to one supplier and if there was a delay in supply because of a major disaster or some shipping problem, their manufacturers were never greatly inconvenienced. The other suppliers could make up the shortfall.

Peter also got used to the fact that Chinese weights and analysis of ores and minerals were final, so it was pointless to argue. Indeed, because he wanted to establish a good name for quality, Peter always made it a rule to buy on a better specification than he sold and to sell on less strict figures. That didn't please everyone though. John Hart back in England remembers buying some Chinese manganese from Peter that proved to be of too high a quality for the job he wanted.

Trips to China remained memorable even after the death of Mao Tse-Tung. When Peter visited at the beginning of the rule of the 'Gang of Four', he was amazed to see all the decorated statues of Chairman Mao disappeared overnight.

Darby Johns, then working for Associated Minerals, recalls one trip he made to China with Peter. 'It was wintertime and snowfalls prevented us visiting the Great Wall but we were able to explore the Forbidden City that was not then open to the general visitor.' When it came to the business side of the trip, 'we were greeted formally in the Great Hall of the People in Tiananmen Square. I recall one elderly Chinese leader who had been with Chairman Mao on the "long march". What fascinated me was that he had a spittoon alongside his chair and he used it frequently and with amazing accuracy.' Peter, who had long grown used to the presence of a

42. 'During the Cultural Revolution red paint and bikes were everywhere in China,' Peter recalled.

spittoon in every Chinese room during his previous visits, was completely unfazed by the performance.

By the early 1970s Peter's trading links in China involved the firm of JH Little. Another of their employees at that time was Tony Wright and he takes up the story.

> JH Little and Co had a very active agency business in China, including that for Metal Traders Ltd, at that time a major London trading company. John Little and Peter therefore had a common interest in Chinese metals and minerals. They decided to merge these interests into one company and thus JH Little Metals was formed. Peter and I were two of the directors. Supported by the charming and very efficient Suzanne [Suzanne Stubbins was Peter's secretary during the 1970s and became secretary of the Bermuda Society on its formation in 1986], whom Peter had persuaded to follow him to this new venture, we shared an office in Bartholomew Close, in the rather mixed immediate vicinity of 'Bart's' Hospital, the ancient church of St Bartholomew the Great, John Betjeman's London residence in Cloth Fair and the Smithfield Meat Market.

> The arrangement was mutually beneficial. It expanded the existing JH Little activities—I was introduced by Peter to a previously unknown area of business, including the Derbyshire mining industry and minerals such as graphite, talc,

mica, barites and fluorspar. Peter was able to continue his interests in trading and China, but with sufficient flexibility for him to give sufficient time to his increasing involvement in the City of London.

During his mayoralty, Peter was keen to play a major role in fostering Anglo-Chinese relations and trade. As he explained in a speech at a dinner given in his honour by the Mayor of Beijing:

> We in Britain earnestly desire to help you to achieve your commitment to economic modernisation in the following areas: Agriculture, Industry, Science and Technology and National Defence. ...To help China expand exports, we offer you the financial facilities of the City of London, British technology and engineering experience. We welcome your students to our universities, your technicians to our factories and technical universities, we offer you experience in the fields of shipping and insurance, and the use of our commodity markets. We wish to exchange our experience in the field of production, distribution and marketing.

All of these, he said, were offered to promote trade on the basis of 'equality and mutual benefit'.

In December 1979, Lord Mayor Sir Peter Gadsden chaired a discussion at the Mansion House on metals trading with the China trade delegation headed by the Chinese vice-minister of trade. A few months later the Chinese ambassador gave a dinner at the Chinese Embassy in the Lord Mayor's honour and this was followed by an invitation from the Chinese Government to pay an official visit to their country in August.

This was a visit Peter was keen to make because he knew it would be advantageous for British trade. It was also without precedence as *The Times* observed: 'Sir Peter Gadsden, Lord Mayor of that most eminent of capitalist institutions the City of London, is preparing to venture where it is thought no Lord Mayor has ventured before to extol the virtues of the City and its institutions.' When he spoke in the Great Hall of the People on his arrival, Peter acknowledged: 'This is the first time a Lord Mayor of London has visited China as Lord Mayor and I am here to strengthen the bonds of friendship between our two countries.' Peter and his party were made most welcome. Over the years many British businesses have had cause to be grateful to him for the strengthening of trade links between the two countries as a result of his mayoral tour.

Peter recalls with amusement that the 1980 mayoral visit was the first Chinese trip he had undertaken without his 'Canton pack'. On previous business trips to the area, he always made a point of stopping

汉語拼音方案草案
声韵母表

声母 (21)	b	ㄅ 玻	p	ㄆ 坡	m	ㄇ 摸	f	ㄈ 佛
	d	ㄉ 得	t	ㄊ 特	n	ㄋ 訥	l	ㄌ 勒
	g	ㄍ 哥	k	ㄎ 科	h	ㄏ 喝		
	j	ㄐ 基	q	ㄑ 欺	x	ㄒ 希		
	zh	ㄓ 知	ch	ㄔ 吃	sh	ㄕ 詩	r	ㄖ 日
	z	ㄗ 資	c	ㄘ 雌	s	ㄙ 思		
单韵母 (6)		i	ㄧ 衣	u	ㄨ 烏	ü	ㄩ 迂
	a	ㄚ 啊	ia	ㄧㄚ 呀	ua	ㄨㄚ 蛙		
	o	ㄛ 喔			uo	ㄨㄛ 窩		
	e	ㄜ(ㄝ) 鵝	ie	ㄧㄝ 耶			üe	ㄩㄝ 月
复合韵母 (13)	ai	ㄞ 哀			uai	ㄨㄞ 歪		
	ei	ㄟ 欸			uei(ui)	ㄨㄟ 威		
	ao	ㄠ 熬	iao	ㄧㄠ 腰				
	ou	ㄡ 歐	iou(iu)	ㄧㄡ 憂				
带声韵母 (16)	an	ㄢ 安	ian	ㄧㄢ 烟	uan	ㄨㄢ 弯	üan	ㄩㄢ 冤
	en	ㄣ 恩	in	ㄧㄣ 因	uen(un)	ㄨㄣ 温	ün	ㄩㄣ 晕
	ang	ㄤ 昂	iang	ㄧㄤ 央	uang	ㄨㄤ 汪		
	eng	ㄥ 亨的韵	ing	ㄧㄥ 英	ueng	ㄨㄥ 翁		
	ong	(ㄨㄥ)轰的韵	iong	ㄩㄥ 雍				

43.   A teaching aid for the pronunciation of Chinese.

in Hong Kong to pick up luxury items that were unobtainable in China. The shopping list usually included chocolate, soap (because at the time Chinese soap was like carbolic), butter, loo rolls (because the Chinese favoured the coarse scratchy variety), Entroviracalm and whisky. With vodka the standard spirit in China, it was impossible to buy whisky and imports were restricted to one bottle. However, since no size was specified, business travellers stopping over in Hong Kong could be found seeking out the biggest bottle of whisky available.

The mayoral visit was Peter's last to China but his admiration and special relationship with the country has continued.

44. Peter as director of JH Little meets Wang Zhen, Vice-Premier of the People's Republic of China, at a reception given by the Sino-British Trade Council in 1978.

Chapter 9

Combining Business
with Civic Life

In judgement: wisdom,
In action: resolution,
In success: humility,
In all things: courage,
And a sense of humour.

Proud Heritage: A Portrait of Greatness

In the 1960s when Peter left Fergusson Wild, he began his long and active association with the civic life of the City of London. Whilst freely acknowledging such an involvement would always be prestigious, Peter said what he was really seeking was the fellowship of like-minded individuals.

Soon after he began working in the City he was delighted to bump into an old school-friend from prep school days at Colwall—Christopher Rawson. He and Peter reminisced over their various exploits including the scrape they got into at The Elms over the purchase of an old tobacco pipe. Peter had been caught redhanded by 'Ping', the headmaster, admiring this pipe he had just bought from Christopher for sixpence. Knowing that the worst sin in the eyes of his fellow pupils was being a 'sneak', Peter opted for the lesser sin of telling a lie—or, in Ping's parlance, 'a cram'. When challenged to explain where he had got the pipe from, Peter claimed it was his father's which he had brought into school to show the other boys without his parents' knowledge. That misdemeanour earned him a severe telling-off for taking his father's 'dirty old pipe', the loss of his pipe and a waste of sixpence.

It took 40 years for that situation to be rectified. In 1980 the Lord Mayor of London, Alderman Sir Peter Gadsden, visited The Elms to launch their appeal for a new swimming-pool. To everyone's amusement, the chairman

of the governors, Mr Christopher Rawson, began the proceedings by publicly presenting the Lord Mayor with a new pipe in settlement of an old
debt.

In the late 1950s when the two first met up again, there was much
hilarity, not least because Christopher lived in a flat above the Family
Planning Clinic in Sloane Street—always good for a few jokes! Peter
admired Christopher's sociable, outgoing nature and the two men rapidly
became close friends.

'I shall be forever grateful to Christopher Rawson for introducing me to
the civic life of the City of London,' Peter says. 'It was through him that
I became interested.' Because Christopher had a professional interest in
the textile trade, he had become a member of the Clothworkers' Company
at the early age of 24 and indeed rose to become Master of the company
some years later. It was at the beginning of the 1960s when Peter discussed
with Christopher the possibility of joining the Worshipful Company
of Clothworkers and Christopher was kind enough to support Peter's
'Freedom by Redemption'.

A present-day officer of the Clothworkers' Company explained that
the company was pleased to welcome Christopher Rawson's nominee in
1962 because 'these were clearly two young people on the up and up'.
For his part Peter has always been proud that the Clothworkers is his
mother company. This very eminent company, one of the great 12 livery
companies of the City, was originally founded in 1528 as an association
of craftspeople engaged in clothworking. Amongst the many celebrated
members in its history was Samuel Pepys who became Master in 1677–8
on account of his eminence as a senior naval civil servant rather than
for keeping a diary.

The Clothworkers' Company, like all livery companies, undertakes a
great deal of charitable work and Peter has played an active role in this
aspect of its work. The company supports several educational institutions
and, because of its long-standing connections with the Yorkshire textile
industry, is an important supporter of the University of Leeds along with
several charities that provide assistance for blind people.

Around the time Peter joined the Clothworkers' Company, Christopher
Rawson was elected sheriff. Once again this was at the very young age of
32. Peter recalls the kindness Christopher showed him then by inviting
him to the judges' luncheon at the Old Bailey. It is the duty of the two
sheriffs during their shrieval year to take charge of the judges' welfare at

the Central Criminal Court. Historically this included the safety of the judges as well as their hospitality, but today it means responsibility for selecting and inviting luncheon guests. Because the Old Bailey judges spend all their working hours contemplating some of the most horrific actions one human can inflict upon another, a complete break in the middle of the day is vital. The sheriffs, as Peter himself would be required to do eight years later, take it in turns to select and invite a small group of interesting people from many walks of life to lunch with the judges each day. In 1962 Peter Gadsden, a sociable young businessman who travelled regularly to Australia and other far-off locations, received one of these cherished invitations.

In 1963 Peter became a freeman of the City of London through his membership of the Clothworkers' Company and was elected to full livery status in 1965. He was then entitled to vote in the annual election of the sheriffs and of the Lord Mayor as well as attend Clothworkers' dinners. All these experiences added to his understanding of civic life and encouraged him to become more involved in the City.

Peter has been active in Freemasonry achieving LGR in 1971 and PSGD in 1980 and has served on the Council of the Grand Charity. His introduction to Freemasonry arose through his friendship with Christopher Rawson who proposed his membership of the Mount Moriah Lodge No 34 in 1963 (on 9 January 2004 the lodge celebrated its 250th anniversary) and he is now an honorary member. Peter is a member of the Old Wrekinian Lodge No 5481(which was his school lodge); the Guildhall Lodge No 3116 and Shropshire Installed Masters Lodge No 6262. He is honorary member of the Barbican Lodge No 8496, Farringdon Without Lodge No 1754, the Londonium Lodge No 4208, the City of London Installed Masters No 8220 and the City University Lodge No 7962.

One of the strengths of being in the craft, Peter says, is that members of all religions and all social levels can sit down together equally as brothers. 'There are few other places where that is the case,' he explained.

Peter had more opportunity for civic activities after he took up a post with Murphyores. In 1964 they appointed him managing director of the London marketing subsidiary of Murphyores which handled European sales. The Australian mining company, also known as the New South Wales Rutile Mining Company, held major leases along the east coast of Australia that yielded thousands of tons of the mineral sands rutile, zircon and ilmenite.

Even in the early 1960s Peter occasionally found his business and civic life merging. For instance in June 1964 he was invited to the City's reception for AW Munro, the premier of Queensland. This was because the City deemed it appropriate to invite the new MD of Murphyores in London, as the company extracted large quantities of minerals from the shores of Queensland.

When Peter too moved to Murphyores it was on condition that he would be free to undertake other business provided there was no conflict of interest. Out went Fergusson Wild's Standard to be replaced by Murphyores' Austin Princess, but there were far more significant changes to Peter's business life than the company car. From 1964 onwards he began running various strands of business, civic and charitable work simultaneously and successfully. All his activities have been carried out with such attention to detail that few would have guessed how many other things were going on in his life at that moment. As Suzanne Stubbins, one of Peter's secretaries, put it: 'He did so much that people said "that can't be one man, it has to be at least a set of twins!" '

Many people would have stumbled under the pressure and commitments yet Peter thrived on it. He says that he has a mind like a filing cabinet and can keep each section in its correct compartment without permitting it to overflow beyond its allotted space or time. He concedes that 'it was a case of priorities all the time. One lived on essential priorities. I was always conscious of the fact that if people paid a fee for something then they expected something back for their money. My professional life was divided into three parts and generally each part required a third of my time but sometimes the balance shifted slightly. A third of my life was concerned with civic activities, a third with social and charitable activities and a third with business to pay for the other two.'

He cheerfully admits it was a great help working for a company like Murphyores, where the boss was six thousand miles away. This gave him the flexibility he needed to get a huge amount done. Peter Gadsden is not somebody who operates well sitting behind a desk shuffling paper around. From the outset he was clearly a 'mover and shaker' although no one had coined the phrase yet; Suzanne described him as 'a real mobile man who was ahead of his time'.

Working for an Australian company meant at least one trip a year down under. It always amused Peter that as soon as the plane touched down in Australia the crew came round with the bug-spray. They would walk down the aisle with two aerosol cans, directing passengers to cover their eyes and noses as they sprayed all and sundry. You were not allowed off the plane until you had been sprayed. Fortunately the ritual was halted during the bicentennial celebrations in 1988 never to be resumed.

Because Peter had conducted business with Murphyores and other Australian mineral sands companies in the past, he knew all about the fierce rivalry that existed between the companies. Trading protocols had to been learned rapidly if you wanted to succeed in the mining business. Peter had found that quite often your host would happily provide you with transport to your next appointment but if that appointment turned out to be with a competitor, then expect to be dropped off some distance away and walk to the compound. It was more than their pride could stomach to be seen near a rival's mining lease.

Peter always chuckled when he arrived in Australia at the notice pinned to the loo door at Perth airport. Gents departing were instructed to 'Check your valuables!' Yet by contrast during Peter's first stay at the Esplanade Hotel in Perth he noticed that keys were not usually provided for hotel guests. When he asked about it he was told it simply wasn't necessary to lock your room.

As his business trips to Australia increased, Peter had to familiarise himself with Aussie drinking protocol. He recalls at one time a colleague was staying in a hotel and when the waiter brought him a cup of tea, he asked, 'Do you take sugar?' 'No thanks,' the man replied. 'Then don't stir it,' the waiter said.

Murphyores' partners enjoyed refreshments of a different kind. Jim Murphy was a confirmed whisky drinker and Bill Murphy a beer drinker. Appropriate supplies of the true Aussie beer were always sent on ahead to the London office if Bill planned to visit. Not surprisingly, the partners were very proud of Australian wines and frequently arranged for a complimentary case of Australian 'champagne' to be sent to a customer. When the customer was French, this was not a good idea. The first Peter knew about it was a phone call from the customs at Avignon informing him that a consignment of Australian 'champagne' had been refused importation at Marseilles. Helpful as ever, Peter arranged for the case to be transhipped to London to be 'dealt with' by the London office. And very nice it was too!

Drinking in Australia was a serious business. Bars were men-only establishments but extremely clean. Between six and seven in the evening they closed for 'the six o'clock swill' when the drinkers were given a break and the bar received a wash-down with a disinfectant solution.

Australian beer was drunk so icy cold that it set Peter's teeth on edge. However his request for some warm beer was taken as an insult. 'No one has complained about our beer,' retorted a barmaid. ' If you don't like our beer, drink somewhere else.' All of this was said as she carried on dispensing beer from a hosepipe like those used for petrol. Aussie beer was often drunk in 'stubbies' which are insulated cans designed to maintain the teeth-chattering temperature for as long as possible. Peter is now well used to cold beer and prefers it the colder the better.

When drinking with colleagues, Peter soon learned it was not the done thing to offer to buy a round. What usually happened was that everyone put their money in heaps on the counter and left the barmaid to decide whose 'shout' it was and to take the right amount for each round from the drinkers in turn. If the pile dwindled then people put some more money down. It was also *de rigeur* to drink each round, otherwise you risked causing offence. The only way to survive these drinking bouts, Peter discovered, was to choose the size of your glass carefully at the outset, then stick with it.

Peter can still recall his surprise when he was invited for a drink at a Melbourne club only to be confronted by a jug of water and a glass. Seeing the expression on his face, Peter's host leant across and said quietly, 'Feel under the tablecloth.' Tucked beneath the cloth, bizarrely, was a miniature bottle of whisky. The bar, like many others in Australia, was not licensed to serve spirits; nevertheless they managed.

The mines Peter visited were always hospitable places. Breakfast for hungry miners usually consisted of a T-bone steak which Peter learned to cope with but etched in his memory is the time he was also presented with a huge bread-and-butter pudding topped with a prune. Before their marriage, Peter had told Belinda that he could eat anything she prepared with the exception of bread-and-butter pudding and prunes—a legacy of school dinners doubtless. Not wishing to cause offence to his Australian hosts, Peter valiantly battled through the delicacy. As the last mouthful was forced down he heard the words, 'Great! I got another one in the fridge you must have!'

Warwick Bartle, one of Peter's colleagues during the 1960s, employed by Western Titanium (WT) whilst Peter was employed by AMA, captures the flavour of business at that time.

Peter and I were competitors, in a bizarre sort of way. We both represented different Australian subsidiaries of Consolidated Goldfields (CGF)—a London mining conglomerate which was founded in South Africa in 1887 by Cecil Rhodes, and expanded round the Empire in successive years. By the early 1960s the company was very diverse and it had branched into minerals sands—Peter's and my speciality—although the main breadwinner continued to be gold. CGF was an old-fashioned company, to me anyway, with multiple layers of management and lots of specialists in little offices who seemed to be there 'just in case'. I recall there were several dining rooms in the HQ at 49 Moorgate, City of London—and everyone was told which one they might attend, according to rank! 49 Moorgate was intriguing, as it combined several buildings and was a rabbit warren of little passages. It had been occupied by a Soviet Russian company prior to CGF's move there in 1929, which might explain the character of the place. Although in the same building, to get from my office to Peter's was quite a journey—I found it easier to go down to street level and use a different entrance on another street!

Reverting to the curious situation in which Peter and I found ourselves—this was the result of the different paths of acquisition that Goldfields Australia had followed in the 1960s. They had taken a 50% interest in AMA in 1961. AMA was the pre-eminent mineral sands company in Australia at that time, and was the virtual fiefdom of Joe Pinter, its managing director, who continued to run the company with a high measure of independence. Joe was the brains behind the industry—he personally invented some of the special equipment needed to effectively separate the minerals, in particular electrostatic and magnetic separators. He built AMA up out of this success in the 1940s, which led into the boom period of the 1950s and 1960s when the industry was populated by real Australian characters. Most of the deposits being worked at that time were adjacent to the beaches of NSW and Queensland, so quite often it was the farming families who owned the land, becoming miners as a result. Whereas there are less than a handful of mineral sands companies in Australia now, there were 40 or 50 back then, with many petty rivalries over access rights on properties, or even over the title.

The 'Black Gold' in the ground was so valuable that passions were occasionally inflamed. There is a famous story from 1960 where two neighbours had a dispute over access. One dug up the access road of the other, using a D8 bulldozer. The other sent his own D8 bulldozer to replace the dirt removed. This went on for a while and finally, according to one version of this much-embellished tale, one bulldozer was run into the other! Almost a battle of dinosaurs!

A second acquisition by CGF, this time for a 100% interest, was WT which had a mine at Capel, Western Australia, 200 km south of Perth. Here Goldfields Australia took a more hands-on approach to management and supported an innovative process developed by WT to make a synthetic rutile product, which competed with the natural version occurring in AMA's deposits. So the respective European representatives of AMA and WT, Messrs Gadsden and Bartle found themselves chasing the same customers round Europe from the same office building. Proprietary information was closely guarded, I can assure you, but this did not stop a friendship developing. I moved to Perth in 1975 to become Sales Manager for WT and the two companies were combined in 1977, putting an end to the competitive anomaly.

Visits to the Australian mining companies have provided Peter with many an anecdote for civic speeches. One that has always caused laughter concerned the manager of a mine who telephoned his head office saying, 'We've got two of cases of beriberi here this morning. What do you want me to do with them?'

'Send them to the canteen,' came the reply. 'Those miners'll drink anything.'

Peter's sense of humour always went down well in Australia. His colleague, John Allen, recalls a speech Peter made in Perth, Western Australia, in the presence of the Western Australian Premier, Charles Court and many other dignitaries. Peter opened his speech with 'Premier, my lords, ladies, gentlemen…and mineral sands traders'.

45. This Australian mining operation was photographed by Peter on one of his visits down under.

Responsibility for marketing AMA's mineral sands in Europe took Peter behind the Iron Curtain at times. His colleague Darby Johns gives an interesting insight into journeys in Poland at this time.

> We went by train from Warsaw to Katowice to visit a customer. The trains were chaotic and bookings were ignored. No such thing as first class of course. We spent a lot of the time crammed in the corridor but as the journey progressed people started chatting. It was surprising how well we could communicate despite an almost total language barrier. We were offered seats to share in turn with others and even managed to have a meal (mainly soup and bread) in the 'dining car'.

Drinking was a significant part of Polish hospitality too and that meant vodka. Peter recalls somewhat hazily that after a Polish business meeting he went to bed with the hotel room moving. In the morning he managed to stagger into the customer's office only to be greeted with a new bottle of vodka in the centre of the table and the proposal that they carry on where they had left off. To the disappointment of his hosts all Peter could do was to sip at his morning drink.

'Last night you very good drinker. This morning you not so good.'

'Yes. This morning, I not so good,' he agreed with sore head.

Warsaw had other traps for the unwary business traveller as Peter found out on a subsequent visit. He fell into bed after a hard day's bargaining and went straight to sleep. Some time in the night the phone rang and he fumbled around in the dark trying to locate the instrument. When he did find it, to his amazement a little female voice said, 'I come to your room now.'

'No, I'm tired,' he said trying to put her off politely.

'I make you less tired,' she persisted.

Peter firmly, but politely, kept refusing until the caller eventually gave up.

He related the story to his elderly colleague the next morning, who felt insulted not to have received a similar nocturnal call himself! Invitations like this were not uncommon in eastern Europe where western businessmen were perceived as very wealthy. There were plenty of people keen to get their hands on some of that money. Stories circulated about business travellers who had landed up being photographed in compromising positions only to find themselves blackmailed.

International travel could have honey-traps of another kind too, Peter discovered when travelling on a plane in another part of the world. He got into conversation with a very amiable passenger who handed Peter his card when they parted, saying, 'If you visit the city where I live, give me a call. We'll go out to dinner.'

This Peter did and they met at the man's apartment for a pre-dinner drink, a gin and tonic so strong that Peter was obliged to tip it into a nearby plant when his companion wasn't looking. After drinks they set off in a taxi to the restaurant. On the way Peter was taken aback when his companion lent across and took Peter's hand, affectionately interlinking fingers with him.

The unexpected turn of events caused Peter to freeze in horror. He decided the safest way to handle the situation was to be as nonchalant as possible and avoid any confrontation. He left his hand there and con-

46.   Peter and Bill Murphy at the Titanium Space Monument in Moscow.

tinued chatting as normally as possible. The restaurant meal passed without further incident but as soon as his companion went off to the loo, Peter ordered a taxi to take him back to his hotel. He mentioned this casually to his dining companion, saying he must be going as he had a full day of meetings to follow.

'I've cancelled your taxi,' came the reply. 'No need for two taxis. You can share mine.'

Peter's protestations were swept aside as the other man began assuming control. The only concession Peter gained was that the taxi would go to his hotel first. Once there the man also got out, dismissed the taxi and insisted he needed a brandy.

Leading the way into the hotel bar Peter went to order him a brandy, but his companion became unpleasant and demanded to see Peter's room.

'No, no,' Peter said breezily. 'All hotel rooms are the same. Have your brandy here in the lounge.'

Eventually in the very public surroundings of the hotel lounge, Peter was able to make it abundantly clear that the man's attentions were unwelcome. Brandy finished and nothing else on offer, the man stormed out of the hotel in a fury.

Peter slumped down into his seat extremely shaken by that encounter. Needing someone to talk to he remembered a person he had met on board an Air India Super Constellation (the one that returned to Calcutta with engine trouble) who worked on the night news-desk of a newspaper, so he phoned her. She could sense what a state Peter was in and asked her husband to drive over and pick Peter up to take him to their flat for a good stiff drink. Peter said that for the first time in his life he understood how frightening it must be for a woman who is afraid she is going to be assaulted.

Peter paid fewer visits to the Iron Curtain countries than might be expected considering the volume of trade he was engaged in. The main reason was that businessmen from these communist countries were only too willing to travel to the more affluent West where they knew they would be well entertained. There were however occasions when Peter did stay in eastern Europe. Sometimes it was with a family in Leipzig and then he undertook to do the shopping. The reason for this was that many goods like chocolate and other small luxuries were unobtainable by locals yet existed on the shelves of the 'foreigners only' shops. Whilst Peter was happy to oblige his hosts, the idea of shops that reserved the best for Westerners whilst denying their own people was an anathema to him.

On one trip in eastern Europe Peter travelled in his business suit with a gold watch chain to see the Mayor of Warsaw. When he came to check in for the flight home, the airport official stared at Peter's watch chain then promptly accused him of attempting to take gold out of the country, which was illegal. Peter's watch chain was immediately confiscated. Protestations that he had been wearing it when he arrived in Poland the previous day were swept aside. It was only Peter's quick thinking which saved the day and his chain. Reaching in his pocket for the Mayor of Warsaw's card, he said, 'Will you ring the mayor and tell him what has happened.' An instant change came over the official's face.

'We are very sorry. There has been some mistake,' he said handing the watch chain back.

Interestingly a few years later when Peter was Lord Mayor he received personal requests from people in Poland who were under the impression that the Lord Mayor was in line to become Prime Minister. Letters came asking for Peter's help to obtain visas to visit the UK.

When Peter travelled with Bill Murphy of Murphyores, he had the advantage of his assistant on hand to deal with the mundane and the unexpected, but that was not always foolproof. Peter recalls the time they travelled from Düsseldorf to Warsaw via Vienna. Norm Carstens, Bill's assistant, was on hand to make sure all the baggage arrived in Warsaw ready for their next meeting. But when they arrived in Warsaw there were no bags in sight. Carstens was promptly sent back to Vienna and told not to reappear until he had found them. Before he left Norm went in search of essential supplies to tide him over the trip but in a communist country they were not easy to find. There was little to buy in the Polish shops. All he found was a toothbrush which he claimed he used to clean his teeth, brush his hair and clean his shoes—in that order! Bill and Peter remained in Warsaw looking dishevelled and unshaven because their personal possessions were missing. Since most of the vital paperwork was in their cases, they could do no business either. Instead they spent the three days they had planned to be in Poland sightseeing, then boarded the flight they had booked to Rome. Predictably it was on their final day that the luggage turned up and was immediately transferred to the hold of the plane to Rome.

The two men walked onto the concourse of Rome airport with three days' growth of beard to be greeted by a well-dressed, smiling Carstens, confident his mission had been successfully accomplished. This was more than the scruffy duo could stand so they pretended their bags had not been found.

Despite the many pitfalls that lurked, Peter was successful in gaining business. The terms of his engagement with Murphyores permitted him to work for other companies. Over the next few years Peter added in the directorships of the Siamese Tin Syndicate, South Crofty, JH Little, Thomas Hill-Jones (a chemical manufacturer in London), LRC (later named SSL International) and several other companies.

In addition to visits to Australia, China and Africa, Peter's directorships of Guthrie Corporation, St Piran, LRC and Pahang Consolidated frequently took him to Malaysia and Thailand which he enjoyed greatly. He also visited India on many occasions to buy minerals for Fergusson Wild. Nagpur, in the centre of India, was the location of one of the largest producers of manganese. In those days there was a nightly air service on DC6s from all the main Indian cities to Nagpur. The planes carrying mail arrived around midnight. They returned whence they had come carrying the outgoing mail which resulted in mail deliveries to all main Indian cities arriving the next day, a postal service truly ahead of its time.

Seldom at home was becoming a feature of Peter's life in the 1960s. In 1969 he spent two months in Egypt seconded to the Egyptian Black Sands Company by the United Nations International Development Organisation (UNIDO) as a marketing economist. It was Peter's job to assist the Egyptians to find new markets for their mineral sands. Two others went with him, one an expert in mining, the other in the financial costings of an operation.

Peter was based in Alexandria and reported to Dr Jimmy Naguib, chairman and managing director of the Egyptian Black Sands Company, who was a wonderful man. In fact Peter worked extremely closely with Dr Naguib and the two became the greatest of friends, a friendship which continues to this day.

Because of the heat their working day began at eight and finished in the early afternoon. During the day Peter travelled to sites where the sands were produced, sometimes in Egyptian army helicopters. He examined the products, which were only being produced in small quantities in those days, reported on the grade required, the potential markets for their rutile, ilmenite and zircon, and advised on how the country could develop its processing of natural minerals.

Peter and Naguib played golf in the afternoons since the golf course was one of the few places where they could talk without fear of being overheard. Peter confesses to being no golfer and those who saw him in action in Egypt agreed. Hussein, the golf pro, commented that Peter used his club like a cricket bat. 'Let the club do the work!' was his frequent cry. Hussein had great respect for the British officers who played golf. It was the Russians he disliked because they didn't play.

Hussein told the story of one British officer at the golf club who gave him some money to place a bet on a horse for him. As he was departing, Hussein overheard his colleague remark that it was a pretty stupid thing to do because he wouldn't see his money again. However, the horse he had backed won and Hussain confounded their predictions, and proved his honesty, by turning up and handing all the winnings over.

Dr Jimmy Naguib remembers Peter as a charming man who became extremely popular with them all during his time in Egypt. 'He is the world expert on beach sands,' Dr Naguib said, 'yet he has the ability to simplify things for everyone to understand.' This was especially appreciated when Peter gave a lecture at the university to the captains of industry in Egypt.

47. For two months in 1969 Peter was seconded to the Egyptian Black Sands Company by the United Nations International Development Organisation to help them develop their mineral sands. Dr Jimmy Naguib and his wife Dora looked after him well during his stay. Dora Naguib here sits by a bemused Peter during an evening's entertainment.

Peter too has fond memories of his time in Egypt and the friendliness of the people. This was demonstrated by the wonderful hospitality shown him by Jimmy Naguib and his wife Dora, a descendant of the Egyptian royal family. Only too aware that Peter would be missing his wife and daughters, the Naguibs were there to look after him at weekends. (Egyptian weekends, Peter recalled, could last three days if you wanted them too—Friday was the Muslim day of worship, Saturday the Jewish one and Sunday the Christian.) The Naguibs also extended their hospitality to Belinda when she came for a holiday during Peter's stay. They were pleased to show their English friends Aswan and Luxor, but for Peter and Belinda the most memorable part of that holiday was the two nights spent at the Naguibs' holiday home. It was in the desert where there was no sound and even the air seemed still. Under the clear sky Naguib arranged for the Bedouin to produce a lamb roast on a spit for his guests.

As is so often the case with Peter, the wonderful hospitality he received was reciprocated. The Naguib family have been to stay with the Gadsdens both at the Barbican and at their seaside home in Wittering. Since Jimmy and Dora moved to the USA, there have been more opportunities for the two families to meet up which have been greatly valued by both parties.

As the Sixties progressed Peter Gadsden became a well-known face around the City at both evening and daytime events. Murphyores had an office in the Barber Surgeons' Hall so if Peter knew he would be very late back from an evening engagement he made up a bed in his office. That was not always as straightforward as he hoped either. One night when he was staying over, he popped outside to throw the rubbish away only to hear the door blow shut behind him. Clad in his shirtsleeves with no key and no wallet, it was far too late to contact a key holder to let him in. Eventually he went to a nearby hotel and booked himself in for the night.

Next morning when the cleaner arrived at the Barber Surgeons' Hall she found Peter waiting for her. 'And where did you spend the night?' she asked with a knowing wink. Reunited with his jacket, Peter was able to return to the hotel and settle his bill.

As it became increasingly difficult to juggle a rapidly developing civic life with family commitments, Peter and Belinda decided to look for an apartment in the Barbican to make life more congenial for them all. Speed House had opened and Gilbert House was well on its way towards completion. When they moved on the 1 January 1970, Belinda recalls that the Barbican was quite literally a building site. 'You had to climb over things to get around the place and there were only six other people in Gilbert House at that time.'

Geoffrey Finn and his wife have fond memories of the Gadsden family moving in to Gilbert House.

I first met Peter soon after we moved into 605 Gilbert House. I arrived home from my office, which was within walking distance from the apartment, at 5.30 one afternoon and was greeted by my wife Miriam saying, 'We have four lovely visitors.' She was referring to Belinda and Peter's four daughters Juliet, Caroline, Clare and Elizabeth who had been entrusted to Miriam's care for a couple of hours while their parents were out on some civic duty. I was of course enthralled to meet four such pretty young ladies. Miriam explained they were our new neighbours' daughters and their parents had moved into 606 across the corridor, and they would be here shortly to pick up the children.

Peter and Belinda duly arrived and almost immediately after formal introductions, Peter enquired about my line of work. He then followed this up by asking me whether or not I belonged to a livery company. When I said not, he asked whether I would be interested in joining one. I replied that I had often thought about it but was unsure as to how one proceeded. Peter said that if I were to join a livery company it ought to be one that has a hall and it I were to allow him he could probably arrange for me to meet the immediate past master (Sir Gilbert Laithwaite) of the Tallow Chandlers' Company.

Well that was the first memorable meeting between the Finns and the Gadsdens and we have been bosom friends ever since. I mention all this as one example out of thousands where Peter has helped countless numbers of people.

Living in the City certainly made Peter's life easier and enabled him to become more involved in civic life but it challenged Belinda's housekeeping skills to the limit. After the convenience of life in Carshalton Beeches, there was a pioneering spirit about life at the Barbican, indeed for those living anywhere in the City in those days. Most shops closed down at the weekends leaving only a scruffy little grocer's shop for the growing band of residents. A small Tesco eventually appeared and then two years later the arrival of Safeways signalled the beginning of civilisation for the residents. The City of London Girls' School, which the two younger Gadsden girls attended, was down at Blackfriars in those days and involved an interesting morning walk.

Peter Gadsden relished the idea of building a civic career as well as a professional one. 'This is,' he said, 'because if you are an achiever you can't sit around and let things be done. You want to get involved.' As the family arranged to move into the City, Peter joined the Ward Club of

Cripplegate and for the first time met Sir Peter Studd, a person he is proud to call his mentor. The late Sir Peter Studd remembered Peter Gadsden mentioning to him that if ever a vacancy arose on Common Council, he would be interested. And the more Sir Peter Studd saw of this young man, the more convinced he was that here was someone who would go far and someone he was pleased to assist.

Sir Peter Studd was not the only person to have been impressed by the abilities of Peter Gadsden. Ernest Parker, another member of Common Council, had also noticed him.

> In no time it became obvious to me that an introduction to Cripplegate Ward was desirable and it transpired that he would welcome the opportunity of meeting my colleagues and friends having applied for the tenancy of a flat to live within the Ward of Cripplegate. We had already taken business premises within the Ward and I spared no effort to bring him into a circle of Cripplegate Ward activities. His response was to undertake the secretaryship of the Ward Club at very short notice, a service that proved invaluable and reinforced my view that we had gained the friendship of one who would not only prove his ability in the Ward Club but could make a serious contribution to the Ward in the more eminent Civic activities of the City Corporation.

History proved Ernest Parker's prediction to be correct. In a short space of time the new secretary transformed a rather sleepy club by organizing functions, encouraging residents to join and providing them with a membership list.

Sir Peter Studd recalled how he advised Peter Gadsden about taking things slowly.

> I gave him some friendly advice on the best way to proceed. I told him that when he became a member of Common Council he might go on to be an alderman. I said you will in due time find yourself up for election for sheriff. But don't be in a hurry to be a sheriff. You want it to happen two to three years before you become Lord Mayor. Take your time. Then you can trail your Lord Mayor. You will get to know who is who in all the positions you have to deal with as Lord Mayor—places like the Foreign Office, the Church, Parliament, the Palace and so on. That's the right way to do things.

Sir Peter Studd chuckled as he related the advice he had been so keen to impress on 'the new boy'. The reason for that chuckle was that within a matter of months he would be urging the young Peter Gadsden to do totally the opposite—to stand for shrieval office during Sir Peter Studd's mayoralty.

Following the death of Bert Toye, of Toye Canning Spencer, Peter stood for the vacancy that now arose and was elected to the Court of Common

Council for the Ward of Cripplegate. On 22 May 1969 Mr Peter Drury Gadsden MA JP was summoned by the Swordbearer to attend the Court of Common Council at the Guildhall. The Lord Mayor, Sir Charles Trinder, took the chair and introduced Peter Gadsden as the new member for Cripplegate. He was appointed to the Spitalfields Market and Housing Committees. This date marks the official beginning of a civic career that would last 30 years and take Peter to its pinnacle within ten.

Chapter 10

Mr Sheriff

(The City of London's coat of arms with motto 'O Lord guide us')

At the beginning of 1970 Peter was invited to speak at a banquet at the Painters' Hall for 90 South American guests to celebrate BOAC's inaugural flight from Miami to London. They said they had chosen Peter to speak because 'he is a much travelled mining company director and much involved in the City'. Coming at a time when Peter had only recently become a member of the Court of Common Council it was a sure sign that people believed he was destined for higher things. Peter used the opportunity to act as an ambassador for the City of London calling his speech 'The City of London—four sides to the square mile—historical, traditional, commercial and residential'. He opened by saying that 'travel has played and will continue to play a vital part in the breaking-down of national barriers, racial prejudices and misunderstanding'—something he remains fervently convinced of today.

At one stage Peter's aspirations to a civic career looked close to being scuppered by the thoughtless actions of a chef. As secretary of the Cripplegate Ward Club, Peter was responsible for arranging a luncheon in Cutlers' Hall in honour of the Lord Mayor. Outside caterers had been engaged for the occasion but unfortunately their chef swore at the beadle of the Cutlers' Company. Peter was held responsible for the gross insult that had taken place and the beadle said he would be reporting Peter to the Master of the company, none other than Alderman Lord Mais, Lord Mayor in 1972. Although Peter was personally blameless, some feared this signalled the end of a promising civic life. Fortunately they were wrong and years later Lord Mais joked about it with Peter. But at the time it was thought to be a close call.

Soon after the BOAC speech, Peter was faced with a dilemma. Should he act as he had been advised or be an opportunist? After the eminently sound advice Sir Peter Studd had given him about doing things in the right order, the mayoral candidate now asked him to do the complete opposite.

What had happened was that as Sir Peter Studd was preparing for his mayoral year, a problem arose with the preferred candidate for sheriff. Only six weeks before the election, he had decided that he could not leave his business for a whole year. Hugh Wontner, chairman of the Savoy group, would still stand as the aldermanic candidate, but who could be his brother sheriff? 'There was only one person I could think of who was capable of stepping into the gap,' said the late Sir Peter Studd. 'That was Peter Gadsden. Having advised him not to consider becoming a sheriff because it was too soon, I had to swallow all that and ring him. I rang him on a Friday and asked him to ignore what I had previously said and to consider over the weekend whether he was prepared to put his name forward for the office of sheriff.'

That Sunday Peter was on his way to Cornwall because he was due to visit the South Crofty tin mine in Camborne the next day. As he travelled on the overnight train, he considered Sir Peter Studd's proposal. It must have been Maxie's advice to Peter from those distant days at Wrekin College which helped him make up his mind. 'Take advantage of all your chances and opportunities' Peter had been taught and that was exactly what he did.

The following morning Peter rang Sir Peter Studd to say, 'Yes. Yes because it is you. And yes because it is Hugh Wontner.' Evidently the *Evening Standard*'s comments about the post of sheriff had not discouraged Peter even though they had said, 'The job is onerous and expensive, but offers to its holder the consolation of having his timetable called a hymn sheet.'

So out of the blue at the beginning of February 1970, Peter and his supporters found themselves launching a campaign from scratch for him to be elected sheriff. There was little time to spare because tradition dictates that shrieval elections are held on Midsummer's Day in Guildhall.

The office of sheriff is the oldest office in the City, older even than that of Lord Mayor, because shire reeves have existed since Saxon times. They were the king's representatives responsible for enforcing royal justice and collecting royal revenues. Today the liverymen of the City of London elect two sheriffs, a right granted by King Henry II. He permitted one sheriff to represent the County of London and one to represent the County of Middlesex, but after 1888 both came to represent the City of London.

Tony Hart, a distinguished architect, was immediately appointed secretary and he assisted Peter in gathering supporters who included 'some powerful names', one newspaper was quick to spot. Notably there was Bunny Morgan, past president and honorary secretary of the City Livery Club with a reputation as the 'Sheriff maker' and a great influence in the City. Sir Cullum Welch, a past Lord Mayor and chairman of Peter's shrieval election committee, was a valuable supporter as he had recently retired from the aldermanic bench. The deputy chairman of Peter's election committee was Stanley Wells from Peter's own Ward of Cripplegate and another well-known City figure, a member of Common Council and past Master of the Worshipful Company of Tallow Chandlers. One other notable figure who declared his support for Peter was the Chief Commoner, George Vine, a City chartered surveyor and liveryman of the Clockmakers' Company. In their opinion Peter was 'a young active person with the right background'.

By May the campaign was in full swing. Peter received a useful insight into what life as a sheriff might hold for him when he was invited to the luncheon for the judges at the Old Bailey. This was the second occasion Peter had the honour of being a guest.

The two serving sheriffs share between them the duty of supporting the Lord Mayor at home and abroad, and of looking after Her Majesty's judges. This latter role involves one sheriff being on duty at the Old Bailey every day and presiding at the luncheon. Within months Peter would be presiding at these luncheons himself, but in May 1970 he was an invited guest along with AF Rogers, Harry da Costa and Stanley Cohen.

Plenty of people were convinced that Peter would make an ideal sheriff and one who might well take his turn as Lord Mayor in the future. As one of his supporters wrote:

> During the past four years it has become apparent to me that Peter Gadsden has a personal charm, is devoid of self-aggrandisement with spontaneous generosity and possessed of innate ability with sound judgement. All that with the support of his devoted wife Belinda renders him admirably suited to fill the high office of Sheriff to serve the Mayoralty of the City of London especially during the ensuing year. His commercial experience and world travel with a varied and valuable educational background coupled with his highly successful business career of the past eighteen months in the City should most certainly prove Mr Peter Gadsden to be socially acceptable within the ambit of Civic activities usually associated with the Mayoral and Shrieval twelve months' tour of service.

Peter was immensely grateful to the hardworking team that quickly formed to support him because his own diary for the first half of 1970 was full. Many of his national and international appointments had been arranged months before. Peter continued his business throughout the campaign and, to the amazement of many, succeeded in maintaining it, on only a slightly reduced scale, throughout the shrievalty. It was just a case of being organised he said. Many felt they were seeing organisation *par excellence* and behind it the support of excellent secretaries and a wonderful wife.

Arriving at Common Hall on the Midsummer Day to watch the shrieval elections, the *Evening Standard* reported Mr Peter Gadsden was 'looking bronzed from a family skiing holiday following a business trip to Hong Kong and the Far East'. The election drew an unusual amount of media interest. It is always one of London's spectacles because the aldermen arrive in full regalia and carrying little nosegays (or posies), in a tradition dating back to medieval times designed to distract the worthies from the smell of the 'great unwashed' as well as to ward off the evil plague.

The 1970 campaign differed from others because it was a stiffly fought contest, causing more than 2,000 liverymen (double the usual number) to turn out for the election. Even the *Daily Express* observed this to be 'the largest assembly since the war'. The reason for all the interest was that three candidates had put up for the two offices. Hugh Wontner stood for the post of aldermanic sheriff and Peter Gadsden was the well-supported candidate for sheriff, but standing against him was someone the newspapers described as 'a surprise runner, an insurance man Eric Bales of Farringdon Without'.

In accordance with tradition, the liverymen decide by a show of hands at Common Hall: Mr Bales was seen to be soundly defeated. However, no candidate is obliged to accept the outcome of this method of election and they can demand a poll, which Eric Bales' supporters promptly did. This not only extended the campaign, but heightened media interest even further because there had only been three shrieval polls since the war. 'One of the first seriously contested elections for the office of sheriff of the City of London for many a long year,' reported a journalist excitedly.

The poll in early July 1970 was decisive:

Hugh Wontner 1209 (the highest number of votes any alderman had received since 1948)

Peter Gadsden 1014

Eric Bales 330

Peter was amazed by this resounding victory, but he stated calmly, 'I regard my election as a job of service.' Even though he would not take office until September, there was much to do. Sir Peter Studd, who was pleased by the outcome of the poll, was on hand to advise on practicalities. 'Strangely enough buttons for footmen and chauffeur's uniforms take ages and this may well prove to be one of the first actual jobs you should put in hand,' he wrote to the new sheriff elect.

Peter had clothes to order to a design unchanged for the past 200 years. Sheriffs require two different sets, their Old Baileys and their court dress. Some people might have had qualms about donning archaic garments like stockings, jabots and knee breeches but Peter was cheerfully prepared to do whatever was required of him. 'The British love dressing-up,' said Hugh Wontner and endorsed by Peter, one-time winner of Wrekin College's dramatics prize. Peter was fortunate in that Sir Guy Bracewell Smith, who was an old Wrekinian, gave Peter his father's court dress which after alteration fitted perfectly. His father had been Lord Mayor in 1946.

Some months later there was much amusement when the two sheriffs were standing side by side in their Old Baileys (the costume that comprises three-quarter-length breeches, stockings and buckled shoes). A guest at a Mansion House reception murmured as he passed, 'I do so admire you men of the cloth'. The parson's son was quite happy to be mistaken for a bishop but told Hugh, charitably, that he could be taken for an archbishop since he looked more venerable.

Besides the clothes there was the badge of office to arrange. Sheriffs have always worn a chain of office since the days of Elizabeth I, which today takes the form of a triple gold chain. Dating from 1850 the triple chain is worn with a badge of office on the front. Traditionally both are paid for by one's fellow liverymen, friends and supporters. Peter's beautiful shrieval chain has since been made into five necklaces, a gift for each of his daughters and his wife, Belinda.

In 1970 there was no time to spare because badges have to be designed and made during July and August, ready for the sheriff to put on when he takes office on Michaelmas Day. Peter chose Norman Harding of Asprey's to design his badge and they decided on the form of an antique scroll which would display Peter's coat of arms in the centre. The badge also had smaller shields or escutcheons to represent different features of his life. In Peter's case there were so many things to include. The final design displayed a teasel to represent the Clothworkers' Company, over the top the badge of the City Livery Club and below the badge of the KSLI flanked by a maple leaf for Canada and a kangaroo to represent his many links with Australia. The arms that surrounded the badge were those of the Ward of Cripplegate, Jesus College Cambridge, the Haggerston family, Wrekin College and the Worshipful Company of Clothworkers. When Peter was presented with his badge and chain of office, he replied he thought the year would be as easy as ABC—Angela(Studd), Belinda, Catherine (Wontner).

The chain of office was hung around Peter's neck by the outgoing sheriff on 28 September 1970. The Sheriff's Inauguration Breakfast followed the ceremony in Goldsmiths' Hall and the Bishop of London proposed a toast to the new sheriffs, commenting that Peter, the minerals expert, would have no difficulty in 'sorting the gold from the dross'.

Further merriment followed when some 'poetry' was declaimed in honour of the new sheriffs:

Two gentlemen of City fame
Now claim your kind attention
Being an old hand at this game
Their names I shall not mention.

But one is an hotelier
And one a man of metal.
And both stride in from day to day
In very finest mettle.

Both well deserve their golden chains,
And both having charming spouses.
One boasts a metal-trader's brains
The other, five-star houses.

But: Claridges, or the Savoy;
Or Tins, or Lead or Copper.
Both are pure gold without alloy
Which is extremely proper.

May the Lord Mayor and they combine
In harmony together,
At play or duty, work or wine,
Nor ever meet foul weather.

These, Hugh and Peter, you may guess
(and Catherine and Belinda),
Lord Mayor and Lady Mayoress,
Are the last words of Trinder.

48.   Sheriff Peter Gadsden and alderman and Sheriff Hugh Wontner greet Sir Peter Studd (Lord Mayor 1970–71) at the Sheriff's Breakfast on 28 September 1970.

Hugh Wontner, the aldermanic sheriff, was Peter's senior by 23 years. As chairman of the Savoy group, he lived 'over the shop', as he put it, at Claridges. The two formed a wonderful friendship during their term of office, as did their wives, all of which made for an exceptionally strong working relationship.

Hugh's association with the Savoy group proved immensely useful on one occasion when a misunderstanding occurred in the dining arrangements. As they had been instructed, the two sheriffs' wives presented themselves, alongside their husbands, at a dinner in Sadlers' Hall. To everyone's embarrassment, the clerk had to tell the Lord Mayor that ladies were not expected. Belinda promptly issued an invitation to Catherine Wontner to go back with her to the Barbican flat where she would rustle up something for them to eat. However, Hugh gallantly stepped in and arranged for the Lady Mayoress and the sheriffs' ladies to dine at Claridges instead.

During their year together the sheriffs acquired various nicknames. 'First we were Tweedledum and Tweedledee, then Gog and Magog, and at one point we were known as Steptoe and Son because of my metal trade connections, then Ping and Pong and even George and Bill,' Peter muses. The aldermanic sheriff Hugh Wontner had on one occasion been referred to as 'the automatic sheriff' and someone suggested they were called sheriffs because they drank sherry.

Following the Sheriffs' Breakfast, their official duties began and, as is customary, the two sheriffs spent the first six weeks supporting the Lord Mayor (in this case Lieutenant-Colonel Sir Ian Bowater) who was nearing the end of his term of office. He was a gentleman of the old school and Peter, 'the youngest sheriff for many years' as one newspaper described him, found it took him time to settle into the rigid formality expected of his office. Even a year later when Sir Ian Bowater saw Peter dashing to a meeting of the Court of Aldermen, he stopped him. 'Aldermen don't run!' came the advice.

On another occasion at a reception the sheriffs were awaiting the Lord Mayor's departure. Eventually much to Peter's relief, Hugh Wontner came over to him and said, 'We can go now.' So Peter went up to the Lord Mayor to take his leave and knew in an instant that he had made a mistake. 'You're not going,' the Lord Mayor said, making it sound more like a statement than a question. As Peter began explaining, his words were cut short: 'Your brother sheriff is leading you astray. You don't leave before I do.'

49. The two sheriffs, Peter Gadsden and Hugh Wontner, with their chaplains before the Sheriffs' Breakfast in 1970. Peter's chaplain was Canon Guy Pentreath who had been his headmaster at Wrekin College (see page 31).

No matter how hard they tried, the two new sheriffs managed to fall foul of protocol several times in those first six weeks. There was the time when they were due to receive the Lord Mayor at the Old Bailey and found themselves delayed so they arrived after him. He greeted them in the Recorder's room with the words, 'I missed you, Sheriffs'. They apologised profusely and Hugh Wontner followed their apology up with a letter explaining that no discourtesy was intended by their late arrival. At their next meeting the Lord Mayor indicated the apology had been accepted by saying, 'Thank you for your letter.' No more was said.

The atmosphere changed immediately when Sir Peter Studd took office in November 1970. At 54, he was the youngest Lord Mayor for many years 'and promises to be the most active', one newspaper predicted. This young team epitomised the energy of the new decade by undertaking an unusually large number of high-profile engagements.

Sir Peter Studd loved being with people and was always reluctant to leave a function. As protocol demands that nobody leaves before the Lord

Mayor, the host and other guests were often enquiring of the sheriffs and the Household Officer on duty, 'When is the Lord Mayor going to leave?'

The first big event in Sir Peter Studd's mayoralty was naturally the Lord Mayor's Show and the sheriff, resplendent in his robes, travelled with his chaplain, Canon Guy Pentreath of Beaulieu. It is debatable who derived the most pleasure from that day. Peter remembers how much the former Wrekin headmaster enjoyed riding in a coach in the Lord Mayor's Procession alongside his ex-Head of School.

The late Sir Peter Studd spoke warmly of his time with Peter Gadsden and Hugh Wontner saying: 'We were a very strong crew. We had such a wonderful experience of friendship that year—quite unexplainable and so personal that no one can take it from us. I can't tell you how enormously it helped and certainly no Lord Mayor and Lady Mayoress has ever had more wonderful sheriffs and sheriffines.'

His happiness in the team was shared by his sheriffs though they were rarely given the opportunity to speak in public, 'Like children in Victorian times, sheriffs are normally seen but not heard,' Peter once said. However at the City Livery Club Annual Luncheon in May 1971 they took the opportunity to mention their exceptional relationship. 'We don't believe there has ever been a happier team than the present Lord Mayor and his two sheriffs. Not until today have we had the chance to say that in public and to acknowledge our gratitude to the Lord Mayor for sweeping us along with such infectious gaiety and enthusiasm,' Hugh Wontner told assembled guests.

The office of sheriff brought with it the first of many royal duties that Peter has been honoured to undertake in his public life. The first came in February 1971, when The Queen visited the Old Bailey to lunch with the judges, the Lord Mayor and the sheriffs to mark the completion of the £7 million rebuilding programme of the Central Criminal Court. What was remarkable about this visit was that no reigning monarch had visited the courts since they were opened in 1907. Peter, seated opposite The Queen, was surprised to hear her say that she had actually attended the courts before. It transpired that in 1947, as Princess Elizabeth, she and Princess Margaret had sat in on a murder case as part of their education.

A few weeks later, Peter played his part in a large royal pageant that brought the City to a standstill and attracted major television coverage. Crowds lined the route to see Prince Charles and Princess Anne ride from Buckingham Palace to Guildhall in an open carriage to be received by the

Lord Mayor and his sheriffs. The occasion marked the Prince of Wales being granted the Freedom of the City of London. At the luncheon which followed, he caused laughter and applause when he said, 'The greatest British quality is the ability to laugh at ourselves, otherwise how would we all have dressed up like this today!'

As if shrieval and business duties were not enough, in the middle of all this, Peter found himself campaigning for the office of alderman. Indeed the day of the rehearsal for Prince Charles' visit saw the Lord Mayor and sheriffs hurrying off to the Wardmote immediately afterwards to attend the aldermanic elections.

Once again events did not happen in the order Sir Peter Studd recommended. In December 1970, Sir Frederick Hoare announced his retirement which meant there was a vacancy on the Aldermanic Bench in the Ward of Farringdon Without. Moves began behind the scenes to find a successor. Mr Peter Gadsden and Mr Philip Syrett were the two names that came forward.

So a year on, Peter was once again involved in campaigning. One journalist commented admiringly that Peter's message to the electorate was 'short and to the point'. In his letter to voters Peter stated: 'As one of the sheriffs I have had the opportunity to study the duties and responsibilities of the Lord Mayor and Aldermen at first hand. My aim in serving this Ward in the City can be summed up in the school prayer, "May its foundations ever stand firm".'

Both candidates faced keen questioning about their aims and intentions. It is interesting to note that as early as 1971 Peter was speaking publicly about the value of having a Barbican Arts Centre. He was realistic about it, knowing that people would want to know how it was going to be paid for, indeed he was a Barbican resident and ratepayer himself. It was highly appropriate eight years later that, as Lord Mayor, Sir Peter Gadsden should be the person to attend the first function in the new Barbican Arts Centre before the official opening by The Queen. On that occasion he said, 'The completion of this huge Barbican project will be the completion of an immense undertaking that represents the City's faith in the future.' He also accurately predicted that 'the citizens of London will discover what a wonderful centre they have'.

At the aldermanic poll in 1971, the electors showed their unequivocal approval of Peter's application. He polled 302 votes compared to his opponent's 60. His official title now became Mr Alderman and Sheriff

50. Alderman Peter Gadsden

1. The Coat of Arms of Sir Peter Drury Haggerston Gadsden GBE, AC, FREng. They are quartered with those of Haggerston as Lady Gadsden is the heraldic heiress of the 11th Baronet. The maple leaves in Sir Peter's arms allude to Canada where he was born, while the teasel alludes to the Clothworkers' Company of which he is a liveryman. As a Knight Grand Cross of the Most Excellent Order of the British Empire, Sir Peter is entitled to supporters to his arms; the dexter supporter, a lion guardant, is holding a cross-crosslet fitchy in allusion to the Ward of Farringdon Without, while the koala bear symbolises Sir Peter's many connections with Australia and the geologist's hammer which it holds refers to his mining interests.

2. The new Lord Mayor leans from the golden coach to shake hands with his brother David before joining the procession to the Law Courts on Lord Mayor's Day, 1979.

3. Peter waves from the chuckwagon at the Mannville Homecoming, Alberta, in 1980.

4. The Lord Mayor and Lady Mayoress surrounded by their daughters at the Mansion House. From left to right: Elizabeth, Clare, Juliet and Caroline, who were Maids of Honour to the Lady Mayoress at the Lord Mayor's Banquet.

5. Peter and Belinda with their grandchildren at Harelaw in 1999 when the family gathered to celebrate Elizabeth's marriage at Ellingham. Since this picture was taken the family has grown and Peter and Belinda are the proud grandparents of seventeen.

6. A private dinner party at the Mansion House given by the Lord Mayor and Lady Mayoress to celebrate the 80th birthday of Her Majesty Queen Elizabeth, The Queen Mother in 1980. Present were their four daughters, Peter's brother David and his wife Judy, and Sir Hugh and Lady Wontner.

7. The luncheon held at Guildhall to celebrate the Golden Wedding of Her Majesty The Queen and HRH The Duke of Edinburgh in November 1997. Peter, as the senior alderman, stands third from the right and Belinda fourth from the right.

8. As Founder Master, Alderman Sir Peter Gadsden receives the Letters Patent for the Worshipful Company of Engineers from the Lord Mayor, Sir Anthony Jolliffe.

9. Peter accompanied Prime Minister Margaret Thatcher around the British Pavilion at Expo 88 in Brisbane, Australia, as part of the bicentennial celebrations.

10. One of many marches by the Red Guards captured on film by Peter during his business travels in China during the days of Mao Tse-Tung.

11. One of many signs Peter saw by the road on his business trips to China. Peter was also given many propaganda leaflets and copies of The Little Red Book, the thoughts of Chairman Mao, which he has kept out of interest.

12. Peter at St Paul's Cathedral wearing the robes of the Knight Grand Cross of the Most Excellent Order of the British Empire (GBE).

13. Sir Peter Gadsden by Leonard Boden painted in 1991. The portrait was commissioned by PPP, of which Peter was chairman.

Peter Gadsden. The Lord Mayor found himself in the most unusual position of having two aldermanic sheriffs and of holding a luncheon at the Mansion House to honour the new alderman, who was also a sheriff. Peter too would join that very small group of Lord Mayors who had become a sheriff first and an alderman later. His election as alderman now set him firmly on the road that would lead to becoming Lord Mayor. As he once explained in a speech, 'The members of the Court of Aldermen's approval of a new alderman is really to ensure that no person becomes an alderman unless in the opinion of his colleagues he has the qualities and attributes to occupy in due course, the great office of Lord Mayor of London.'

As alderman of the Ward of Farringdon Without, it was necessary for him to resign as secretary of the Cripplegate Ward Club. Because Farringdon Without is the largest of the City wards, it is in the unique position of having three beadles. However, Peter did not often get the chance to process with all three of them because he was often asked if he would loan a beadle to another alderman whose own beadle had failed to turn up!

51.   As alderman of the Ward of Farringdon Without, Peter had three beadles. This was unusual but very popular with his colleagues because it meant an alderman whose beadle had failed to turn up could look to Peter to borrow one.

Peter's shrieval year was even busier than many predicted but made manageable by the Gadsdens' move into the Barbican the previous year. It now meant that Peter could always get home each night even after late dinners. With Hugh Wontner living at Claridges, the sheriffs' Old Bailey flat was not used as much as it might have been during their shrievalty. Nevertheless it was vital for the many swift changes of clothes which engagements required.

The sheriffs accompanied the Lord Mayor on his overseas tour to Thailand and Iran in August. In Tehran they were surprised to discover how much their visit was genuinely appreciated. Sir Peter Studd recalled one Iranian telling him 'you have no idea how much good you have done. We were seen as lame ducks before but now we are top of the pops.'

During the year, Peter was often glimpsed dashing around the City slotting business meetings into the spaces in his 'hymn sheet'. Ever the master of organisation, he also managed to dovetail some of his overseas visits into the schedule for the mayoral tour. Their visit to the Far East

52. As sheriff, Peter accompanied the Lord Mayor, Sir Peter Studd, and his brother sheriff, Hugh Wontner (Lord Mayor in 1973), on the mayoral tour to Thailand in 1971.

offered Peter an opportunity to visit some of the mining operations of which he was a director in Thailand and Malaysia. Amusingly this caused some consternation amongst the customs officers at Bangkok airport when businessman Mr Peter Gadsden arrived. They examined his hand luggage only to find it contained an ornate and evidently expensive badge and chain of office. Peter was also obliged to execute some swift costume changes between going down a mine in the morning and appearing alongside the Lord Mayor of London at a banquet in the evening.

The civic visit to the Ulster '71 Exhibition presented different challenges and was hailed as a great success. The exhibition set out to provide a showcase for everything made in Ulster ranging from shipbuilding, engineering and aircraft engines through to tobacco products. It was the largest exhibition since the Festival of Britain 20 years before.

There were many who had misgivings about such a high-profile civic party visiting the Province in those troubled times. Indeed on the day of their arrival newspapers carried reports about the troops in Belfast coming under machine-gun fire for the second time in three days. Sir Peter Studd was determined to give the people of Ulster the spectacle they deserved and so agreed to the party riding through the streets in procession, though he admitted afterwards he was fearful of being shot at any time. Sheriff Peter Gadsden rode alongside the Mayor of Belfast in an open carriage, aware of the risks but determined to do his public duty.

Whilst in Northern Ireland, Peter took the opportunity to visit his old prep school at Rockport and take tea with them; this was the first time he had returned. This official visit to the school by an ex-pupil, now the sheriff of London, was much appreciated and forged links which have been maintained ever since.

As the sheriff's lady, Belinda found her time fully occupied with official duties as well as looking after their four daughters. Fortunately the two eldest were of an age to assist with looking after the younger ones when their parents were attending an evening engagement—which was almost every night. 'Seldom at home it definitely was,' one of Peter's daughters agrees!

Shortly before Peter became sheriff, Belinda was honoured to become a member of the Guild of Freemen of the City of London. This was indeed a great honour because she was only the fourth woman to join the Guild, the first being Mary Donaldson who went on to become London's only lady Lord Mayor.

Belinda did much to assist Angela Studd, the Lady Mayoress, with the 'Save St Paul's Appeal'. A survey of St Paul's in 1969 had revealed that 250 years of pollution and traffic vibration had taken their toll. £3 million were needed to weatherproof the roof and overhaul every mortar joint and stone. Lord Mayor Sir Peter Studd made fund-raising for the appeal a high priority and his chosen charity. Both Peter and Belinda devoted a great deal of their time and influence to supporting this cause.

At the end of the shrieval year in September, the City livery companies gathered to bid farewell to their sheriffs. The tribute paid to Peter on that occasion speaks volumes: 'Mr Alderman Peter Gadsden is a man of the City, works in the City, lives in the City and is steeped in City traditions. He is a man dedicated to the service of others, as has been shown by his civic activities during the last year.'

This was high praise for a man who has always understood and upheld everything the City values. In one of his speeches a few years later, Peter explained, 'We keep traditions not because we are backward-looking, but because they are the foundations upon which we build the future.'

Chapter 11

'Trader Gadsden'

We're Purchasers, the Purchasers,
Who always play the game,
A Band of Brothers one and all,
And worthy of the name.
The cause of charity is our aim,
To provide for others' care,
So raise a toast to the Purchasers,
Who are sportsmen everywhere.

From the 'The Purchasers' Song'. (Peter is a member of the Almost Modern [AM] Order of Purchasers which was formed in 1921.)

The Seventies were a busy decade for Peter. Once he had completed his shrieval duties he picked up the reins of his businesses which had been set aside slightly. Now that the family were living at the Barbican Peter found it easier to run a complex business life and enjoy family life to the full. In order to simplify his business operations Peter vacated his office in Barber Surgeons' Hall and set up two new offices to deal with different aspects of his business. This meant Peter was seen on the move even more than before. Suzanne Stubbins, one of his secretaries at this time said, 'Peter would rush round the City without an overcoat in all weathers. He knew all the walkways through the City and walked fast between everywhere. He covered huge distances. In fact he connected a pedometer to his trouser leg one day and found he had travelled seven miles that day.' Hilary Machtus who ran Peter's other office said, 'No sooner had Suzanne phoned to say "Peter's left" than he appeared at the door. I was convinced he must be on roller skates! Only traffic lights and pedestrian crossings held him up.'

Both offices were run by eminently competent secretaries. Peter's colleagues admired the fact that over the years he had a very small number of incredibly loyal staff. The only reason his secretaries generally left was because they had married and were starting a family. All kept in touch with Peter and the family and have remained personal friends.

Hilary wrote to him saying

> I just wanted to thank you firstly for all your generosity through AMA, but principally for being such a nice person to work for and for making my job such a pleasure over the past four years. I have enjoyed it all very much and shall miss you. However, I'm looking forward to being a "Mum" and Peter [her husband] and I hope to see you, Belinda and the girls again before too long,

> Yours affectionately, Hilary
> (To distinguish between Peter her husband and Peter her boss, Hilary referred to her husband as 'Little Peter' and her employer as 'Big Peter'.)

Another secretary, Mary McLeish, decided to give Peter a reference rather than the other way around. She wrote:

> He is a man of action rather than inaction. He works at great speed and, quite frankly, it is not always easy to keep pace with him. He crams into a week what another would cram into two or even three, yet he is always relaxed.

> He rarely uses motor transport during the day in the City—he prefers to keep fit by walking at great speed from appointment to appointment (at 140 paces to the minute no doubt, which perhaps is not surprising since he once served in the King's Shropshire Light Infantry!)

> He never wears a coat or a raincoat, even in the depths of winter, or on the wettest days—his daily 'walks' around the City keep him 'glowing' and in the best of health.

> He enjoys a challenge—he never says: 'No, it cannot be done.' He will find a way to do it and it will get done. He is a very positive person and in no way negative. He never puts off until tomorrow what can be done today. From this you will gather he is altogether very much a 'live wire' and those of us who work closely to him go home completely exhausted and in need of rest to face another day—he, no doubt, will have another engagement, which will probably finish late in the evening and yet he will be as 'bright as a button' the next morning.

> He has a fantastically accurate memory—he never forgets to do those little things he has promised to do, such as sending a piece of helpful information to that one, or copying an article of interest to another, or making sure that those 'in the picture' receive a copy of the photograph, etc etc. These little 'services' are always performed—THOROUGHLY WITH ENTHUSIASM.

Suzanne Stubbins ran the office in Bartholomew Close which handled Peter's business connected with JH Little (part of the Inchcape Group) and Pahang Consolidated between 1971 and 1977 until she left to start a family.

Hilary Machtus worked on Peter's Australian business from the office in Coleman Street between 1971 until 1975 when she too left to have a baby. In fact the baby came rather early, she left one day and the baby arrived very soon after. 'So Peter got off lightly,' she said, 'He was very nearly faced with delivering it himself!' Hilary recalls 'what a lovely man Peter was to work for' adding, 'there wasn't a time when I didn't enjoy working for him. It was busy but fun.' Soon after she began working for him he helped her out when Hilary unexpectedly received a huge bouquet of red roses from an admirer, delivered to the office. Having recently got engaged, there was no way she could take those flowers home, beautiful though they were. Peter nobly stepped into the breach. 'Don't worry,' he said, 'I'll deal with them for you.' Then he added with a grin, 'It's Belinda's birthday, I'll give them to her as a present!'

After working for the Australian mining company Murphyores, Peter went to work for Associated Minerals Consolidated (AMA) and undertook several other appointments along with his aldermanic and magisterial responsibilities. Running the Australian end of the business required careful planning to accommodate the time differences. The day in Coleman Street always began with the morning telex from Australia. In order to make it easier to accommodate their working day with that of the London end of the operation, Peter installed an answer phone in this office and Hilary recalls it caused a great deal of interest because it was one of the first answerphones in the City. The messages they received were amusing because people who rang were often taken aback by a recorded message and would say 'I really can't talk to a machine'.

Peter also arranged for an extension of the office telephone to go to the flat in the Barbican. This enabled him to take business calls at any time of the day or night. His customers were greatly impressed; unaware that he was actually at home, they thought he worked very long hours in the office.

Telephone calls were expensive in the 1970s and those across the world extremely expensive. In an effort to keep down the cost of communicating with his office when he was in Australia, Peter devised a number code. Hilary recalls that if she sent through the message 01 01 that meant that she had despatched one telex and one letter and had not received either from him. Peter might reply 1110 which decoded, meant he had received one telex but not the letter but he had sent one telex and one letter to the London office.

Peter rarely phoned the office when he was travelling. 'I think it was only once and that was because someone had broken into his hotel room and stole cash and travellers' cheques from his briefcase,' Hilary remembers. That Peter could function so effectively at such a distance without regular contact with his base seems amazing in these days of emails and mobile phones, but says much for his meticulous planning and organisation.

The nickname 'Trader Gadsden' was given to Peter by William Foster, a fellow Clothworker who sat opposite him at dinner. Foster asked Peter what he did for a living, to which he replied, 'Marketing minerals'. Following the meeting Peter was invited to join the board of the Siamese Tin Syndicate and South Crofty as a non-executive director. The sobriquet 'Trader Gadsden' proved to be a brilliant summary of Peter's business activities at this time.

Siamese Tin certainly sounds exotic and the company indeed owned mines in Malaysia and Thailand which Peter visited on his travels. Because the company had taken over the Cornish South Crofty tin mine, they changed their name to St Piran, the patron saint of Cornwall. Visits to Camborne might sound tame compared to Peter's other destinations but they were frequently entertaining and often furnished him with stories to amuse colleagues back in London. Cornwall was only at the tip of England but sometimes Peter thought he had stumbled on a different planet. At the time decimal currency came in, Peter remembers Charlie Williams, employed at South Crofty, saying, 'I don't like it meself. Don't think it'll take on in these parts.'

Although the towns were only a short distance apart there was intense rivalry between the miners from Redruth and those from Camborne. Peter was there when one of the workers in the offices at South Crofty, Camborne, was bemoaning the fact his daughter had just married someone from Africa. He received scant commiseration from his colleague who said, 'You're lucky. My daughter married a man from Redruth!'

Peter usually travelled down to Cornwall on the overnight sleeper from London to be wished 'Good morning' by the station master at Camborne. On one occasion Len Thomas, a director of South Crofty, asked the station master, 'How's yer aunt? I know she's bin ill.' To which the station master replied. 'She's dead Mr Thomas. They cremated 'er.' Adding, 'Yer know, that cremation. It's an 'orrible death.'

The Cornish accent took a while to tune in to and not everyone was clear what was being said sometimes. Shortly after Christmas one of the miners was telling Len Thomas about his son. 'He's got a goi-tar,' he said looking suitably glum.

'Oh I am sorry. A goitre is pretty serious isn't it,' Len sympathised.

'What? No, a goit-ar is just noisy,' the miner said, surprised Mr Thomas had misunderstood him.

Over the years much has been penned about integrity in business dealings and today people are most concerned that they do not accept any gifts which could be construed as bribes. Peter, who has been in business for many years, feels some of these concerns have been overplayed.

> I never came across bribery personally. It was all done on trust. Entertaining done in business cements a friendship. If you get a man's trust and confidence he'll do business with you on the basis of friendship. But you can only persuade people to buy from you if the price is right.

> A lot of people gave Christmas presents in the early days in the City. It oiled the wheels but I don't believe they would give you business unless the price and the quality were right. You'd not get a contract because of a gift.

Peter's business required various skills. There were the trading skills, the need to make sure you were buying and selling at the right price. Even employing all his wits, Peter could still come unstuck. To this day he has a clear memory of a sapphire he purchased in Ceylon (Sri Lanka). On his return to the UK Peter was eager to have it valued but, horror of horrors, he was told by a reputable gem dealer in the City it was worth nothing like he had paid for it!

Whilst some goods might not come up to Peter's expectations, others could exceed them dramatically. JH Little and Co had purchased some wine from eastern Europe and gave a case to a director of Inchcape. The new owner stowed the case up on the luggage rack when he got on the train that evening. As he travelled home anticipating a quiet evening by the fire sampling his new acquisitions, a secondary fermentation was going on in the bottles. Havoc ensued when they began exploding.

Even when trading in materials Peter knew well problems could occur. Not only was there the price and quality to consider but also the integrity of the supplier. He did his utmost to ensure that the supplier would deliver on time but ships sink and mines have accidents so there were plenty of unforeseen problems to factor in. Even when the goods arrived with their purchaser, there might be problems. If the quality was not up to scratch, Peter had to renegotiate a settlement—a penalty. Clearly it was not viable to return the minerals to the mining company overseas if a problem had arisen but it was imperative that the purchaser was happy in the end. As Peter said, 'You knew each other and they trusted you. Unfortunately whilst you can insure against many problems, quality is not one of them so a settlement was needed.'

According to John Allen, one of Peter's business colleagues, Peter's politeness worked like a charm. 'He is an extremely intelligent man and has a very quick mind with a very eloquent turn of speech. I have heard customers telephone with quite legitimate complaints about minerals and at the end of the conversation they were apologizing to him for complaining in the first place!'

By the 1970s Peter had become recognised as one of the leading authorities in the country, and further afield, on mineral sands (rutile, ilmenite and zircon). In 1979, shortly before Peter became Lord Mayor, he was made a Fellow of the Fellowship of Engineering later to be called the Royal Academy of Engineering (FREng), an honour of which he is extremely proud because it is recognition of his mining expertise. He received invitations to give lectures on minerals sands and marketing, to publish papers and to write for journals. In 1969 after his two month secondment to Egypt, he prepared a report for the United Nations on 'Mineral sands: world market survey'. In 1971 at a meeting of the Institution of Mining and Metallurgy, he gave a paper on 'The marketing of minerals'; his lecture was later published in their transactions.

Barry Millard who worked with Peter during the 1970s recalls his extraordinary quick wit.

> My fondest memory which highlighted the quickness of reply and repartee of Peter occurred at the Industrial Minerals Congress held in Paris in 1978. Peter was at that time the European representative of AMA, then the largest global producer of rutile and zircon.

> Peter had delivered a paper on behalf of Darby Johns of AMA who could not attend the Congress and the following paper was delivered by Warwick Bartle who had been with Western Titanium in Perth and who had recently joined Quebec Iron and Titanium as Marketing Manager for zircon to be produced at Richards Bay Minerals (RBM), South Africa. The impact in the market place of added production of zircon both from RBM and new producers in Australia was immense with the prospect of significant oversupply occurring when the new operations came fully on stream.

> Warwick's paper covered the development of the RBM project with production rates outlines as well as other details relating to mineral reserves, product specifications, price projections and generally outlined how this project would be the largest supplier into the global market at the expense of other producers both existing and future.

Following delivery of the paper it was question time. Peter rose to the occasion and enquired how much bulk storage was being built and where, to store this zircon which he considered could not be sold in competition with others already established.

The question as put with the accompanying wit in the delivery brought the house down and it took some moments for Warwick to be able to recover his thoughts and reply.

Amongst Peter's published articles was one on 'Invisible exports and the role of the City of London in providing expertise and finance in support of the minerals industry'. It was a great honour to be invited to give the 'Fourth Distinction Lecture' to the Fellowship of Engineering in September 1980 about 'The minerals industry and the City' and this was subsequently published as a paper. It is amazing that Peter found the time to give this lecture because he was Lord Mayor of London at the time. It was also during the mayoralty that Peter co-authored an article on 'The role of the City of London in support of the textile industries in Great Britain: a historical review'.

During the 1980s when Peter was President of the Ironbridge Gorge Museum Development Trust and assisting the museum with fund-raising, he linked his own engineering background to their history and gave several prestigious papers. The first was entitled 'The perspective of the past, indications from the history of the Industrial Revolution in Britain'. When he was asked to give the 33rd William Menelaus Memorial lecture to the South Wales Institute of Engineers in 1983, Peter chose to speak on 'The origins of the iron and steel industry'.

The following year he attended a conference in Rome where he delivered the first Marston Fleming Memorial Lecture on 'Reagents in the minerals industry'. His chosen subject was 'The Ironbridge Gorge: the birthplace of the Industrial Revolution'. By this time Peter was Governor of the Imperial College of Science and very knowledgeable about the important role Shropshire had played in the Industrial Revolution.

In addition to his many business commitments, Peter had to juggle being an alderman and a Justice of the Peace. All aldermen are magistrates (although Peter had been a magistrate since 1969 sitting at Greenwich and Woolwich) and on the bench in the City of London at the Mansion House and Guildhall courts. The Mansion House court has since closed but it was still active during Peter's mayoralty. In those days there were also cells at the Mansion House and one which had gained notoriety was known as 'the bird cage' because Emily Pankhurst had frequently been held there. Thanks to Emily's sojourn, it was also the first cell in the country to have its own lavatory.

Peter took his duties as a magistrate seriously and enjoyed being on the bench even though it could be very time-consuming. He was given a useful piece of advice when he became a magistrate which was 'Don't explain your judgement because your explanation could be wrong but your decision right'. So he never did. Peter said, 'It could be irritating when you might have spent ages hearing a case where the defendant had pleaded "not guilty" all the way through, then you find the case proved. You then decide on the appropriate punishment. After the sentence had been handed down the defendant would say so politely "Thank you your worships". Then you knew he was guilty and you had probably given him a lighter sentence than he expected!'

For one so steeped in City traditions, it was natural that Peter should have played his part in the reincarnation of Rennie's London Bridge in Arizona. This episode in the life of London Bridge actually began in 1967 when the Corporation of London was faced with mounting bills for the complete renovation of the bridge. Controversially they sought the required Act of Parliament to enable the bridge to be offered for sale by tender and hoped they could raise enough money to pay for a new bridge. To their amazement the McCulloch Oil Company put in a tender for just over £1 million ('an offer we cannot refuse') to buy Rennie's bridge of 1831 and rebuild it 7,000 miles away in the heart of the Arizona Desert at the newly created Lake Havasu City.

The City of London (Arizona) Corporation was set up to handle everything connected with the acre of land which McCulloch Oil gave to the City of London; Peter joined the board of directors in 1970. Quite soon after he became deputy chairman and served as chairman of the board between 1985 and 1988.

Once contracts were signed things moved very quickly. The first stone from London Bridge was ceremonially lowered in September 1968 by the Lord Mayor, Sir Gilbert Inglefield. After that 10,000 tons of granite were carefully removed, numbered and shipped to Long Beach California to be moved by truck to Lake Havasu City. The erection of the bridge was completed in the autumn of 1971 and formed the centrepiece of Lake Havasu City, which had been designed by CV Wood, junior, President of McCulloch Oil and planner of Disneyland. The city had a population of 8,000 at the time but was planned for 75,000. Sir Peter Studd and the sheriffs were invited to the opening ceremony at the beginning of October 1971 along with members of the City Livery Club, members of Common Council and their ladies. Peter had actually completed his shrieval term by then but had shown so much personal interest in the venture that the organisers wanted him and Belinda to be at the official opening.

Stanley Heather, in his capacity as attorney and general counsel of the City of London (Arizona) Corporation, also made up the party and remembers the event well. 'The company was large enough to fill a chartered aeroplane, and the evening before we set out, there was a briefing gathering at the City Livery Club which developed into a memorable "send-off" party with everybody excited at the prospect of going to America for this special occasion.'

The opening ceremony, he recalls, was a 'truly unforgettable spectacle' which led on to a banquet and an evening firework display. The hosts had planned several days of hospitality for the party from London which some of the older members of the party found very demanding on account of the heat in this desert region. Stanley Heather says that for him 'the most enduring memory, if one was forced to choose, was a flight from

53. Peter has been a good friend to London Bridge in Arizona ever since the bridge was first erected there in 1971. He has attended many anniversary celebrations and is seen here with Belinda during a recent visit.

Las Vegas up the Grand Canyon in a small eight-seater aircraft belonging to Frank Sinatra and being served with Bloody Marys. Sir Peter and Lady Gadsden were members of that adventurous party, and I am sure that they were as much impressed by that spell-binding spectacle, as were my late wife and I.'

Many friendships developed between the members of the two parties which have lasted to the present day, strengthened by reciprocal visits. The year after the opening of the bridge, Peter and two colleagues from the City of London (Arizona) Corporation returned for a business meeting to resolve a few outstanding issues. However they discovered on the evening of their arrival there was a large gathering of local residents waiting at the bridge to greet them. Stanley Heather, who was there as the legal arm of the group, recalls how each of them found themselves manoeuvred in front of the microphone with the invitation to 'say a few words'.

The following day they were invited to attend a parade to celebrate the first anniversary of the bridge in Arizona. Stanley Heather said:

> We three from the City [Leslie Prince was also with them] were announced over loudspeakers as honoured representatives of the City of London, and again I began to experience the nerve-racking premonition that we were going to be expected to 'say something'.

> A large stand had been erected for spectators to watch the parade, which included majorettes, vintage American motor cars, cowboys on horseback and elaborately uniformed marching bands of varying sizes. In front of the packed viewing stands something that looked very much like a saluting base had been erected and, horror of horrors, we were invited to occupy this and 'take the salute' as the parade marched by.

> We made our way from the seats in the stand we had been occupying and, whether by accident or design, Sir Peter and Leslie Prince got themselves submerged in the enthusiastic crowd, and did not succeed in getting to the 'saluting base' by the time the head of the procession arrived. So I found myself alone 'like Patience on a monument, smiling at grief' until the last float or posse of wild west characters had passed by. My influential colleagues apologized to me later, but I shall always remain unconvinced that their reluctance to press forward with me, with the odd 'beg pardons' to the crowd, was caused by the natural observance of innate good manners.

The following year the roles were reversed and the American delegation were guests of the City of London at the opening of Britain's new London Bridge (which Peter commented 'was erected at no cost to the ratepayer or the taxpayer') by The Queen. The guests from Arizona were taken to visit some of the special treasures of the City, including calling at Guildhall Library to see their most prized possession, a signed first edition of Sir Thomas More's *Utopia*.

The president of the board of trade in Lake Havasu City, Mr Lester Galst, was only too aware that the City has special dress for some occasions, so he phoned to enquire what he should wear. He was advised to go and talk to Moss Bros in Covent Garden who would 'see him right'. In the event Mr Galst created a splendid impression by being the only person at the opening ceremony wearing a black top hat and a pearl-grey cravat with his morning coat.

Peter has made numerous visits to Arizona to represent the Corporation of London. He has always taken a close interest in the development of Lake Havasu City and been present at more events and meetings connected with London Bridge than anyone else from Britain. So it was with great pleasure that he attended the 10th anniversary of London Bridge in 1981 and the 25th anniversary celebrations in 1996. State Senator, Linda Binder, (a freeman of the City of London) who had originally entertained the City delegation in the 1980s, was delighted to resume her former role for the silver anniversary of the bridge because, she said, 'I made many life-long friendships and Peter and Belinda have been the most marvellous and considerate of friends ever since we first met in the 1980s.'

Sir Peter Studd joined Sir Peter Gadsden, and the two former Lord Mayors of London were joined by the governor of Arizona. 'We had a wonderful celebratory dinner along with fireworks off the bridge,' Linda Binder recalls. 'Then the next day we had the London Bridge Day Parade along with a cake baked by the locals that was a whole street long! There were evenings spent on the Lake with wild rides up to the Palms Restaurant for huge drinks called "Green Things" and lots of lovely food. Very casual but such fun,' she remembers.

Chapter 12

Becoming Lord Mayor

My soul is for my God,
My heart is for my lady,
My arm is for my king,
My honour is for myself.

(The inscription is from a French sword in a museum in Warsaw and was quoted by Peter in his speech in Guildhall on his election as Lord Mayor.)

In the past when a person became an alderman he had a fairly good idea when he might be elected Lord Mayor of London. As Peter put it, 'In those days there was an element of Buggin's turn, which depended on your seniority within the Court of Aldermen.' In Peter's case, all things being equal, he hoped that the honour might be bestowed in 1980–81. However events moved more quickly than he expected.

It was August 1978 when *The Times* business section ran with the story that they had heard a whisper Alderman Peter Gadsden would follow Sir Kenneth Cork as the next Lord Mayor of London. Sir Kenneth and his wife Nina were close friends of Peter and Belinda's and Peter was delighted to follow someone so much admired. Amongst the advice Sir Kenneth gave Peter was: 'Don't worry about your enemies as you know where you stand, but worry about your friends as they too can do you down.' Another one of his memorable comments came when he was told a certain parson was left-wing. Sir Kenneth replied, 'No more left-wing than Christ was.'

To ensure Peter knew what he might be letting himself in for, *The Times* helpfully gave him a quick résumé. They said it would be a seven-day-a-week job beginning at 7am and often ending at 2am. He might have as many as ten engagements a day, and during the year give 300 speeches and shake 100,000 hands. Just in case that sounded too tempting, they ended up by saying that he need not expect any holiday during the year either. This might have sounded daunting to all but the most determined! Actually Peter was to confound all their predictions because he regularly undertook 12 engagements a day, sometimes 16, and made about 800 speeches.

Mayoral elections are traditionally held on Michaelmas Day unless that falls at a weekend when they are moved to the Monday after. 1978 was particularly unusual because not only did Michaelmas fall on a Saturday, but the following Monday was Yom Kippur, the holiest day of the Jewish year. This resulted in the mayoral election in 1978 being moved to Tuesday, 2nd October.

As hoped, the liverymen shouted 'All! All!' in response to the question 'All of those who would have Alderman Kenneth Cork for Lord Mayor for the year ensuing, please signify'. When the same question was asked with Alderman Peter Gadsden being named they shouted 'Next year!' which meant Peter was the prospective Lord Mayor for 1979–80.

Because there is barely six weeks between the mayoral election and taking office, the alderman who receives the 'next year' vote has to begin preparations immediately and trust he will receive the necessary support in 12 months' time. The planning of the Lord Mayor's diary with his engagements and overseas visits takes nearly 12 months to organise. If something goes awry and the anticipated candidate is unable to take office then the 'unexpected' Lord Mayor has to enact a diary of engagements and state visits which he has had no hand in planning. In Peter's case all went to plan and he was elected the Lord Mayor in September 1979.

The year before Peter took office was dominated by preparation. There was not only his mayoral diary to organise but his business one as well. He said at the time:

> you don't go into this to get something out of it. You do so because you have probably made a reasonable success of your business affairs and it's an opportunity to put something back into the community. By the end of October [1979] I will have given all my businesses up to devote myself full-time to being Lord Mayor. I will leave my business alone for a year. I have, fortunately, people to take care of all the activities I am involved in. I just hope I will be wanted back afterwards! I've got one year to put my personality and experiences at the service of the City.

There was another aspect of preparing to be Lord Mayor of London which amused Peter and reminded him of his school days: the clothing list. Just as being sheriff and alderman required regalia, so being the Lord

Mayor included ostrich feathers for your hat. Peter was asked to name his favourite soap and also received a list which began '20 pairs of pants, 20 handkerchiefs, 20 shirts...'

Peter has always been sure that pomp and circumstance does matter. 'Behind the ceremonial is a very good reason for it all. We all love ceremony and as a country we do it rather well,' he said. 'It would be a poorer place without it, and most importantly—if we ever got rid of it, we could never get it back again.' For all the pomp and circumstance, Peter wanted to keep the common touch. 'I hope we are going to be natural, you've got to enter into the spirit of the occasion—it's a party, after all,' he said of the forthcoming Lord Mayor's Show. Peter certainly succeeded in being himself. At the end of his mayoralty one of the comments that pleased him the most was: 'Sir Peter Gadsden was the unstuffiest Lord Mayor ever.'

For Belinda this was also a year of preparation and that meant lists and more lists. There was a list of guests to be invited to the Lord Mayor's Show and another list of guests for the Lord Mayor's Banquet, and the Lord Mayor's Christmas card list topped 500! She admits that she was extremely nervous about how she would cope and chatted with several previous lady mayoresses in an effort to gain some idea of what she could expect. All she discovered was that everyone did it differently!

As Peter began sorting out the traditional regalia of the office, Belinda was faced with the far more difficult task of preparing a wardrobe to cover all manner of engagements from the formal to the pits (quite literally, because the Lady Mayoress was scheduled to go down two mines). She decided at the outset to go to a dressmaker rather than purchase ready-made gowns. 'And I seemed to be in the dressmaker's every week for 12 months,' she remembers. This did ensure that Belinda never arrived at a reception to see her dress being worn by another lady. It also meant gowns could be designed to suit the particular occasion and Belinda had noticed the Lady Mayoress spent a large amount of time standing on a platform receiving lines of guests. Another thing she noticed was that the Lady Mayoress's dress was often seen from the back as she processed past. With infinite wisdom, Belinda also took into account the fact she would be obliged to consume a large number of lunches and dinners most days, and decided dresses without a waistline might be an advantage. They were!

'There comes a time when you wonder if you can keep on eating,' she said, 'especially if you've already been to two receptions before an official dinner—but somehow one manages.' Sir Peter Studd had warned Peter and Belinda about the eating problem and his advice had been to take a small amount no matter how much was on offer and push it round the plate a bit.

By the end of that year, however hard she had tried to eat the smallest portion of the rich foods served, Belinda had nearly two stone to shed! She remembers with horror on a state visit to Brisbane in the summer of 1980 one concerned lady coming up to Lady Mayoress and asking, 'When's the baby due?'

Not only were there her own clothes to arrange, but the Lady Mayoress was required to have Maids of Honour in those days. It was usual for the Lady Mayoress to have four young lady attendants which, in the case of the Gadsden family, presented no problem. Their four beautiful daughters were perfect for the occasion. Traditionally the sheriffs' ladies each had two attendants. Sheriff John Hart had two daughters who were Maids of Honour as well and Sheriff Christopher Leaver had a niece to accompany his wife. That enabled Peter to ask his god-daughter, Amanda Jane Barnes, to be the other Maid of Honour. She was the daughter of a friend from Cambridge, who had shared the same digs in 71, Jesus Lane (in fact he was one of those who had appeared before the tutor hunting the mystery pee-er!).

Gowns were needed for them all. Fortunately Belinda had met Maureen Baker, designer of Princess Anne's elegant wedding dress, at a function in the City, so Belinda was able to turn to her for assistance with the Lady Mayoress's gown for the Lord Mayor's Banquet.

Amongst Peter's business colleagues there was great interest when it emerged that he would hold the highest office in the City of London. The magazine *Industrial Minerals* immediately reported the next Lord Mayor of London would be 'Mr Peter Gadsden, the well-known mineral sands figure and London Manager of the Associated Minerals Consolidated of Australia whose activities have led him into a more wide-reaching interest in the minerals industry. Don't be surprised if the Lord Mayor's theme for 1979–80 is mineral orientated,' they predicted.

Their prediction was not wide of the mark. When Peter came to consider his theme for the year, he decided 'National Resources and the Environment' would be appropriate and give the proceedings a lively, cosmopolitan flavour. 'Natural resources include not only minerals, coal and oil but also the products of farming, horticulture and forestry which provide essential food and clothing,' he said. 'The theme stresses the vital role that natural resources must play in our future survival, and the part the City of London has played in providing the essential finance and expertise in the development of natural resources in this country and overseas, particularly the Commonwealth.'

It is interesting to see that Peter's attitude towards conservation in 1979 was ahead of his time in many ways. He believed it was possible to develop natural resources, whether oil, minerals or forestry, without spoiling the environment. 'We cannot ignore the wealth below our feet. We can mine today and still protect the environment. The coastal lines of today won't be the coastal lines of, say, a thousand years time,' he said. 'I believe in "controlled mining". In Australia they have actually improved the environment in some cases. If you want to benefit the earth, you have to disturb it sometimes. The important thing now is to rehabilitate it once you have finished disturbing it.' He also said that alternative sources of energy ought to be explored and more attention paid to recycling.

Once it became known that Peter was the Lord Mayor Elect, congratulations flooded in from family, friends and colleagues alike. Some made entertaining reading like the telegram from his mineral sands colleagues in Australia who wrote with typical Aussie succinctness: 'Congratulations! Get yer head out the sand!' Peter could not resist responding in similar vein saying that since his name was Peter and he was built on a rock, he'd have no problem.

Business associates at Sierra Rutile Limited were amazed and delighted. David Fraser wrote to say:

> I must admit that I was really quite surprised when I saw the announcement in the *Financial Times* about five weeks ago. I did not think mining engineers, however eminent, became Lord Mayors. You are probably the first to achieve such 'transformation'. I can assure you that we who can claim to be acquainted with you in Sierra Leone feel very proud at your elevation, and those of us in the mining fraternity particularly are proud and are honoured not only to be acquainted but also to be in the same profession as yourself.

Other congratulations came from people who had known Peter in the past and felt happy to have played even a small part in his great achievement. One lady wrote that 'it came as such a happy bolt from the blue to see you and such magnificent achievements on TV. You have no doubt forgotten that I ever existed but I not only remember you and your brother but the gracious and charming hospitality of your parents when invited to tea at their Rectory in Shropshire. It was so enjoyable I

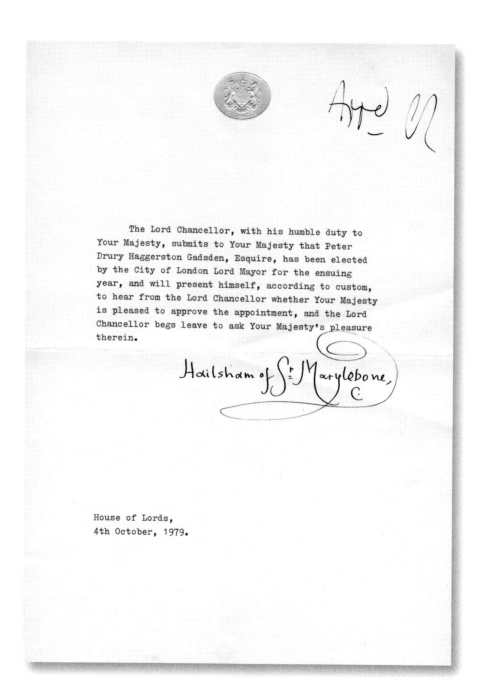

The Lord Chancellor, with his humble duty to
Your Majesty, submits to Your Majesty that Peter
Drury Haggerston Gadsden, Esquire, has been elected
by the City of London Lord Mayor for the ensuing
year, and will present himself, according to custom,
to hear from the Lord Chancellor whether Your Majesty
is pleased to approve the appointment, and the Lord
Chancellor begs leave to ask Your Majesty's pleasure
therein.

Hailsham of St Marylebone, C.

House of Lords,
4th October, 1979.

54.   Letter of Approval as Lord Mayor.

missed the last of very few buses back to Wellington and received further hospitality by staying the night!' The lady revealed herself to be 'your old Tudor House matron at Wrekin College' who 'felt cheered and proud to feel that thirty-six years ago I was for a very brief period a minute cog in the wheels of your highly successful career and amazing achievements for one still in the prime of life. Thank you for bringing a real bit of joy into my life.'

Another voice from the past came from even further back. 'I wonder would you remember Miss Bryan, your Fourth Form Mistress at Rockport?' a letter from Northern Ireland began. Along with her good wishes, she added, 'Mr and Mrs Bing would have been so very pleased to know that you are giving such wonderful unselfish service for the benefit of Britain— I remember your Father's visit to Rockport and the interesting lectures and the wonderful bird calls he did for our pleasure.' She was also able to send good wishes from Miss Dickinson, the now elderly school matron who had fond memories of escorting little Peter back to Shropshire at the end of term and putting him in the ladies' waiting room at Wolverhampton railway station to await collection by his mother and father.

Shortly before Peter and Belinda were due to move into the Mansion House, one of the household officers appeared rather like a fairy godfather, telling Belinda he was prepared to grant her one wish. It seemed that the Lady Mayoress was permitted to order something that would make her life more comfortable in the Mansion House. To the officer's surprise and amusement Belinda requested an automatic washer-drier. The staff at the Mansion House had never supposed that the Lady Mayoress would be doing her own laundry anyway. It is hard to know how she was expected to cope since a Lady Mayoress was not assigned any help with domestic or secretarial matters in those days. By contrast the Lord Mayor had three footmen to assist him and the full secretarial team of the Mansion House. The only person Belinda could turn to was the girl who cleaned the Lord Mayor's private apartment. She was very willing but Belinda noticed she had an unerring knack of ironing holes into garments and washing clothes a different colour. In the event the Lady Mayoress's washer-drier did sterling service. 'It was one of the best moves I ever made,' Belinda said, 'Especially when the children descended on us at the weekends with suitcases full of dirty clothes!'

In October 1979, just a month before Peter took office, he told a journalist that:

the Lord Mayor's diary for the next year is very nearly complete. The Lord Mayor will attend lunches and dinners every day. He will visit schools and give prizes away; he will visit hospitals and old people's homes; he will meet prominent persons visiting London; he will preside at state banquets given in Guildhall in honour of visiting heads of state and he will work six or seven days a week from first thing in the morning until he retires to bed at night. It's an endless procession of people.

Peter was under no illusions about the amount of work involved in his year of office nor that he would be paying for the privilege. He felt it was correct as he told another journalist:

> The Lord Mayor does of course contribute to the cost of the mayoralty, I've no idea what the figure is because I haven't been Lord Mayor before, but it's right and proper. It's an office where you serve and I think it's not a bad thing if you have to make some personal financial sacrifice whilst holding that office. My father always told me—work hard and save for the future. That's what I've done—I suppose I have been almost puritanical about it—and I'm happy to say that now I'm in the position of being able to give something back to the community.

One area that required a lot of forward planning was the Lord Mayor's Show. It might only be a one-day show but Peter considered it would be 'the biggest party of my life and I want everyone to enjoy it. This is a time for happiness and fun,' he said. 'It's a jolly good excuse for a party. It doesn't cost the ratepayers or anyone who comes to see it a penny. It's paid for by the Lord Mayor who hopes the contributions by participating commercial companies will cover the cost. It should be self-financing. This year, our theme is "Natural Resources and the Environment" and I'm delighted that both Canada and Alberta will have floats in the show.'

Because he understood only too well the significance of tradition in the life of the City, Peter commissioned some research into the history of the Lord Mayor's Show and that enabled him to revive former events. He discovered that the usual funfair in Paternoster Square had its origins in the medieval Newgate fayre so for his Lord Mayor's day the area took on the appearance of medieval street theatre with morris dancing and pipe bands complete with the tantalising aroma of roast lamb from two spits. It was the biggest fair anyone could remember on the site and local papers were delighted that the new Lord Mayor had 'revived the spirit of "Merrie England" '.

Research also uncovered the fact that some 500 years earlier a river pageant had played a central role in the Lord Mayor's procession. Peter thought it would be an exciting idea to revive this tradition in the form of a 'Firework Spectacular' on the river during the evening. 'I have always loved fireworks so I decided to have them because it always seemed to me that there was such an anti-climax after the procession,' he explained. The fireworks have now become such an established part of the Lord Mayor's Show over the past quarter of a century that many people have forgotten it was actually Peter's idea in the first place

LRC, of which Peter was a director, were proud to sponsor the 'Firework Spectacular'. To mark the event, the chairman presented the Lord Mayor with a commemorative sword with the inscription:

> *My soul is for my God,*
> *My heart is for my lady,*
> *My arm is for my king,*
> *My honour is for myself.*

The sentiment had impressed Peter. 'After I had been elected Lord Mayor in Guildhall, I referred in my speech to a sword which I had seen in Poland bearing those words, never dreaming that this would be taken up,' Peter said. 'I mentioned that if I had a sword I would like to have those words inscribed on it. I was, therefore, surprised and delighted when LRC, together with Paines-Wessex, presented me with a beautiful Wilkinson sword inscribed with those words.'

On the morning of the procession the Lord Mayor spoke from the golden coach and told the world: 'I am particularly delighted that the procession is really international with floats from Canada and New Zealand, and a town crier from Perth, Australia.' He went on to say: 'I send special greetings to you all, especially those of you watching in Shropshire and Northumberland,' which delighted friends and relatives in both counties.

Belinda watched the first part of the procession from the balcony of the Mansion House and saw her husband set off in the gold coach for the Law Courts in the Strand. A little later the Lady Mayoress was summoned to go and get in her car along with her two guests to join the Lord Mayor at the Law Courts. Belinda had chosen Juliet and Caroline, their two eldest daughters, as her guests but when they were due to go, Juliet was missing. Caroline immediately went to fetch her but in the meantime the Mansion House officials were insistent that the Lady Mayoress must leave because the crowds were so large. Belinda pleaded for a few more minutes but these were not granted and so she ended up leaving in the official car on

55.   The Lord Mayor, Sir Peter Gadsden GBE, and the Lady Mayoress.

her own. All was not lost though because a police car brought the two girls to join their parents at the Law Courts.

The city section of the Lord Mayor's procession was led by Chinese lion dancers, which was most appropriate. Not only do they drive away the past and bring in good luck for the coming year, but they celebrated the new Lord Mayor's friendship with China and his intention to promote closer trade and cultural links between the two countries.

In one newspaper's opinion 'Sir Peter Gadsden, London's new Lord Mayor, symbolises the international side of trade and expertise within the City'. That was certainly evident in the Lord Mayor's Show because most of Peter's foreign contacts were only too happy to participate.

The Canadian Prime Minister, Joe Clark, was quick to telegraph his congratulations to London's new Lord Mayor saying:

> Your years of service to the community have earned you the respect and confidence of all your colleagues and associates, and I join them in wishing you well in the future. Canadians are especially proud that this honour has been bestowed upon a native Albertan. We are certain that you will approach all the challenges of your new responsibility with vigour and dedication.

One of the Canadian newspapers was more direct: 'a breath of Alberta freshness has blown into the City of London,' it announced. Both the Canadian High Commission and the Alberta Government took part in the Lord Mayor's Show. The High Commission sent two Royal Canadian Mounted Police, who rode horses graciously lent for the occasion by Her Majesty The Queen. Alberta sent a covered wagon driven by the Honourable Al 'Boomer' Adair, Minister of Tourism for Alberta. The traditional chuck wagon made such a big impression on the crowds that the minister and his wagon were invited to appear on the children's television programme *Blue Peter* a few days after.

It seemed that everyone who had been connected with Peter's life at various stages was eager to play their part in the big procession. Wrekin College wrote to inform the Lord Mayor Elect: 'Our cadets have put in a great deal of effort to reach a standard which they hope will reflect the pride we all feel in being asked.' The KSLI also took part, but their march of 140 paces to the minute caused the organisers some concern. In order that the regiment could take part in the Lord Mayor's procession and not overtake the float in front, special arrangements were made. It was agreed that the procession would come to a halt in front of the Mansion House to permit the KSLI to march past at their traditional pace and when the

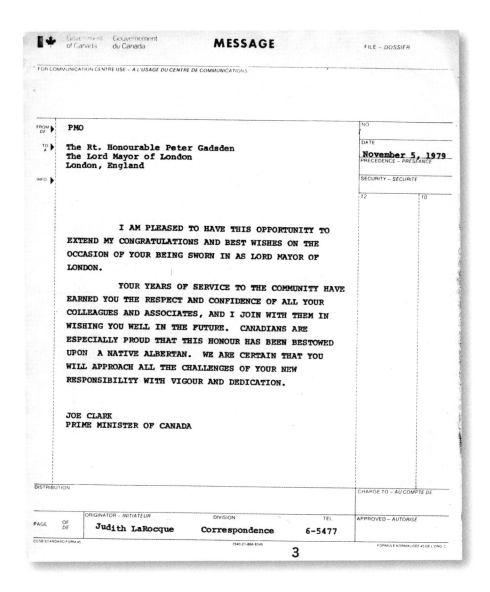

FOR COMMUNICATION CENTRE USE – A L'USAGE DU CENTRE DE COMMUNICATIONS

FROM DE	PMO	NO
TO A	The Rt. Honourable Peter Gadsden The Lord Mayor of London London, England	DATE **November 5, 1979** PRECEDENCE – PRÉSÉANCE
INFO		SECURITY – SÉCURITÉ
		12 10

I AM PLEASED TO HAVE THIS OPPORTUNITY TO
EXTEND MY CONGRATULATIONS AND BEST WISHES ON THE
OCCASION OF YOUR BEING SWORN IN AS LORD MAYOR OF
LONDON.

YOUR YEARS OF SERVICE TO THE COMMUNITY HAVE
EARNED YOU THE RESPECT AND CONFIDENCE OF ALL YOUR
COLLEAGUES AND ASSOCIATES, AND I JOIN WITH THEM IN
WISHING YOU WELL IN THE FUTURE. CANADIANS ARE
ESPECIALLY PROUD THAT THIS HONOUR HAS BEEN BESTOWED
UPON A NATIVE ALBERTAN. WE ARE CERTAIN THAT YOU
WILL APPROACH ALL THE CHALLENGES OF YOUR NEW
RESPONSIBILITY WITH VIGOUR AND DEDICATION.

JOE CLARK
PRIME MINISTER OF CANADA

DISTRIBUTION   CHARGE TO – AU COMPTE DE

PAGE OF DE	ORIGINATOR – INITIATEUR Judith LaRocque	DIVISION Correspondence	TEL 6-5477	APPROVED – AUTORISÉ

CGSB STANDARD FORM 45   7540-21-866-6545   FORMULE NORMALISÉE 45 DE L'ONG C

3

56.   A message from the Prime Minister of Canada. Peter received messages
of congratulations from all around the world when he became Lord Mayor of
London.

KSLI caught up with the procession, they would resume marching at normal speed.

Business colleagues from all over the world joined the celebrations. The Australian mining interests arrived along with a contingent from Jabez Gadsden's company. In all there were 55 floats and, it was estimated, 3,500 people took part in the procession assisted by 25 bands to keep the whole procession moving at 2.7 miles an hour, someone was careful to note. Peter confesses that he can remember very little detail of the procession. It took four hours and was one long glorious blur of smiles, hand-shakes and waves.

'By Gadsden, what a show!' the evening headlines read. The verdict on the Lord Mayor's Show came from a 79-year-old lady who had never met Peter but felt moved to write. She began 'My Lord Mayor, I feel I must thank you for a wonderful show. I watch it every year and this year surpassed all others!... I hope you have a very happy year and all goes well and peaceful for you. You looked so happy when you spoke from the coach.' Another person wrote saying 'The whole show radiated a spontaneous happiness that was most infectious.'

The Lord Mayor's Banquet received extensive television coverage because it was a first—not just a first for Peter, but also a first for Margaret Thatcher. In his speech, the Lord Mayor, Sir Peter Gadsden, said 'I am delighted to have the honour of welcoming the first woman Prime Minister of this country to her first Lord Mayor's Banquet,' and he added 'I am lucky to have such an attractive Prime Minister sitting next to me—my predecessors have not been so fortunate.' This was to be the beginning of an excellent partnership between Lord Mayor and Prime Minister. 'You and I share a background of chemistry which enables us to take a practical approach in our separate tasks,' Peter said to Mrs Thatcher in his speech that evening.

Perhaps the final accolade for the Lord Mayor's Day came from Sir Ian Bowater, who had been Lord Mayor ten years earlier when Peter was still learning the ropes as sheriff and committing the odd faux pas. A colleague reported to Peter that Sir Ian spoke 'in glowing terms of the Lord Mayor's Show. In fact he said, "The Lord Mayor's Show was 3,000 yards long and must have been the most extensive and magnificent that the City has had in its history." He was also highly complimentary about the banquet and Mrs Thatcher's speech. He also said that you spoke splendidly and that one could hear your voice from one end to the other of Guildhall without

57. The Lord Mayor's Banquet in 1980 was not only a special occasion for Sir Peter Gadsden but also for the Prime Minister, Margaret Thatcher. This was the first time a woman prime minister had been present and spoken at the banquet.

any difficulty whatever. He went on further and said, "Peter and Belinda and their maids of honour, who were most charmingly dressed, looked quite beautiful. Altogether it was a great Lord Mayor's Banquet and I am sure they are going to make a most successful couple." And they did.

Chapter 13

Thoroughly with Enthusiasm

TO LONDON'S LORD MAYOR

Bridgnorth—historic, ancient,
Hard battles fought and won,
Its green and pleasant beauty,
Where dire deed were done.
But in this country town of ours,
Of men and women, strong of heart,
Some with strength to lead.
Now one, 'Lord Mayor of London',
The local famous son,
Just like London's Lord Mayor of old,
He's turned again—for once
Bridgnorth has claimed your heart,
This Sir—you know 'tis true,
Because Lord Mayor of London town,
Bridgnorth is proud of you.

(This tribute to Peter appeared in the local paper, the *Shropshire Star*, in June 1980 and was penned by Bridgnorth resident, Joan Winwood.)

For Peter this was a year like no other and undertaken at a pace like no other. Those who worked alongside him felt the year was well summed up by his personal motto: 'Thoroughly with enthusiasm'. Sheriff Sir Christopher Leaver has vivid memories of Peter's energy. 'During his mayoralty, he threw himself into everything with a jolly enthusiasm. The already exhausting mayoral programme was not enough for his year. He accepted every suitable engagement that he could around the country, not just in the City, often seven days a week. In addition to all this he travelled widely. I never saw him tired. It was his influence that really geared up the number of diary entries from "busy" to "non-stop" and so it remains to this day.' Sheriff John Hart is in no doubt that 'Peter approached the mayoralty at 140 paces to the minute! We were never closed, day or night. Peter was very good at being always available. He just loved selling the City.'

Halfway through the year Alderman Jolliffe (who would become Peter's aldermanic sheriff during the final weeks of the mayoralty) remarked with some amusement that 'the Lord Mayor must live by the maxim "if you keep moving you are not going to be hit" because he never seems to stop'.

Even The Queen was struck by the pace of the mayoralty and remarked to Peter, 'You have a very busy life, Lord Mayor, even busier than mine.' To which he replied gallantly, 'Yes, Ma'am, but yours is a lifetime's job.'

At 50, Peter was one of the youngest Lord Mayors for many years and the first since the Second World War who could not have seen active service on account of his age. At 41, Christopher Leaver was thought to be the youngest aldermanic sheriff. The sheriff, John Hart, was a couple of years older than Peter but the *City Recorder* noted that, 'If fitness and stamina are essential ingredients for the gruelling task of sheriff of London, then the new sheriff, Mr John GM Hart, 51, is well qualified on that score alone.' The paper went on to mention John's impressive sporting achievements as a former international rugby player and a hurdler. This was a youthful trio and 'a happy team of kindred spirits. We all got on famously and still do,' Sir Christopher Leaver says.

The harmonious atmosphere created by this mayoralty was noticed by the City. 'I am told this is one of the happiest years in the Mansion House which is a glowing tribute to the conviviality that Peter Gadsden and the sheriffs have generated among the staff there,' the Upper Warden of the Wheelwrights was heard to say. Certainly Peter's normally good-humoured approach to life carried people along with him. Others noticed that too. One newspaper commenting on London's new Lord Mayor reported, 'Sir Peter Gadsden is relaxed and his manner informal. He is not the stuffy plum-in-the-mouth sort of chap you might expect for one aspiring to one of the most rigidly formalised posts in the land. In fact he has the appearance and jolly charm of a High Street family butcher.'

'This is the year of the mug!' the Lord Mayor announced. What he was actually talking about was a consignment of 5,000 mugs he had just received bearing the Lord Mayor's coat of arms and those of the City of London, which would be given as gifts during his term of office. The newspapers loved it and ran with headlines like 'Lord Mayor mugged'. Peter said that 'the year of the cork' (when Sir Kenneth Cork the previous

58. All agreed they made a happy team. Sheriff John Hart on the left and the aldermanic sheriff Christopher Leaver presented the Lord Mayor with a lion and a koala since both animals appear as supporters on his coat of arms.

Lord Mayor of London had given cork cigarette-lighters as gifts) had now become 'the year of the mug'.

A youthful Lord Mayor taking office at the beginning of a new decade gave this mayoralty the feeling of a new dawn. Peter felt it too. 'My mayoralty spans the end of the 1970s and the beginning of the 1980s,' he said, 'and it would seem an appropriate time to reflect on the 70s and to decide that in the 80s people will all work together in a spirit of co-operation.' People who have made a study of the office of Lord Mayor believe that Peter's term of office did herald a change in the character of the mayoralty. He quickened the pace, undertaking a much larger number of engagements than had previously been the case and was responsible for the office shifting away from being purely ceremonial towards a more ambassadorial role.

The late Sir Peter Studd remarked that 'one of the strengths of the job is that it is bigger than any human being can encompass. No two human beings are quite the same and the greatness of the office is created by you putting your small amount of dust on top of that deposited by the previous person to hold the office. Each person has their own personal gifts which come out in the handling of the office and that keeps it lively.' Peter Gadsden's own perception of this high office is an interesting one; he remarked that, 'The Lord Mayor has a lot of influence but no power.'

During Peter's 12 months he undertook so many engagements it would be impossible to comment on a fraction of them but there were some clear highlights. He is in no doubt which he would put first: the celebrations for The Queen Mother's 80th birthday. Peter said it was 'a moment of history and certainly the most important event in my mayoral diary'. The Queen Mother chose St Paul's Cathedral for the thanksgiving service because she was president of the Friends of the Cathedral. This focused the national celebration of her birthday on the City of London.

On 15th July crowds lined the route between Buckingham Palace and St Paul's to cheer The Queen Mother as she travelled in an open landau accompanied by Prince Charles in a ceremonial parade to the City. To everybody's delight the sun shone despite the weathermen pronouncing the summer of 1980 to be the wettest since 1907.

Tradition required the procession to stop at Temple Bar so The Queen could touch the hilt of the pearl sword, the symbol of the City's authority, which would be presented to her by the Lord Mayor. However, Her Majesty asked if this custom could be waived in order that nothing should interrupt her mother's special day, the City was happy to oblige.

When Their Majesties arrived at St Paul's, the Lord Mayor received them and carried the pearl sword in front of the Sovereign. This particular honour was one Peter has never forgotten. During his mayoralty Peter was honoured to carry the pearl sword in front of the The Queen on four occasions.

A few days after the service of thanksgiving for her 80th birthday, The Queen Mother graciously accepted the Lord Mayor's invitation to a small private dinner party at the Mansion House. She mentioned a few friends she would like invited and particularly asked that Peter's family be there and that his daughters bring their boyfriends, or in Juliet's case, her husband. Another request was no speeches and no mention of it being an *eightieth* birthday.

A few days before the dinner Sir Hugh Wontner called on Peter to tell him about something that had happened during his mayoralty in 1974.

59. The Lord Mayor, Sir Peter Gadsden, stands with the royal family on the steps of St Paul's to await the arrival of Her Majesty Queen Elizabeth, The Queen Mother, for the thanksgiving service on the occasion of her 80th birthday.

60. The Lord Mayor of London carried the pearl sword in front of The Queen into St Paul's Cathedral for the Order of the British Empire Service. Peter was honoured to carry the sword in front of the sovereign on four occasions during his mayoralty.

On that occasion The Queen Mother had lunched at the Mansion House and asked if she might see the magistrates' court there. Hugh had been happy to oblige and was amused when Her Majesty said she would like to stand in the dock to see what it felt like. At the time Hugh said, 'I'll sit in judgement with the Recorder of London,' and accordingly they moved to their appropriate seats. 'But the decision of the court was never announced,' Hugh told Peter. 'Can I announce it tonight?'

Peter explained to Hugh that Her Majesty had made a point of saying no speeches so all they planned was for the Lord Mayor to wish her a happy birthday without mentioning her age. However during the dinner Peter enquired of Queen Elizabeth whether she would like to hear the decision of the court following her previous visit to the Mansion House magistrates' court. She replied, 'Oh yes. What fun!'

At an appropriate moment, Peter looked across catching Hugh's eye and signalling that this was an appropriate moment. Hugh stood up and reminded Her Majesty of the time she had been in the dock, adding, 'The decision of the court has never been given, but I will announce it now. Your Majesty, we found you guilty,' he said to everyone's astonishment. Then he added that this gracious lady was 'guilty of stealing the nation's heart'.

For the Lord Mayor, there were other royal engagements during the year like the State Banquet at Buckingham Palace in honour of the President of Indonesia's state visit. Belinda remembers the sumptuous gold plate that decorated the table and the music from a pipe band.

Another enjoyable, though totally different, event in the Lord Mayor's calendar was the children's Christmas party at the Mansion House. Peter, and indeed the whole Gadsden family, put a lot of effort into making it an exciting event for the young guests. Peter's daughters had been to several Lord Mayor's parties when they were younger and so they were in an ideal position to offer practical advice. His daughter Elizabeth used her artistic abilities to design an eye-catching invitation featuring just the sort of characters she knew children adored. On the day there were Punch and Judy shows, cartoon films, a performance by Smartie Artie together with music from the band of the Light Infantry. The children received a special gift to take home with them at the end. It was a jigsaw with a picture of the Lord Mayor, whom they had all met, waving from the golden coach.

As ever it is the children, all 700 of them, who really made this event. Despite the large number, Peter has a clear memory of one boy in fancy dress who walked straight up to him saying, 'Who are you?'

To which Peter naturally replied, 'Well, I'm the Lord Mayor.'

He was taken aback when the little lad replied scornfully, 'Yes, but you're not the *real* Lord Mayor though, are you?'

When Peter asked him why not, the boy pointed across the room saying, 'See that Father Christmas over there? Well, he is a fake. And you're not the *real* Lord Mayor either.'

All was not lost though because one little girl came bouncing up to him later in the afternoon and said admiringly, 'I like your suit very much. It is even nicer than my costume'—praise indeed!

Belinda received a most unusual Christmas present that year. A phone call came through telling her that the International Stores had bought the prize bull at the Smithfield Market and they wished to present it to the Lady Mayoress. 'I thought, gosh, is the prize bull going to arrive on the doorstep of the Mansion House? What will I do with it? But I was told to donate it to my favourite charity. Now that taxed everyone's ingenuity because what charity could use that quantity of meat?'

Peter's daughters were proud of their father's elevation to the mayoralty but at the same time somewhat embarrassed by his eminence. Juliet, who was married, said she was grateful that she had a different surname! Clare was a student at Exeter University at the time and was asked if she was related to the new Lord Mayor. 'Oh, I shouldn't think so,' came the shifty reply. Between themselves the girls vowed they would not move into the Mansion House, and said politely at the outset 'I hope you won't be offended if we stay at the Barbican.'

'Well it would be easier, darlings, if the whole family was together the first weekend. It would make us feel more at home,' their mother tactfully suggested, so they agreed. Thereafter with the exception of Juliet, who had her own home, the other three were regular weekend guests at the Mansion House and they loved it. 'It was like staying in a five-star hotel,' Elizabeth said.

That first weekend other members of Peter's family also stayed at the Mansion House. His brother David and wife Judy joined his sister Daphne and husband Norman. Daphne was taken aback to discover the Mansion House held an extra surprise. She recalls waking up in the early hours and seeing a ghost walk towards her bed. The room was fairly light because of the street lights, so there was no mistaking what she saw. Daphne said that she sat bolt upright in bed and screamed—she couldn't help it. That woke her husband instantly but the spectre had disappeared. In the morning at her husband's suggestion, Daphne mentioned her night visitor to one of the staff. The way in which he shut up like a clam and refused to talk about it convinced her that she was not the first person to have had that experience.

Fortunately Peter and his family never saw any apparitions during their stay. The first evening the three of the girls were on their own, and because their parents were dining downstairs, the girls' supper was brought into the Boudoir on a trolley. In the centre of the trolley was a silver bell so they could summon the footman as soon as they had finished their first course. However, when they had finished eating, they looked at each other, reluctant to ring for a footman whom they knew to be waiting outside the closed door, but who was no older than themselves. Within a few weeks the Boudoir door was left wide open and the footman could be seen leaning against the door-frame chatting happily to the Gadsden girls as they ate their supper.

Initially the girls were concerned that staying at the Mansion House might restrict their social life because they feared their every move would be observed. If they came in late they had to ring the bell to get Security to let them into the Mansion House. However they soon learned that Security were willing accomplices. If the Lord Mayor happened to ask whether one of his daughters had arrived home late the previous evening, he was always reassured that they hadn't and no times were ever divulged.

Among Peter's more unusual mayoral engagements was his appointment down a sewer. This was a first. As the newspapers were keen to point out, 'No other Lord Mayor has stooped so low'. 'I like to see all aspects of life in London,' the mining expert told them, 'And this, although hidden, is one of the most important. People living in London often don't realise that others are working day and night to look after their interests.' When asked what he had seen below ground, the Lord Mayor replied, 'Nothing more sinister than two surprised toads!'

Some of Peter's engagements read more like the exploits of an action hero than the Lord Mayor of London. There was the occasion when he entertained Billy Beaumont, captain of the England 1st XV, at the Mansion House. The press wanted a photograph of the Lord Mayor kicking a rugby ball and Peter was happy to oblige. Unfortunately he kicked it with rather more enthusiasm that was required so the ball ended up in the middle of the Bank intersection. The household officer, Colonel Brooke-Johnson, then had to risk life and limb ducking and diving between the traffic to retrieve it.

Peter's engagements also took him inside a nuclear reactor at Dungeness Power Station, flew him out to visit the Forties Alpha oil rig in the North Sea, and dressed him up in Geordie pitmen's gear to go five miles out under the sea to view the world's biggest undersea mining complex.

It is worth remembering that, as Lady Mayoress, Belinda also accompanied Peter on many of these expeditions. Visits down mines and out to oil rigs were completely new experiences to her, but she took them all in her stride. One of the things she remembers vividly about that year was the frequent changes of clothes she was required to make if she had six engagements in one day. She concedes that was nothing compared to Peter's marathon 16 engagements in one day, many of which required a costume change.

One unique event recorded in Peter's mayoralty gave him particular pleasure as the son of a clergyman. It was the occasion of the annual dinner of the Archbishops and Bishops of the Anglican Communion at the Mansion House. Peter asked the Archbishop of Canterbury, Robert Runcie, whether he might invite the Cardinal Archbishop of Westminster and his chaplain. The newly enthroned Archbishop of Canterbury was delighted with this ecumenical idea and with Peter's suggestion that the doxology be used instead of the grace that evening. As Peter said in his speech, 'We all pray and long for Christian unity. Christianity should unite us and not divide us. We can witness for ourselves how much unhappiness and tragedy has been brought about—and, sadly still being brought about—by ignorance, bitterness and sometimes even hatred between Christians.'

The presence of the head of the Roman Catholic Church in England made this a unique event. The Lord Mayor said in his speech, 'Your Eminence, you were the first Cardinal to take part in the enthronement of an Archbishop of Canterbury since the Reformation, and this evening you are the first to attend the dinner which the Lord Mayor gives each year to the Anglican Archbishops and Bishops.' Another first that evening was the attendance of the Moderator of the Free Church Federal Council and the Moderator of the General Assembly of the Church of Scotland.

Being Lord Mayor involves receiving a great deal of hospitality but, as Peter explained, 'Usually in return for the hospitality you are expected to make a speech. The most I have had to give in one day is six, but it was usually three.' This called for the tightest organisation and Peter remembers going out in the morning with a different speech in each of his waistcoat pockets. Fortunately the Lord Mayor is ably supported by a team of people who have many years' experience between them. Things still go wrong occasionally as Peter recalled. 'On one occasion I had with me at luncheon the speech that I was giving at dinner that day. Fortunately the lunch was in a hotel not far from where I was staying, so the household officer on duty was able to nip back and fetch the right one.'

There was a system at the Mansion House whereby those asking for a photograph of the Lord Mayor or his autograph are sent one, and there are many people around the world who collect them. Peter was surprised, however, to receive a letter requesting his autograph from a little girl aged six who added a PS—'Please send 2 copies so I can swop one.'

In addition to the many high profile foreign guests it was his honour to entertain, Peter wanted to pay tribute to the many people and organisations that had played a part in his path to success. In some ways Peter's year in office was a personal pilgrimage. Occasionally the places he visited had links far back like the thirteenth-century house of John of Gaddesden, in Little Gaddesden. It was still a private house and, at that time, the home of Sarah Brightman's parents. They were as pleased to welcome the Lord Mayor of London as he was to see this home of his distant forebear. 'My family always used to say we came from Little Gaddesden,' he told them, 'and there are still some of us in Buckinghamshire.'

Peter was also able to view an exhibition in the church that featured material about John of Gaddesden's life and his seal of office. This was an object of particular interest to the Lord Mayor who possessed his own seal of office. During this official visit to Buckinghamshire Peter went to Aylesbury Grammar School to present a cup in memory of his father. Taking another step forward in time along his personal path, Peter went to St John's Church, Wembley. He attended morning service there much as his mother would have done as a young woman. Then she had listened to the inspiring sermons of the Reverend Basil Gadsden and fallen in love with him. Sixty years later her eldest son stood at the lectern to read the second lesson.

During the mayoralty Peter took the opportunity of visiting all his former schools so he could give pupils a better understanding of the role of the City of London and, he hoped, inspire them to aim high. Arriving at his first prep school, Rockport in Northern Ireland, to open the school's new all-weather pitch, Peter was surprised to meet several former classmates. The visit was much appreciated by the present-day pupils. As one of them told a local journalist, 'I think we will remember him as the man who gave us an extra day's holiday at half-term!'

61. As Lord Mayor, Peter was delighted to visit The Elms Preparatory School near Malvern where he had been a pupil many years earlier.

His visit to The Elms near Malvern was memorable for a different reason—namely that the Lord Mayor was delivered to the school by the police! The official Rolls-Royce Phantom Six (registration number LM 0 which some assumed stood for Lord Mayor's Own) expired on the way there just outside Oxford and the local constabulary had to be called up. They managed to get the Lord Mayor to his engagement only half an hour late.

That was not the last of LM 0's problems. Three weeks later the Lord Mayor travelled in the Rolls-Royce to Canterbury to witness the enthronement of Dr Robert Runcie, the new Archbishop of Canterbury. The journey there was eventful because a log dropped off a lorry travelling in front and bounced onto the bonnet of the Lord Mayor's car. Fortunately it did not break the windscreen but it smashed the lights as it fell off.

After the ceremony the civic party bid the Lord Chancellor and other officials goodbye, then got into the mayoral car. The chauffeur started the engine. Nothing. The Rolls had broken down again. With another engagement waiting for him back in the City all the Lord Mayor could do was thumb a lift back with the Lord Chancellor, Lord Hailsham. He was more than happy to oblige because he admitted that he had brought two cars to Canterbury anyway, one for him and one for his regalia! Irritating though these problems were, Peter took it with good humour, remarking that 'Riding in different cars from the police's to the Lord Chancellor's has given an unexpected variety to the mayoralty which I rather enjoy. And it tests the ingenuity of the household officers.'

Although travelling around in a Rolls-Royce might be many people's dream, for Peter it was one aspect of the mayoralty he found hard to accept. He was used to rushing round the City on foot, in all weathers, without a coat. Such an august personage as the Lord Mayor of the City of London was obliged to wait at the Mansion House until the Rolls was driven round to collect him—even if the Lord Mayor was only going as far as Guildhall. For Peter that took some getting used to.

From The Elms Peter had moved to Wrekin College. By a wonderful stroke of fortune the school's centenary year coincided with Peter's term of office so their speech day that year was a grand occasion with the Lord Mayor of London presenting the prizes. It was also a perfect opportunity for Peter to involve the school in his mayoralty. Wrekin College Chapel choir took part in the Fleet Street Club's Christmas festivities in London where it was reported they 'sang like angels' at the Connaught Rooms.

Thanks to Peter's personal intervention the school was able to hold its Centenary Dinner at Guildhall. This was something Peter was delighted to arrange because, as he said in his speech, 'I owe much to Wrekin.' Seven hundred guests attended and included three of Wrekin's headmasters, Canon Guy Pentreath amongst them. It was a memorable occasion for everyone and one that was later immortalised in a large picture that hangs in the school today. This was created from a photograph, presented to the school by the Old Wrekinians' Association and unveiled by Peter in 1981.

From Wrekin, Peter had moved to Jesus College, Cambridge. During his mayoral year he not only dined at the college but arranged for the Jesus College Cambridge Society and the Jesus College Dining Club to hold their dinners at the Mansion House. This is but one of the many actions which have led people to say, 'Peter is a great enabler and facilitator'.

There was a point when it looked as if Peter would be unable to fit in a Jesus College dinner at Cambridge because his previous engagement in the City did not finish until early evening. That would only have given him half an hour to get from the City to Cambridge. Fortunately Peter remembered sitting next to someone at dinner some weeks earlier who had said, 'If ever you need a helicopter, you just have to say the word.' At the time it had seemed a kind but unlikely offer. But Peter suddenly thought perhaps he could use a helicopter and phoned his dining colleague up.

The answer which came back sounded rather like a cryptic message for James Bond. 'Be at Blackfriars Bridge at 6.45pm. You'll see a barge moored there. Get on and we will pick you up.' Dressed for an official dinner, the Lord and Lady Mayoress boarded the barge as instructed and waited. There was a whirring sound and to their amazement a small helicopter came into sight, landed on the barge and collected them.

The flight to Cambridge was swift and easy. Peter sat at the front next to the pilot and Belinda recalls her amusement as they came into Cambridge. Peter was sitting there with an Ordnance Survey map on his lap saying to the pilot, 'Turn right at this bridge.' At 7.30 promptly the Lord and Lady Mayoress stepped from their helicopter onto the lawn at Jesus College to be greeted by the master and fellows.

One personal highlight for Peter and Belinda in the mayoral year was their silver wedding anniversary on 16 April 1980. The pressure of public engagements meant that they had to postpone their celebrations to the following day but it was well worth it. Daughters and boyfriends joined family, bridesmaids and ushers to sit down to a dinner for 35 guests in the Salon. Peter Drury, who was the steward at the Mansion House, went to great lengths to lay the most splendid table with silver from the vaults. The centrepiece of the table was a cornucopia decorated with fresh fruits.

Another family event came right at the end of the year in office when Peter decided to hold a ball in honour of his four lovely daughters. Each of the girls could choose 50 friends to invite to the Mansion House ball. The Lord Mayor arranged to have his own bar in the Venetian Parlour for the 25 'oldies' he had invited! The idea of holding a ball in honour of your family was thought to be such a lovely one that the next Lord Mayor copied it and this has led to many more family parties like it. What made the event particularly special for Peter and Belinda was that Juliet, their eldest and only married daughter, had recently given birth to her first child, Nicholas, Peter and Belinda's first grandchild.

A letter which appeared in the *Daily Telegraph* right at the end of Peter's mayoralty gives an idea of how his period in office was regarded as one of the busiest the City had ever seen, although today the path Peter blazed would be regarded as normal for a Lord Mayor of London.

At this time of year, when a new Lord Mayor of London takes office, your readers may care to pause for a moment to consider what a physical, as well as gastronomical feat of endurance his term will be, if that of his predecessor, Sir Peter Gadsden, is a suitable guide.

During the past twelve months Sir Peter, according to the Lord Mayor's engagements recorded in the City's local newspaper, attended the following official functions in London: 123 luncheons, 153 dinners, 11 banquets and 83 receptions. In addition, he was present on 48 religious occasions, of which the service in St Paul's Cathedral in celebration of Her Majesty The Queen Mother's 80th birthday was the undoubted highlight of his year; he received over 80 distinguished visitors to the Mansion House; he presided at over 90 meetings of various descriptions, including 20 school or university speech day ceremonies. He also presided, in his capacity as Chief Magistrate of the City, at over 40 Court sessions, and he was in attendance at 30 Freedom of the City of London ceremonies.

Outside London he visited United Kingdom cities as far apart as Belfast, Aberdeen, York, Sheffield, Cambridge, Cardiff, Portsmouth, Hereford and Truro. He flew over to Dublin for lunch and his other activities were as diverse as going down into tin and coal mines, sewers, and submarines, flying gliders and helicopters, as well as visiting North Sea oil and gas rigs, sludge boats and an atomic power station. He found time to donate a pint of blood and to be a spectator at many of the country's annual sporting occasions.

However, Sir Peter Gadsden will probably be best remembered as a much travelled roving ambassador for his country; he was not only the first Lord Mayor to go to China, but also visited countries and states as varied and far apart as Luxemburg, Tunisia, USA, Canada and Australia.

Peter was also delighted to receive the Speaker of the House of Commons, George Thomas, at a meeting of the Court of Common Council and to invite him to sit on the dais with the aldermen. But out of all this, Peter says four major events stand out during his year of office. There was a visit to his birthplace in Canada; the enthronement of the Archbishop of Canterbury; their silver wedding anniversary dinner at the Mansion House and the thanksgiving celebrations for Queen Elizabeth, The Queen Mother's 80th birthday.

Chapter 14

'A Good Job Done, Gad!'

You and I must keep from shame
In London streets the Shropshire name;
On banks of Thames they must not say
Severn breeds worse men than they;

AE Housman, *A Shropshire Lad*

One thing which characterised the 652nd Lord Mayor of London's time in office was the huge amount of travel he undertook. For a person accustomed to covering 30–40,000 miles a year on business, the mayoral travels probably seemed small fry by Peter's standards. However, he was in no doubt that travel should play a significant part of his mayoralty. 'Part of my effectiveness is that there will be a lot of people all round the world who will read about the Lord Mayor and say I've met him.' One newspaper headlined an account of his travels with the words 'Ambassador at Large'.

It is traditional for the Lord Mayor to visit a Commonwealth country during his summer tour and this was a tradition Peter was keen to uphold. 'The Commonwealth has a very important part to play in the world,' he said. 'There are so many things that unite us—our background, our heritage of language and way of life. The Commonwealth has evolved from history and is still a force for good.' The Canadians appreciated his views. 'It's a quirk of fate that has given the City a head of government solidly rooted in the Commonwealth—and this shows in the breezy informality of the man and his family,' they said, adding: 'Sir Peter Gadsden is the embodiment of the spirit of London.'

During his travels, Peter gained a few unusual titles given him by well-meaning foreign hosts keen to pay the Lord Mayor of London the respect due to his high office. This meant on one occasion he was addressed as Lord Gadsden, since the host assumed a Lord Mayor must be a lord. There were others who thought Lord was his title or his first name, and Mayor his surname! In one country he was called Sir Gadsden and his spouse Lady Belinda. As ever Peter graciously took it all in his stride, making no comment. Possibly that was because Peter had reached the stage where he had almost forgotten his real name since he was always addressed as 'Lord Mayor'.

For the first few weeks in office Peter found it disconcerting. In fact he recalls sitting at the table on one or two occasions and hearing someone say 'Pray silence for the Lord Mayor'. He looked around for a second to see where the Lord Mayor was sitting only to realise 'It's me!' and got to his feet smartly!

Although Peter might have been given some strange titles during his year in office, he was honoured several times with awards. Most notable of these was the GBE, Knight of the Grand Cross of the most Excellent Order of the British Empire. He was also elected an honorary member of the Guildhall School of Music and Drama. The same year he became a Knight of St John, having been an Officer of the Order of St John since the time he was sheriff. As Chancellor of City University during his mayoralty, Peter was awarded an Honorary Doctorate of Science (DSc) in 1979 'by virtue of his achievements in public affairs, his contribution to civic life and his endeavours to promote the prosperity and progress of the City of London'. Receiving a Hon DSc alongside Peter was Sir Freddie Laker, the pioneer of cheap transatlantic flights.

Belinda received an honour in 1982 when she was made a Dame of Honour and Devotion in the Sovereign Military Order of Malta. This is a special honour which can only be awarded to someone from an established Catholic family such as the Haggerstons.

Taking into account the travels of Basil Gadsden and Peter's country of birth, it comes as no surprise that Canada should have loomed large on the Lord Mayor's itinerary. 'Canada is there always in my background,' Peter said, 'It's something that is unusual in the City—I travel as a Canadian and it's something I'm proud of.' By fortunate coincidence the province of Alberta was celebrating its 75th anniversary in 1980 and Albertans abroad, or elsewhere in Canada, were invited to come home and join in the celebration. Peter had been handed a personal moosehide-covered invitation to the 'Homecoming' by the Honourable Al 'Boomer' Adair, the Minister for Tourism who drove the Albertan chuck wagon in the Lord

Mayor's Show. Peter relished the idea of returning to his birthplace and also to Edmonton where his brother and sister had been born and where he had lived for a while. Although Peter had travelled to Canada before, he had never returned to Alberta.

The Lord Mayor's visit to Alberta is remembered with pride by Maureen Mackay who was very privileged to be asked to be the escort for Sir Peter Gadsden and his party during his visit to Alberta for the celebration of the 75th anniversary of the province. 'We had a very busy programme planned for Sir Peter during his six-day visit,' she recalls.

> Myself, and a colleague Don Smithson, flew to Vancouver, British Columbia in two of our government aircraft to meet Sir Peter and his party on their arrival from Hawaii. The welcoming party on arrival in Edmonton, to Sir Peter's amazement, included his brother David and sister-in-law Judy. They were also met by the Honourable Al 'Boomer' Adair, Minister of Tourism for the province of Alberta. Much to Sir Peter's surprise we had a police escort to the hotel—six city police on motorcycles.

> Sir Peter's first day in Edmonton started with a civic parade to City Hall to be officially welcomed by the Mayor of Edmonton. He was escorted to City Hall by the Gurkhas. The Mayor hosted a dinner that evening in Sir Peter's honour and approximately 250 people attended.

In his speech at the dinner, Peter said: 'It is seven years since a Lord Mayor of London made an official visit to Canada and I am delighted to have this opportunity of renewing the bonds of friendship between us.' Unusually, as Peter pointed out, 'I am here as 652nd Lord Mayor of London and the first to be born in Canada' which was something his hosts were delighted to celebrate with him. As a Canadian newspaper put it: 'One of the biggest local boy makes good stories of the last 25 years.'

Maureen Mackay recalled, 'It was protocol for Sir Peter to leave the function before anyone else but he was having such a good time he dismissed his party, who were still very tired from their journey, and he carried on dancing and socialising with the guests in attendance.'

Despite being late to bed after the Edmonton dinner, Peter was up and about promptly the next day. Maureen Mackay resumes the story:

> The following day was the official 75th anniversary celebration for the province of Alberta. It was held at the provincial Legislature Building in the grounds. Sir Peter was met by the Honourable Peter Lougheed, Premier of the Province of Alberta, and the Right Honourable Pierre Trudeau, Prime Minister of Canada. Thousands of Albertans and visitors assembled and joined in the festivities.

One amusing incident occurred in the days that followed when Sir Peter and his party spent one and a half days in Jasper National Park, a treasured mountain resort in Alberta and stayed at the Jasper Park Lodge. It was in Jasper the Royal Canadian Mounted Police tracked Sir Peter down. Sir Peter and his party were to attend a Western Barbeque in Calgary and appropriate clothing had been purchased for the occasion (denim jeans and skirts for the women). The tailor had been at the hotel prior to departure for Jasper to take measurements for the alterations that were required. Much to the tailor's horror, he had mixed up the jeans that were to be altered and thought he had made a mistake with the Lord Mayor's. The tailor called the hotel in Edmonton only to be told Sir Peter was not in the hotel and for security reasons they could not divulge where Sir Peter was. The tailor, in a panic, called the Royal Canadian Mounted Police indicating it was urgent he contact Sir Peter. The RCMP in Edmonton knew Sir Peter was in Jasper and had the local RCMP contact Jasper Park Lodge asking him to contact the tailor in Edmonton right away as there was an emergency. 'Not knowing what had happened I called the tailor,' Maureen recalls, 'and the dilemma was solved. We all laughed hysterically and I am still laughing to this day over the incident.'

In complete contrast to the hilarity at Jasper, the following day Peter moved to Mannville which was a very emotional experience. This was the first time he had returned to his birthplace and he summed up his feelings to the hundreds who had turned out to welcome him home, when he said: 'There are four very special milestones in a person's life—the day you are born, the day you are married, the birth of your children and the day you return to your birthplace.'

The civic party from London laid on a miniature Lord Mayor's Show for the Mannville inhabitants, parading up the main street with a gurkha band. They also walked behind the same chuck wagon that had been sent over for the Lord Mayor's Show the previous November. Maureen Mackay recalls that Sir Peter was dressed in his official Lord Mayor's regalia and all the people of Mannville and the surrounding area were on the streets to greet Sir Peter and his party. There was a covered wagon pulled by horses for the parade as well as several men on horseback. One of the media requested Sir Peter get on one of the horses for a picture which of course he did. Unfortunately he had sneezed the night before and put his back out. That did not stop him. He had a full day ahead of him and he was not going to let his sore back disrupt the festivities. But

62. Peter obliged the crowds who turned out to greet him in Mannville by mounting the horse. Those close by heard Sheriff John Hart say, 'That hurt, Lord Mayor, didn't it?' as Peter hopped up. This was because John knew Peter had injured his back with a sneeze the previous night.

as he was mounting the horse, sheriff John Hart was heard to murmur, 'That hurt, Lord Mayor, didn't it?'

A full day it certainly was. There was a visit to Christ Church where Peter's father had been the minister, followed by a visit to the local school to address the students and teachers. He also declared open the local reservoir and this was followed by a fly-past of the Royal Canadian Airforce.

The official dinner laid on in Mannville was a personal tribute to a favoured son because it was all planned and carried out by the inhabitants themselves. Maureen recalls that 'several hundred people were in attendance at this very special occasion—one that will never be repeated for this small community'. Amongst those waiting to be presented to Sir Peter were two people from his past, Ella and Elsie. As they presented a bouquet to Belinda, they revealed that they had been bridesmaids at Peter's parents' wedding. Elsie proudly displayed the brooch given her by May Gadsden on that day in 1927.

As Belinda recalls, 'It was, as you can imagine, a very emotional time, everyone was mopping their eyes. Peter was so touched by the whole thing and they were so thrilled to see him.'

Dr Heaslip, the doctor who had delivered Peter, was not well enough to travel from his home in Florida, but he had ensured that his daughter and son-in-law were there to represent him. In the letter they brought, Dr Heaslip recalled the strong friendship that had developed between both families. 'My wife and I visited your father and mother in Ireland and also in Shropshire. Your father and I played many games of tennis at Mannville,' he wrote. Later in the year, Peter made a point of travelling to Florida to be reunited with Dr Heaslip once more which gave them all immense pleasure.

63.   Peter was delighted to meet Ella and Elsie during his visit to Mannville, Alberta, in 1980. These two ladies had been his mother's bridesmaids in 1927 (see page 9).

Other faces from the past were waiting to greet Peter though he was too young to remember them. 'Spud' Croft, the neighbour who had been Peter's babysitter, was proud to see her young charge transformed by his robes of office. Edith Johnson, who as Miss Rutherford had played the organ in the Reverend Gadsden's church, was also presented to the Lord Mayor of London along with former neighbours of the Gadsden family. Others came up saying, 'Mind if I give you a cuddle? I did when you were a baby!'

Mannville is a small town of 850 inhabitants (350 more than when Peter was born!), which one journalist described as 'based on one street, one hotel and a set of railroad tracks' but they were determined to do their son proud. Not only did everyone turn out to welcome the Lord Mayor of London but a special commemorative postmark was issued by Mannville Post Office on 2 September 1980. The commemorative envelope for the Mannville Homecoming '80 carried a portrait of Sir Peter in his mayoral robes and underneath said 'Commemorating the visit of the Lord Mayor of London Sir Peter Gadsden 2 September 80'. 'It was a very special day

64. Mannville welcomed their son home in true style with a 'Homecoming Banquet' for the Lord Mayor of London.

for many and one that will be remembered for a long time,' Maureen Mackay said.

The last part of Peter's Alberta Homecoming took place in Calgary where he was made an honorary Calgarian. The blue denim jeans that had caused such problems earlier fitted perfectly and were part of the official dress for the Lord Mayor of London at the Western Barbeque in Heritage Park. To complete the costume the Mayor of Calgary presented the Lord Mayor of London with a white cowboy hat—the official symbol for the city of Calgary—which he immediately put on.

The final words on the Canadian tour have to go to the Lord Mayor's official escort, Maureen Mackay, who concluded, 'It was a wonderful trip not only for Sir Peter but for all the people who met him. Sir Peter has made visits back to Alberta since 1980 renewing friendships. He has been a wonderful ambassador for Alberta and has many friends here. I, for one, hold Sir Peter and Lady Belinda very close to my heart. They are very warm and kind individuals and will always be very special in my life.'

In May 1980 the Lord Mayor managed to squeeze in a brief official visit to Atlanta, Georgia, and to Gadsden, Alabama. In Atlanta, Peter attended the fourth Industrial Minerals Congress. As a mineral trader he had

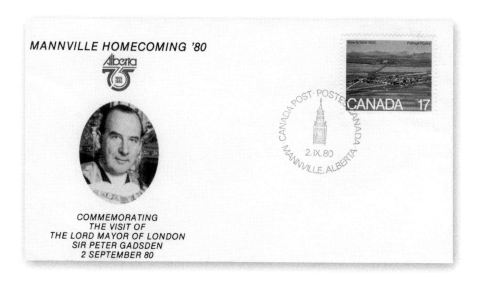

63. The envelope with special Mannville cancellation stamp was issued to commemorate the Lord Mayor's visit to Mannville. The Queen graciously accepted this for inclusion in the Royal Philatelic Collection.

attended the three previous congresses in London, Munich and Paris but on this occasion, as the Lord Mayor of London, he was there to open the congress. He was delighted to do this and in his opening speech reminded the audience of the wonderful float that *Industrial Minerals* and the *Metal Bulletin* had displayed in the Lord Mayor's Show only six months previously. From Georgia, Peter took the opportunity to make a flying visit to the city of Gadsden, Alabama, named after his ancestor James Gadsden. There the Lord Mayor of London was greeted by the Mayor of Gadsden. After the reception, Peter went on to visit a mining operation not far away.

There were other parts of the Lord Mayor's overseas tour that had personal connections. In the case of Australia, these were both family and business. When planning the Australian leg of the itinerary more than a year earlier, Peter learned that Adelaide had not received an official visit since 1975 so he was keen to incorporate the city into his schedule. It enabled him to visit the Collegiate School of St Peter, where Canon Guy Pentreath, his mentor from Wrekin College days, had been Principal.

The 18-day mayoral visit to Australia in the summer of 1980 was definitely not for the faint-hearted. The maximum number of visits were slotted into each day to avoid disappointing people. Belinda recalls that part of their summer tour as being the most gruelling. They came from China, stopped 24 hours in Hong Kong, then flew into Perth feeling jet-lagged but facing five receptions on their first day. By the fourth reception, she said, things had rapidly turned into a blur of faces, but they soldiered on for three days at this pace.

A request from the Public Relations Officer in Perth that the Lord Mayor of London bring the golden coach with him when he made his official visit to the city had to be refused. However, the Worshipful Company of Goldsmiths stepped into the breach and mounted an exhibition of ceremonial gold plate. The visit included a blend of official dinners (one of which the newspapers described as being 'like a page from *Who's Who*. All the diamonds were out along with the gossip columnists') and visits to familiar mining operations like AMA's near Bunbury.

Continuing his personal pilgrimage, Peter undertook a private visit to his father's church at Buchan. It was on the way to this church that an incident occurred which brought Peter's father to mind.

When the Honorable Peter Nixon, the Australian Primary Industry Minister and Federal member for Gippsland constituency, arrived to collect the Lord Mayor from his motel, he heard a commotion going on near the swimming-pool. He raced to the scene and found a four-year-old boy in difficulties. Peter Nixon pulled him out of the water then set about giving the child heart massage and mouth-to-mouth resuscitation. An ambulance was called but by the time it arrived the boy had regained consciousness. The child owed his life to the prompt action of the minister, who was modest about his achievement. 'I just applied mouth-to-mouth and kept going until the little boy came round,' he said. 'I was quite thrilled to feel his heart start to beat.' In fact if the child had been unconscious a moment longer he would have suffered brain damage. After that incident Peter Nixon maintained contact with the boy for some time.

The episode took Peter back to his childhood when he had been paddling in the River Severn under his father's supervision. Their attention was caught by a child in difficulties in the river. Without a second thought, the Reverend Gadsden jumped into the river and swam out to rescue him. It was an exceptionally brave thing to do given the force of the river and Peter always believed that his father deserved a medal. The rector, however, sought neither recognition nor praise for his action.

Unlike the Reverend Gadsden, who was able to go home and get changed, the Australian minister had to carry on with his duties because time was of the essence. Peter remembers that on the way to their next engagement they had to seek out a shop to buy some strong peppermints to mask the sick smell that lingered around the Australian minister.

Fortunately the rest of the tour passed without further incident and the mayoral party enjoyed a little official tourism that included a cruise in Sydney Harbour followed by lunch at the Opera House before they departed for Hawaii. Because they crossed the International Date Line the civic party succeeded in arriving the same day as they had left, but more amusingly the Chief Commoner was able to celebrate his birthday for two days. On the second day his wife was heard to comment that these birthday celebrations had gone on too long.

Peter knew all about the advantages of crossing the International Date Line. During his business travels whenever possible he planned his itineraries so he enjoyed a three-day weekend, unbeknown to the office back in London.

The Lord Mayor's tour was judged a huge success in Australia and William Murphy, Peter's former boss at Murphyores, sent a telegram that neatly summed it up—'A good job done, Gad!'

During his mayoral year Peter also made other official visits to Tunisia and Luxemburg at the request of the Foreign Office. Although Peter had travelled abroad extensively, nothing prepared him for the grand manner in which the Lord Mayor travelled. The chauffeur of the Rolls-Royce LM 0 drove the Lord and Lady Mayoress directly to the VIP lounge at Heathrow. All the official paperwork was processed without them ever being aware of it and then 15 minutes before take-off someone appeared saying, 'Lord Mayor, I think we'd better move now.' That was the signal to get back into the car and be driven to the steps of the plane. Belinda said she thoroughly enjoyed it and was sorry when their year was over and they had to revert to being normal passengers.

In Tunisia the British Ambassador managed to secure an invitation to an official luncheon with the President. This was an unexpected honour and extremely good for relations between the two countries. Peter believes that during this visit he contributed to good relations by saving President Bourgiba from serious injury. It happened when the President took the Lord Mayor out on to the terrace to show him the gardens and tripped in the process. It was only Peter's quick action which saved President Bourgiba from falling headlong down a flight of steps.

In Luxemburg the gentlemen in the mayoral party were taken on a tour of the Arbed Steel Works, which Peter found particularly interesting. The part of the visit which remains etched in his memory though occurred when the manager, who spoke fluent English with a strong accent, stopped alongside the iron ore stockpile. 'And zis is ze bed where we keep ze hores,' he told a surprised civic party. A few thought it fitting since they had heard Peter marketed virgin metals and common (wh)ores!

The countries who received the mayoral party were appreciative of the honour bestowed on them and went to great lengths to welcome their guests and ensure events went smoothly. Sometimes British protocol took the hosts by surprise. When the party arrived at the hotel in Canada, Colonel Milo, the household officer, efficiently took charge of collecting the Lord Mayor's luggage. A few moments later he was bemused to find someone pressing a dollar into his palm as a tip. It required some tactful handling to avoid offence and explain what was appropriate and what was not.

Peter was amused at the way some people thought that normal life should be suspended if the Lord Mayor was around. When he arrived at a hotel near Gatwick airport to spend the night (because there was no direct flight between Luxemburg and Gibraltar) the manager immediately went over to a couple locked in a passionate embrace in the corner of the lounge. They were oblivious to the rest of the world but found themselves being tapped sharply on the shoulder with the admonishment, 'Please behave! You can't do that here tonight, we have got the Lord Mayor staying.'

Peter made a particular effort to use his influence to encourage friendly relations between China and Great Britain. In 1979, as Lord Mayor he attended a reception and dinner at Guildhall held in honour of His Excellency the Premier of the State Council of the People's Republic of China. The following year the Lord Mayor attended a dinner at the Chinese Embassy given in his honour by the Ambassador and on this occasion Peter was invited by the Chinese Government to pay an official visit. The mayoral visit to China at the end of July 1980, whilst not part of Peter's personal pilgrimage, was very significant for both countries. Sir Peter Gadsden was the first Lord Mayor to pay an official visit to the People's Republic of China, although for Peter it was his 15th visit to the country since 1959.

In addition to the many commercial meetings that took place, the mayoral party were given the opportunity to visit notable heritage sites like the Ming Tombs, the Summer Palace, the Forbidden City and walk on the Great Wall of China.

Their stay outside Canton (now called Guangzhou) was fascinating on account of the hot springs. Peter had been before so he knew what to expect but Belinda was amazed to discover that even their hotel room had its own hot spring plumbed in. 'It was rather like a miniature swimming-pool,' she said. 'You filled it up with this special hot water that was brown and smelling like iron. It was all rather fun.'

The City had high hopes that the Lord Mayor's visit would lead to enhanced trade and commerce but, based on his own experience, Peter urged caution saying his four-day visit might not lead to contracts in the short term. 'It is really too early to say. All sorts of things were discussed and they will be followed up by the appropriate people. The trip went very well indeed. We were very warmly welcomed everywhere. Those businessmen that know China know they have to be patient,' he told City traders. 'Business does not happen overnight. Don't expect to come back on the first visit with enormous contracts but be patient and keep contact with people there.'

Not all Peter's visits were overseas, indeed he travelled around the British Isles more than most former Lord Mayors had done. Whilst he did not quite manage to go from Lands End to John O'Groats, Peter did his best. There was a mayoral visit to Geevor tin mine in Cornwall which required everyone in the party (ladies too) to be kitted out in mining overalls, boots and helmets. Belinda remembers it well not just because it was the first time she had been down a mine, but because the mining company was unused to kitting out women. They did their best and gave her the smallest boots they had (size 9½–10) and an enormous pair of overalls. When the civic party were properly clad they walked three miles underground in the Geevor mine.

Scotland made it into the Lord Mayor's itinerary when he flew to Aberdeen and then out to the Forties Alpha oil rig. There was an official state visit to Northumberland which took Peter and Belinda to Berwick, Alnwick, Seahouses and Ellingham. This caused great interest amongst the townspeople of Alnwick, because it was the first recorded visit of a Lord Mayor to the ancient town and Belinda and Peter were familiar faces. The town square was cleared and a band played to greet the official guests. Belinda was amused to find herself engaged in something akin to a royal walkabout in the market place. 'Normally I park the car here and can be seen lugging the groceries across the street,' she said.

Whilst in the area Peter was invited to inaugurate the roads and sewers contract for a new research establishment next to the A1. Some people may not have thought this was the most glamorous project but for a mining engineer it was a gem. If those present had thought Peter would be content to cut a small turf with a ceremonial spade, they were mistaken. He announced that he would do the job properly and drive the JCB digger to cut the turf. The councillors were slightly taken aback by the Lord Mayor's willingness to do some 'real' work and decided they had better check his insurance and driving licence. When they found all was in order, Peter was shown the controls. Off he went and cut four hefty turfs.

There was another mining visit in the north-east; this time the mayoral party went seven miles underground to reach a coal face under the sea near Newcastle. This was also memorable from the Lady Mayoress's point-of-view because the party travelled by train for 25 minutes, then lay on their stomachs on a conveyor belt to go roaring down to the coal face. 'This is far more exciting than any of the big dinners!' Belinda was heard to say.

Being so close to her ancestral home in Ellingham, it was not surprising that the official visit should take in the little village. The villagers were delighted by the honour and announced that 'Ellingham is very proud to welcome its adopted son as the Lord Mayor of the City of London.' Peter read the lesson at Sunday worship in the parish church and planted a tree outside the village hall.

As the end of the mayoral year drew near one newspaper reported that:

> Sir Peter likens being Lord Mayor to Cinderella. Instead of the ball and the bewitching hour, Lord Mayors have their elections, the Show, the year in office and then, like the stroke of midnight, they disappear when a successor takes office. By the time *his* bewitching hour arrives, Sir Peter Gadsden will have a wealth of experiences to look back upon and, he hopes, the personal satisfaction of a job well done.

What was Peter's view of his year as the Lord Mayor of London?

> I enjoyed it all, every minute of it. It's an endurance test, but I like meeting people. For a year you put everything into it, holding the torch, selling the City all round the world. Communication is the essence of the job. When I go abroad I realise how much people still look to London for leadership. Dick Whittington did the job four times. Luckily nobody can be asked to do it for more than one year now. When it's all over I'm going on holiday until Christmas.

Many marvelled at the sheer volume of work that this Lord Mayor had undertaken. Despite the huge number of luncheons and dinners he had attended, Peter remarked, 'I can remember who sat next to me at many of the dinners, but I can't remember any of the menus.'

Perhaps it is appropriate to let the Archbishop of Canterbury have the last word about the rector's son who became Lord Mayor. In a speech in November, Robert Runcie said:

> I have been able to observe at close quarters the infectious enthusiasm and vitality which he has poured into his year of office. One sign of the energetic way in which he has done his work is visible. After so many banquets and gala dinners, I am told that his girth has not increased by a single inch. He has demonstrated that the ancient office of Lord Mayor has vast potential for breaking down barriers and promoting friendly relations throughout the world.

> Sir Peter has been seen during his year of office in all five continents and simply to list the countries he has been to would take all my time. I am told that in one six-week period of hectic travelling he took off and landed in a variety of aeroplanes not less than fifty-eight times.

> As an ambassador of the City he has been the honoured guest of the Mayor of Peking (now Beijing) and made a highly successful visit to China. He is known as a friend now in Gadsden, Alabama; he has returned to Canada where he has seen his father's old church and gone to Australia. The City of London has trading and commercial links with every part of the world and Sir Peter has built on those connections and on his own cosmopolitan background to

66. The Lord Mayor and Lady Mayoress with their daughters in the Mansion House.

promote the kind of understanding and goodwill which is more than ever necessary in a dangerously divided world.

At home he has been a genial host at the Mansion House and someone who has continued the City traditions of breaking down barriers by conviviality. For the first time since the Reformation, the Cardinal Archbishop of Westminster joined the bishops of the Church of England to be entertained by the Lord Mayor.

So thank you Sir Peter for your enthusiasm, for your avid interest in the most diverse affairs and people, for being a Lord Mayor who has walked the sewers, wielded a pneumatic drill in a Cornish tin-mine and chuckled about my post-box at Lambeth Palace with its admonitory notice from the Postmaster General disclaiming responsibility for any letters posted in it.

Chapter 15

Business as Usual

Be always a good manager of your time, and lay hold of each opportunity that offers for the doing of whatever is necessary to be done. If you neglect a proper opportunity, you may not perhaps meet with it again; whereas, by laying hold of it when it offers, you will be able to dispatch much business in a little time; and if you accustom yourself to rise early, you will find that you have time enough to do all the business that you have to do, and much more than a person who rises late will think possible to be done.

(Rule XXV from *Rules for the Conduct of Life*)

Following the mayoralty it was business as usual for Peter and he picked up the reins of his mineral marketing consultancy. But this soon became only one aspect of an extremely busy life. The 1980s and 1990s were a period when Peter's expertise was in demand. His experiences as a mineral marketing consultant and as a leading figure in the City meant he was in an excellent position to offer an overview in a situation. As a result Peter undertook a large number of non-executive directorships of public and private companies over the next twenty years. He holds firmly to the belief that 'non-executive directors have a contribution to make because they provide a broader picture'.

These included the directorships of Guthrie Corporation; Inchcape International Trading; Private Patients' Plan; Thomas Hill-Jones; Penny and Giles plc; Aitken Hume International and Aitken Hume Bank; W Canning plc; London World Trade Centre Association; City of London (Arizona) Corporation and William Jacks plc, of which he became a director in 1984 and still is today. He was also chairman of the City of London branch of the Institute of Directors between 1995 and 1999.

Although approaching his sixties, an age when many men retire or think about winding down, Peter was still extremely busy with business and charitable activities. He has been involved with many charities including: the Britain-Australia Bicentennial Schooner Trust; the Battle of Britain Memorial Trust; Sir Robert Menzies Memorial Trust; the Metropolitan Society for the Blind; St Bartholomew's and St Mark's Hospitals; the Museum of Empire and Commonwealth Trust; the Industrial Trust; Nuffield Nursing Homes Trust; Phyllis Tuckwell Memorial Hospice; the Britain-Australia Society Educational Trust; the Hereford College for the Blind, and the Hereford Cathedral Perpetual Trust.

He was a commissioner of the 1851 Royal Commission and a member of the Commission's Board of Management from his appointment in 1986 until 1999. The secretary recalls that:

> he attended meetings of the Board in July and December each year, and was usually present at both the annual December cocktail party, held in honour of current holders of one of the Commission's Fellowships or Studentships, and the biennial Presidential Dinner. Characteristically, Sir Peter played a very active part in the management of the Commission, including developing its policy and activities. He made many contributions to discussions on organisations or individuals which the Commission might support through its ad hoc awards scheme. He was one of a party of Commissioners on a specially arranged tour of the new British Library and was instrumental in suggesting and organising a Commissioners' visit, in November 1998, to the Ironbridge Gorge Museum.

Such a vast and impressive list of activities is evidence that Peter Gadsden possessed exceptional skills. It is also worth remembering that alongside many of these business directorships, Peter was also chairman of an even larger project, the Britain-Australia Bicentennial Committee, from 1984 to 1988 and he remains chairman of the Britain-Australia Bicentennial Trust.

Because Peter has been in such demand to be the chairman of various committees, people have studied his style to find out how he is so effective. Observers are convinced he had a distinctive way of chairing and it was one that commanded almost instant respect. Tony Harvey, who knew Peter through the fund-raising activities of the Natural History Museum, summed it up by saying, 'You couldn't ignore Peter!'

An interesting caveat to his comment is that Tony also considered Peter to be a very quiet chairman who never tried to push his viewpoint. Nevertheless Peter had a great presence and was very powerful. He ran his committees like clockwork according to Gill Rides, his secretary for many years. 'He was the best chairman I've ever known. He sat on so many committees and meetings and ruled with a rod of iron. He stood no nonsense and did not let people wander off the point. The result was that you could fit in several meetings in a day without any problem.'

Peter said being a chairman is 'like being the conductor of an orchestra. When I chair a meeting I am, in effect, conducting that meeting, letting people have their say but also having to push it along to a conclusion. You have to be firm but kind. Most of all you have to be good at summing up,' he says. Many of these skills, which Peter honed up so successfully, were learned years earlier from his first bosses, Guy Falla and David Dale.

Others, who have watched him in action, think it all comes down to preparation. Tony Harvey said:

> Peter has done his homework really well. He has familiarised himself with the agenda, considered where the sticking points might be. He then thinks who might have concerns about these areas and goes off to discuss it with them before the meeting. That way, when it comes to the meeting the problems have already been resolved and the meeting can proceed smoothly and efficiently. He has a phenomenal memory and sharp mind. One technique he used to good effect was that of planting a question if he thought it might serve a purpose. He was a quiet worker behind the scenes but with a scrupulous attention to accuracy, particularly when it concerned the minutes of meetings.

Above all he thrives under pressure, yet no one recalls him ever raising his voice or losing his temper, though one person admitted 'he did get uptight on occasions!'

In May 1981 Peter was appointed part-time member of the Board of Crown Agents for Overseas Government and Administration until he retired from the board in 1987. These were what could euphemistically be called 'interesting and challenging times'.

After the 1983 General Election, the Foreign Office became involved in an argument with a Middle Eastern oil state which suddenly withdrew billions from the Crown Agents. Because this state had been the Crown Agents' principal source of revenue, the Agents were technically insolvent so the new Foreign Secretary decided to close them down.

Sir Peter Graham takes up the story:

> As a board we decided to oppose that idea. I think it was Sir Peter Gadsden who pointed out that the Agents had been incorporated by Act of Parliament and therefore had to be closed by Act of Parliament. That was a useful weapon and mainly Sir Peter and I managed to drum up considerable all-party support. That made the Government change its mind and in fact we also received some loan support to keep us in business.

However we still had to restore financial viability and Sir Peter's business experience was invaluable in the making of some pretty hard decisions such as the sale of the opulent office on the Embankment, cutting staff by about 50% and marketing our services to countries and international bodies where the Agents had never worked before. All of this paid off and the organisation has gone from strength to strength ever since.

During his time with the Crown Agents Peter visited their offices overseas including those in Singapore, St Lucia and Barbados when he was abroad on business, although he never travelled specifically for them. The fact that he had taken the trouble to make personal contact was much appreciated. A colleague recalls that Peter was always generous with his time despite having an enormous workload.

When his term of office on the board expired, Chris Patten, the minister responsible for overseas development, wrote of his appreciation for Peter's service through a period that even he admitted had been 'fraught with difficulties for management and board alike. The breadth of experience and advice which you have brought to the Board during this testing time has been warmly appreciated.'

In 1981 Peter became a non-executive director of the UK's second largest private medical insurers, Private Patients' Plan or PPP as they were known. Although his mineral marketing consultancy continued, PPP became his main employment for the next 12 years. During that time Peter was instrumental in expanding PPP's field of operation outside the UK particularly into Malta and Hong Kong. In 1986 he also opened the new PPP House in Tunbridge Wells. 'Everywhere I go in business and public life I'm known as Mr PPP,' he said cheerfully.

From being a director in 1981, Peter was chairman between 1984 and 1996, then in 1996 when the company restructured, he became non-executive chairman of PPP Healthcare Foundation and the first president of PPP Healthcare Group. The directors commissioned Leonard Boden (who had also painted a portrait of Canon Guy Pentreath) to paint his portrait and this can still be seen at their offices in Tunbridge Wells.

In the opinion of Gill Rides, who managed Peter's work for PPP, the secret of his success was that he took a personal interest in the employees at PPP, even quite junior office staff. 'He doesn't forget anybody and could remember their names even though he hadn't seen them for ages. People adored him. They always felt better for being associated with him,' she said.

Working for PPP brought in its wake some interesting conference travel for Peter and Belinda to venues like Jersey, Auckland, Dublin and Boston. Expansion into Malta and Hong Kong involved travel to these countries which Peter, the inveterate traveller, was more than happy to undertake. He was an especially welcome and regular visitor to Hong Kong during the 1980s. He knew the colony well from his mineral trading days and he had also called through as Lord Mayor, albeit briefly en route to Australia.

Peter preferred to be known as 'Mr PPP' in Hong Kong rather than the cheeky nickname 'DSM' he had once earned on a business trip. This sobriquet had been given by an amah (a Chinese maid) who was upset that Peter was attempting to get another day's wear out of one of his shirts. She nicknamed him 'Dirty Shirt Master' which became abbreviated to DSM by his friends in Hong Kong.

Overseas business travel still had a few pitfalls even for someone as experienced as Peter, Ron Fuller recalls:

67. The board of directors of PPP. Back row, left to right: David Rose, Richard Blaxland, Tom Lewis, Geoffrey Kidner, Viscount Boyne, Dr Lotte Newman, Peter Lord, Sir Anthony Grabham. Front row, left to right: Sir Alexander Durie, Clifford Grinstead, Sir Peter Gadsden, Ray Forman, Sir Richard Bayliss.

It must have been around 1983–4. The employer both Peter and I worked for had a major consumer of our mineral products in Avignon. Our counterpart in Avignon was a most courtly gentleman whose name was Loic Petit de la Villeon, one of nature's most pleasant men. I was based then in Australia and together with a colleague, Peter Cassidy, I met up with Peter Gadsden in London and we all three sallied forth to Avignon to have a business meeting with Loic. The visits to Avignon were always welcomed because as well as the pleasure of meeting with Loic we stayed at a lovely old hotel inside the walls of Avignon, the Hotel de l'Europe.

The morning after our evening arrival we duly met with Loic who then took us to a lunch at a restaurant overlooking the vineyards where Chateauneuf du Pape was grown and produced. In fact Loic introduced us to a white Chateauneuf, and we lingered and lingered in the lovely surroundings until finally it came time to leave, when we three found we could hardly stand! We finally made it to Loic's stately old DS23 car, and we were looking forward to getting back to the hotel and a lie-down preferably under running water with the lights off.

Halfway to the hotel, Loic, who too was the worse for wear, announced there was a custom that whenever visitors came from Australia, they had to stop and partake of a particularly fine French beer at a tavern nearby. We groaned our agreement, stopped and drank two glasses under duress of a thick dark beer that I swear would not have run out of the glass if you had turned it upside down!

We finally arrived back at the hotel close to 5 o'clock in the afternoon, struggled out of the car and Loic said, 'Gentlemen, I am so sorry I cannot entertain you this evening, I have another engagement.' We three looked at each other, all with similar visions of lying down in a cool room after about an hour in a cold shower. Suddenly though Loic spoke again, 'However, I am pleased to tell you that Monsieur Shouzenous will call for you at 7 pm and take you to dinner.' No amount of protest was accepted, so we struggled up to our rooms to repair and prepare as best we could.

At a few minutes before seven, I entered the downstairs bar intent on a large coffee to find the two Peters drinking milk!

Monsieur Shouzenous duly arrived and escorted us to a very nice restaurant indeed, the kind you only find in France, and which in any other circumstances would have been most enjoyable. We struggled through dinner, sipped at a fine wine to avoid upsetting our host, and all was well until it came to after-dinner cognac. I flatly declined to partake. Our host insisted and insisted. Finally I looked him straight in the eye and said, 'Monsieur Shouzenous, if I drink one more mouthful of alcohol, the person opposite me will be wearing my dinner, and since you are the person opposite, I do beg you not to insist any further.' He got the message, thank God.

Then we had to get back to the hotel. Avignon is filled with very narrow old streets as befits its venerable age. We all, including by now our host, were having difficulties making our way back to the hotel.

Three very red-eyed, pasty-faced, unsteady Englishmen avoided the hotel breakfast-room next morning and wandered carefully to the town square seeking strong coffee and a firm chair. For the ensuing 48 hours each and every invitation to have a drink was politely, but firmly, declined.

In 1984 Peter also became chairman of the Royal Commonwealth Society for four years then took over the office of vice-president in 1988. This was entirely appropriate for a person with so many personal and business connections with the Commonwealth. Peter did much to foster links between Canada and the Commonwealth and personally visited the provinces of Alberta, British Columbia, Ontario and Nova Scotia to speak at dinners and meetings arranged by the local branches of the Royal Commonwealth Society (now called the Commonwealth Trust). It was Peter's initiative that led to the society's AGM being held in Halifax, Nova Scotia, in 1987 rather than London again. Peter was proud to take the salute at the Commonwealth Night of the Nova Scotia Tattoo. The timing of Peter's appointment coincided with his chairmanship of the Britain-Australia Bicentennial Committee and enabled him to make useful contacts with New Zealand and Australian branches of the Royal Commonwealth Society.

The headquarters of the Society in Northumberland Avenue was trading with a substantial loss and with the help of an expert introduced by Sir Hugh Wontner, Peter instigated a thorough investigation which resulted in many faults in the organisation being rectified.

It was decided to appoint a Grand President and the society was honoured when HRH the Duchess of York accepted the post. An amusing incident occurred when the Grand President met the High Commissioner of Australia, His Excellency, the Honourable Douglas McClelland. Earlier in the evening the Duchess of York was sitting next to Peter at the dinner which he was hosting for the High Commissioners and Agents General of Australia and Canada. She enquired where he would recommend for a holiday in Australia. 'Lizard Island,' he said, 'But I'm no expert. The Australia High Commissioner is here. Why not ask him? I'll present him to you after dinner.' 'What is he like?' the Duchess asked. 'He's charming. Very informal. He doesn't stand on ceremony. In fact he's known as "Call me Doug",' Peter added.

68. Fishing has been one of Peter's pastimes, encouraged by that excellent fisherman, Sir Peter Studd. This splendid catch was made in Nova Scotia when Peter managed to snatch a few days' holiday.

After dinner the High Commissioner was presented to Her Royal Highness and she greeted him with a wonderful Aussie accent saying, 'G'day Doug'. His Excellency was completely taken aback by this and replied, 'Good day, Your Royal Highness.'

The Duchess then went on to enquire where she should spend her summer holidays in Australia. To which he replied, 'Lizard Island.'

'That's exactly what Sir Peter has told me,' she said.

'Well, that shows what good taste we've both got!' he countered.

By that time a crowd was gathering to be presented to Her Royal Highness and she moved on to shake hands. His Excellency the High Commissioner turned to Peter and said, 'She thinks my surname's Doug.'

'No she doesn't!' came the amused reply. 'She knows you like the informal approach.'

During the 1980s Peter was more than happy to put his expertise and influence at the disposal of charitable institutions like the Natural History

Museum. Through a mutual friend Peter was introduced to Tony Harvey, Head of Library at the Natural History Museum and the person charged with helping the museum to raise money.

The early 1980s were a period of great change for the museum because they were suffering a funding crisis. The best way out of this, it was thought, was for the museum to set up a development trust in the same way as some American museums had done, and Tony Harvey was appointed Director of the Development Trust. Although Peter never became a main board trustee of the museum, he helped the museum to get its fund-raising organised because he brought with him experience gained with the Ironbridge Gorge Museum Development Trust in Shropshire. The Natural History Museum Development Trust was actually launched in 1988 but Peter was active behind the scenes from the mid-1980s until the mid-1990s.

As the present Natural History Museum director Sir Neil Chalmers explained, 'Sir Peter was able to help us to operate at the right level. We had no idea how ambitious we should be. But he was able to take a whole institution view and help us to build up a network of contacts.' Tony Harvey offers an interesting insight into the way Peter approached the task.

> He got to know the organisation first, understood its foibles, where it was going and what it needed. He can lead from the front but he is a great power behind the throne and very gracious with it. He wanted to do good and I never heard him say a bad word about anyone. He made things happen through his connections. Peter didn't join anything he did not intend to contribute to and he used everything he had got totally appropriately. He never saw it as a duty and he never abdicated responsibility. Sir Peter was the right person at the right time for the Natural History Museum. He drove it forward and broadened and consolidated its work.

The skills he brought were very practical ones because he knew exactly how a museum could approach outside funding. It was Peter's suggestion that the museum should host exclusive dinners for the captains of industry. These were held at the museum so the diners could be shown around parts of the museum afterwards, enabling them to gain a better understanding of the specific needs of the museum. The guest list for these dinners was totally Peter's and because he was such a good host and good company, the events proved popular and extremely beneficial to the museum. This was also true of the Livery Days at the Natural History Museum which Peter helped organise along similar lines to those he had initiated at Ironbridge.

69.   The Iron Bridge in Shropshire (seen in the background) has fascinated Peter since he was a schoolboy. In later years he became an excellent ambassador for the bridge and for the Ironbridge Gorge Museum. Seen here from left to right: Stuart Smith, Peter, Belinda, Lorna McClelland, Joy Jenkinson and the Honourable Douglas McClelland, the Australian High Commissioner (Barry Jenkinson took the photograph).

It is worth remembering that at the same time as he was assisting the Natural History Museum with its fund-raising, Peter was also working on the Britain-Australia bicentennial celebrations. He had been particularly interested in the museum's collection of eighteenth-century watercolour drawings of plants and animals in Australia. Working with the museum, Peter helped them organise a touring exhibition called 'First impressions: the British discovery of Australia' as part of the Britain-Australia bicentennial celebrations. The gala opening of the exhibition at the Natural History Museum in January 1988 was followed by a 16-month tour of seven major Australian cities. Peter was delighted: 'This is an exhibition for everyone; it tells the story of the British discovery of Australia through the work of those who faced the challenge of the new land: maritime explorers, gentlemen, scientists, convicts, governors and artists. The highlights of the exhibition are the unique and priceless works of art, many never seen before.' Fulfilling his reputation as 'a great facilitator and enabler' Peter arranged for part of the sponsorship for this exhibition to come from PPP.

During these two decades Peter gave a great deal of his time and expertise freely helping all manner of organisations from well-known national bodies to quite small groups. The honour he received from the Royal College of Anaesthetists in June 1994 actually had nothing to do with his chairmanship of PPP despite its medical ring. The college admitted Sir Peter Gadsden as an honorary fellow (FRCA) at a ceremony at the University of London in recognition of his work as chairman of the college's very successful appeal to raise money to enable them to have their own building. Previously they had shared premises with the Royal College of Surgeons.

Continuing the medical theme Peter has supported the St John's Ambulance. He was president of the South-Eastern Division between 1981 and 1986. This arose out of a much earlier association in 1977 when he was made an Officer of the Order of St John and, in 1980, a Knight of the Order of St John. Further medical honours followed for Peter when the Royal Society of Health made him a fellow (FRSH).

Life wasn't all work. In fact Peter and Belinda enjoyed some excellent holidays during this time, not just in Spain and Wittering, but as guests of their many friends. Most holidays were marvellous fun but a few turned out to be memorable for less pleasant reasons. The three-week Geestline cruise on a banana boat, spent with their great friends Sir Peter Studd and his wife Angela, Alan and Annabelle Henn and three other couples, would definitely rank as memorable! The outward voyage went well but the trip back became increasingly uncomfortable as the boat sailed into a tropical storm with a force-ten gale. There were 60-foot waves and the ship rolled at about 40 degrees. 'We had to stay in our bunks the whole time as the gale force winds buffeted us. Even the crew sustained broken bones,' Belinda recalls. 'We were all so thankful to be on land and back with our families again.' That was indeed a cruise to remember!

One of the small organisations Peter gave his support to was the Master, Wardens and Commonalty of Freemen of the Art or Mystery of Drapers in Shrewsbury, to give them their official title. Peter helped them preserve their beautiful medieval hall in the centre of Shrewsbury.

Although Peter knows the county town well, there are so many notable timber-framed buildings in Shrewsbury that he had not been especially

70.   Peter loves travelling whether for business or pleasure. He is seen holidaying in Malaysia with Belinda and his brother David and sister-in-law Judy in 1996.

aware of the Drapers' Hall. In fact, it was the visit of a liveryman of the London Drapers that set the ball rolling. A member of the Worshipful Company of Drapers happened to be passing through Shrewsbury and paid a visit to the hall in the 1980s. He found a sixteenth-century building in severe need of restoration. The Shrewsbury Drapers had been founded in 1576 but 300 years later there were only a dozen freemen whose time was taken up with running their almhouses. What came out of the liveryman's visit was that the Worshipful Company of Drapers offered to buy the Shrewsbury hall and renovated it at considerable cost to themselves.

Afterwards they arranged to lease the building back to the Shrewsbury Drapers for a peppercorn rent. This arrangement continued happily until the livery company's accountant pointed out that this was not a financially viable situation. So it was agreed to sell the hall to the Shrewsbury Drapers for a modest sum. Modest the sum might have been but the Shrewsbury Drapers did not have the money. Enter Peter.

Bringing with him experience gained from the City and from working with various museum development trusts, Peter helped the Shrewsbury Drapers to form a Heritage Preservation Trust for the building which gave them charitable status. After that he worked with them on a three-pronged funding bid. They sought a heritage grant and private loans whilst Peter set about brokering a loan for them through one of the banks of which he had been a director.

By 1988 the Shrewsbury Drapers had their hall back and arrangements were in place for the accommodation to be let, enabling the building to be self-financing. The Drapers are in no doubt as to whom they owe the greatest thanks. In recognition of the major part he played, Peter became a freeman of the Shrewsbury Drapers' Company.

Peter has never forgotten his friends in Mannville and the wonderful reception he received. He along with Belinda, his brother David and sister-in-law Judy returned again during the 1980s. During one visit in October 1987 Peter noticed that the Mayor of Mannville did not have a badge of office, so Peter immediately offered to rectify the situation. Back in London he arranged for one to be designed and executed in silver gilt. The design incorporated local Mannville industries, Peter's own coat of arms, the Albertan tartan and the maple leaf. The ribbons on the badge were in the colours of Canada and the City of London. The reverse of the badge is inscribed 'Alderman Sir Peter Gadsden, born Mannville 1929, Lord Mayor of London 1979–80'.

When Peter visited his birthplace in August 1988 he presented the badge as his personal gift to the village. During that same visit he also set up a charity in memory of his parents, the Basil and Mabel Gadsden Memorial Fellowship, for the benefit of the citizens of Mannville.

Peter has remained in regular contact with the village of Mannville and was invited back in May 1992 for the Yellowhead Caravan celebrations. This event commemorated the official opening of the newly twinned Trans-Canada/Yellowhead Highway #16 across Alberta.

The Gadsdens were part of the VIP group in the 100 car cavalcade that travelled from Lloydminster to Jasper and Peter was surprised that in the leaflets handed out to mark the occasion Mannville was listed as 'birthplace of the Lord Mayor of London'. As Peter was about to leave Mannville he was handed a pool cue. Eddie Eschak bet Sir Peter a dollar that he wouldn't make his first shot. Sir Peter took aim and skilfully directed the ball into a side pocket. Everyone cheered and the astonished Eddie paid his wager which Sir Peter gave to the club funds.

71.   When Peter discovered that the Mayor of Mannville, Alberta, had no badge, he arranged for one to be made in London. The design incorporates local Mannville industries, Peter's coat of arms, the Albertan tartan and the maple leaf. The ribbons are in the colours of Canada and the City of London. The badge was Peter's personal gift to his birthplace in August 1988.

It was during the same visit Peter went to Mannville Elementary School and found time to talk to the children in each classroom. As well as a countryside tour, the party stopped off at Stellaville Church where the Reverend Basil Gadsden had preached and they were able to recognise his father's handwriting on some framed memorabilia on the church wall. At Christchurch, Mannville, they saw the entry on 21 July 1929 for Peter's baptism. When the official party moved on to the local hospital in Mannville Peter also saw a framed record of his birth displayed on the wall. But more surprising was that, despite the passage of 60-odd years, Peter met Walter Hinton who remembered him as an infant he had babysat for in 1929.

THE PREMIER OF ALBERTA

Legislature Building. Edmonton. Alberta. Canada T5K 2B7 / 403/427-2251

June 12, 1990

Sir Peter Drury Gadsden,
   GBE, MA, DSc, FEng.
606 Gilbert House
Barbican
London, England
EC2Y 8BD

Dear Sir Peter:

I am very pleased to have the opportunity to convey to you my warmest best wishes and appreciation for your outstanding efforts over the past many years in bringing your home province of Alberta to the attention of the international business and tourism community.

Your loyalty and generosity to the Province of Alberta, and particularly to the Village and community of Mannville, are very much admired and deserving of recognition.

On behalf of the citizens of Alberta, please accept our thanks for your many acts of kindness, your friendship, and untiring efforts.

Sincerely,

Don R. Getty

72. Letter from the Premier of Alberta, Don R. Getty.

Chapter 16

'Mr City'

(Peter was amused by this notice which appeared on everyone's table at the annual Copper Club dinner in New York. Such a notice was unlikely to appear at a dinner in Guildhall.)

Over the years Peter has been given various titles, some formal and some very informal, but one that has cropped up over and over again is 'Mr City'. As one colleague who worked closely with Peter in the 1980s and 1990s said, 'Peter has done so much to keep the City life alive. He's concerned about history and tradition. Things must be done according to the book. The result is that he is always in demand for his knowledge of city traditions and nothing is too much trouble for him.'

Because Peter has a genuine interest in people he has been able to put a human slant on the City's activities. He brought to the fore the things that were happening in the City, would explain what they were about and why the traditions were worth preserving. 'We keep these traditions, not because we are backward-looking,' he explained in a speech, 'but because they are the foundations on which we build the future.'

The immediate aftermath of any mayoral year takes a bit of getting used to. Not only are the main protagonists exhausted but there is also an understanding that the late Lord Mayor will go into purdah and 'disappear' from the City. He is not to be seen in the presence of his successor until the Easter Banquet nor should he accept any formal civic invitations until then. It is helpful for the new Lord Mayor to be given the chance to make his own mark without the distraction of the previous incumbent. For a person who lived and worked in the City, as Peter did, it was rather difficult to be invisible.

Initially Peter and Belinda took a well-deserved holiday in Florida for three weeks, then after he returned Peter moved around the City with extreme care to ensure he neither bumped into the new Lord Mayor nor appeared at the same function. Inevitably there was the odd occasion when Peter was almost caught out and had to rush up a staircase in Guildhall to get out of sight.

Although Peter's mayoralty was over, several later events were rooted in it. One of these was Peter's admission as an honorary freeman of the Borough of Islwyn in South Wales.

It all began in 1979 when Ken Lewis, Deputy Treasurer of Islwyn, met former colleague John Griggs, then Chamberlain of the City of London, at a conference at Eastbourne. Reciprocal invitations and visits took place between London and Islwyn later that year. When representatives from Islwyn were in London they were given a conducted tour of the Mansion House and had the pleasure of meeting Lord Mayor Sir Peter Gadsden.

One of the next planned events was a London visit by pupils from the comprehensive school in Islwyn to meet the Lord Mayor and tour Guildhall. Gwyn Davies, then Deputy Mayor of Islwyn, remembers the welcome they received. 'The Islwyn coach was met at the City boundary by a City Police motorcycle and escorted to Guildhall. All traffic stopped and our young representatives were met outside Guildhall by representatives from the City of London Girls' School. We were led down to the magnificent Guildhall Crypt. The Lord Mayor of London, Sir Peter Gadsden, joined us at lunchtime.' The Duty Esquire accordingly had allocated 45 minutes for the Lord Mayor to be present before he moved on to another engagement but the Lord Mayor continued talking with the children. Each student was given one of the Lord Mayor's mayoralty mugs. After two hours Colonel Milo, the Swordbearer, was in despair having been reminded by the Lord Mayor that they would leave 'when it suited him'.

The rest of the afternoon was spent touring Guildhall and the Museum of London, then it was back on the coach to return to South Wales. 'As the coach engine sprang to life,' Gwyn Davies remembers, 'who should return but Lord Mayor, Sir Peter Gadsden, and loud cheers resounded from the youngsters.'

Peter's kindness towards the schoolchildren from South Wales was appreciated, not just by the pupils themselves, but by the borough as well. He was invited to call on them any time he should find himself in the area. The following year he did just that as he returned from an engagement in North Wales. Gwyn Davies said, 'Looking out of the window we saw a dirty Range Rover coming down the drive. John Rogers almost had apoplexy and was irately about to sort this driver out and send him to the rear car park. Fortunately we saw Gadsden and his lady get out of the vehicle. They had travelled through mud, muck and water to join us.'

Friendship between the City of London and Islwyn grew and David Morgan in his year of office as Mayor of Islwyn in 1980/81 received the Freedom of the City of London. This privilege has been granted to all the mayors of Islwyn since.

A personal friendship rapidly developed between Peter and Gwyn Davies, as both men had a mutual interest in rugby and enjoyed watching England versus Wales together at Twickenham and Cardiff. In February 1981 Peter was invited to be guest of honour at the dinner held in Islwyn

73. The Lord Mayor with the Mayor of Islwyn and a party of schoolchildren from Islwyn in South Wales. This visit led to a long-standing friendship between Peter and the Borough of Islwyn.

when Gwyn was mayor. The event turned out to be particularly memorable on account of the weather. A blizzard began at 8pm on the Friday night and continued well into the weekend. So bad was it that the dinner had to end earlier than intended so the guests could get home safely. Because Peter was booked into the local hotel where they were dining, Gwyn Davies and his wife volunteered to stay and keep him company.

Gwyn takes up the story:

> The following morning it was still snowing heavily when Peter came down to breakfast dressed for our intended visit to Oakdale Colliery, only to be told that the hotel was completely cut off. The council officers, led by John Parry, obtained a Landrover, and returned my wife Rita to our home. That evening we started a marathon game of cards which was to continue into Sunday and Gareth Pugh, the manager of the hotel, presented Sir Peter with a decanter of vintage port at the Saturday dinner.

> Eventually he was taken to Newport Station in the valiant Landrover. In the evening it had to collect an expectant mother from the mountain village in which she resided. The main road was blocked so the vehicle was needed to undertake the arduous task of taking her to hospital in Newport. Eventually I arrived home at 9.30pm and explained our good deed for the expectant mother. The caustic comment I received was that Peter had telephoned my wife at 5pm from the Barbican. To this day she believes that I had been enjoying myself drinking and playing cards. Dear Boy!!

After such camaraderie between the two men, and between Islwyn and the City of London, it comes as no surprise that the Borough of Islwyn should have chosen to honour Peter 'in recognition of the eminent services rendered' by him and 'as a further expression of the esteem in which he was held by the Mayor and citizens of the Borough, he was granted the Freedom of the Borough of Islwyn on 12th October 1982'.

Peter was delighted to accept the honour and attended a special ceremony the following year with his youngest daughter Elizabeth. When one councillor stood up to introduce the guest of honour, Sir Peter Gadsden, he opened his speech by inadvertently welcoming *Saint* Peter. A voice called out from the back of the Council Chamber, 'We are only making him a freeman. We aren't canonizing him!'

To the delight of the audience, Peter began his reply in Welsh although he had not thought to prepare a response to any quips from the audience.

There was also a further development in the freemen story. When it was enacted in 1994 that Islwyn Borough Council would cease to exist as a local government authority, an Association of Freemen of the City of London in

Islwyn was formed in January 1995. At the inaugural meeting, it was agreed that the president for life would be Sir Peter Gadsden and the chairman the late WH Davies, Mayor of Islwyn at that time. Dinners of the association are still held annually in Islwyn, the City of London or Shropshire.

Although Peter's mayoralty was over, as 'one past the chair' he was still in demand to undertake engagements that the Lord Mayor was unable to fit in. It was on just such an occasion that Peter returned from an overseas business trip one afternoon with a dinner engagement booked for that evening. Knowing how tight the schedule was and that planes can get delayed, Peter had packed his dinner clothes in his overnight bag ready to change at Heathrow the moment he touched down. However a fire at Dusseldorf airport delayed everything and forced the airport authorities to set up a marquee to process passengers. With time running out, Peter was obliged to change in an awning. Then he boarded his connecting flight dressed for the dinner. A fellow-businessman recalls with amusement how the Germans, confronted by this elegant figure in full regalia, were unsure whether to salute him or not!

74. In 1982 Peter received the honorary Freedom of the Borough of Islwyn 'in recognition of the eminent services rendered by him to The Borough'.

The time a distinguished Nigerian Chief was admitted to the Freedom of the City of London is recalled by Peter with amusement and some embarrassment. It was a very important occasion and the gentleman brought with him some 400 supporters. At the dinner in the Old Library at Guildhall it was arranged that the band would play the British national anthem and the Nigerian national anthem. Unfortunately the band had not been told that Nigeria had changed its national anthem so they launched into one that was no longer in use. To rectify the situation, the Nigerian guests stood up and sang their new anthem without any music. It was all taken in good humour, indeed some said they preferred the old tune!

On the same occasion it was the quick thinking of one of Peter's colleagues attending the ceremony that saved the hosts from further embarrassment. John Allen lived in a small village in Sussex called Blackboys and in conversation with one of the visiting entourage was asked where he lived. John and his wife looked at each other then he rapidly replied, 'Tunbridge Wells'.

After the mayoralty Peter felt able to devote more time to livery activities. He was the 28th Clothworker to become Lord Mayor and the following year he became Warden of the Company. From 1981–7 Peter was member of the finance committee and in 1989–1990 served as 470th Master of the Clothworkers' Company, exactly ten years after he had been Lord Mayor. This was a particularly busy period for Peter because it coincided with the completion of his chairmanship of the Britain-Australia Bicentennial Committee. One interesting connection between these two offices is that the Master's chair, made of Australian black bean wood, was a gift to the Clothworkers' Company from Sir Robert Menzies, an honorary liveryman of the company.

During Peter's year as Master, he was approached to sit for a portrait wearing his gown and badge. He agreed to this as he had done to other requests for portrait sittings in the past. This portrait was not an official one, as the young artist had elected to undertake it in the hope that the sitter would purchase the picture on completion. As time went on, Peter and others watched the development of the portrait in amazement. The artist had decided to interpret the Master of the Clothworkers in a similar manner to Velasquez's famous portrait of the very elderly Pope Innocent X. The sixty-year-old Peter saw himself depicted on the canvas sitting in a similar pose with his hands resting on the arms of the chair. Peter's hands were shown disproportionately large and displaying all the wrinkles and

75. As an alderman, Peter is seen meeting President Ronald Reagan in 1988 with the Lord Mayor, Sir Greville Spratt.

prominent veins of a very old man, in contrast to the reality. Not surprisingly, many people expressed dislike of the picture and Peter certainly had no intention of buying it, yet alone hanging it.

This presented an interesting situation because the Clothworkers' Company had no wish to purchase it either and the artist was forbidden to sell it to anyone else. Three years later the Clothworkers' Company decided the best thing to do was to arrange to acquire the painting from the artist, then put it in store, which is where it resides today.

Peter's daughters are all freemen of the Clothworkers' Company and Juliet and Clare are liverymen. They were amongst the first 12 women to be admitted to full livery status and as such appear in a painting specially commissioned to commemorate the admission of women to the company. The painter, June Mendoza, was honoured for her artwork in the 2004 New Year's Honours List.

Caroline and Elizabeth also carry on their father's connections with the livery companies. Caroline is a freeman of the Worshipful Company of

76. 470th Master of the Clothworkers' Company 1989–90.

Gardeners and Elizabeth a liveryman of the Wax Chandlers. Belinda was recently admitted an honorary freeman of the World Traders' Company.

The Worshipful Company of Clothworkers is Peter's mother company, and with their permission he is a member of several other companies. In 1978 he was admitted to the Marketors' Company as an honorary liveryman and an honorary member of the Court only a year after its foundation. This is because he has spent his life in marketing. In addition he is a past master of the Guild of Freemen of the City of London.

Because world trading has been Peter's profession, he was granted permission to join the Guild of World Traders (which is now a livery company) in 1985. He had taken a personal interest in the formation of this company from the outset and during his mayoralty 'Trader' Gadsden was invited to unveil the foundation stone of International House (then part of the London World Trade Centre complex). In 1987–8 he served as the second Master of the Guild and was the sponsoring alderman necessary for the company to achieve full livery status in 2000. The World Traders became the first new livery company to be formed in the new millennium. When he was Lord Mayor, Peter presented the Letters Patent to the Actuaries' Company and was made an honorary freeman of the company.

In recognition of Peter's presence in the laying of another foundation stone, he was made an honorary liveryman of the Plaisterers' Company in 1975. As sheriff, he had accompanied the Lord Mayor, Sir Peter Studd, when the foundation stone of the new Plaisterers' Hall was laid. In 1999 Peter became an honorary liveryman of the Worshipful Company of Fruiterers.

Some people say that Peter's role in the formation of the Worshipful Company of Engineers is the jewel in his livery crown because this company has been one of the most successful of modern livery companies. Certainly the story of Peter's involvement in the company's founding makes for fascinating reading and gives an interesting insight into this man's talents and method of working.

As early as 1974 Peter had been keen to form a new livery company based around mining. He knew this would not only accord with the City's wish to forge closer links with the modern professions but also with the Court of Aldermen's desire to see some new livery companies formed. The Court had pointed to the fact that only seven new companies had been formed since 1900 despite the emergence of many new professions.

Developing his idea a stage further, Peter sounded out the Institution of Mining and Metallurgy of which he was a fellow. Whilst many expressed sympathy with the notion, in practice there were not enough interested members from one institution to create the required numbers. At the same time the word from the City was that they would prefer a company with a broader base. The suggestion was that perhaps engineering might be considered as its base.

Peter also canvassed engineers who were members of other livery companies including Trevor Crocker, Robert McWilliams, Gerald Mortimer, Robert Dunn and Ted West. With the support of the president of the Fellowship of Engineering, Sir Denis Rooke (who later became the Second Master of the Worshipful Company of Engineers), and the secretary, Michael Leonard (who became the first Clerk of the Company), Peter was invited to address their AGM in March 1983. This led to the fellowship passing a resolution 'supporting the formation of an unincorporated association to be called the Company of Engineers which will then petition the Lord Mayor and Court of Aldermen of the City of London for recognition as a Livery Company of the City of London'.

On 29 June 1983 the Company of Engineers was formed with six officers and Bunny Morgan (known to many as 'Mr Fixit' of the City) and Stanley Heather, recently retired City solicitor who was able to give the embryonic company valuable legal advice about setting up. Amongst the company's first officers was the Honorary Chaplain, Hugh Rom, priest-in-charge of St Katherine Cree, who unusually had an engineering background. The main objective of the company was defined as 'affording the means of professional and social intercourse and mutual information between its members, those who practice engineering and those who benefit therefrom, so as to promote the development and advancement of the science, art and practice of engineering in the City of London and elsewhere'.

Many people would have been satisfied to know that the Engineers had achieved so much and allow events to continue their leisurely progress through the various stages towards full livery company status. In the past this took 14 years: seven years after foundation the Engineers' Company could expect to approach the Court of Aldermen with the request they be permitted to become a company without livery. Seven years later they could apply to become a livery company.

Peter knew other companies were working towards petitioning the Court of Aldermen and he feared that if the Engineers did not move swiftly they would join a queue. There was also a possibility their request might be delayed if the Court of Aldermen chose to space out the number of new companies being formed. Peter was also aware that in a year's time new rules came into force that would necessitate the Engineers seeking Guild status prior to forming a company. This too would slow things down. So, guided by Stanley Heather, it was full speed ahead on the legal front.

Knowing how supportive Lord Mayor Sir Anthony Jolliffe was for the creation of an engineering livery company, Peter wanted him to be the person to present their Grant. There was an added personal dimension to this request because Sir Anthony had been the aldermanic sheriff during the final six weeks of Peter's mayoralty. Only too aware that the cogs in the City can grind at a stately pace at times, Peter decided to get things moving.

He made an appointment to see the Lord Mayor. Knowing the office from the inside, Peter was able to sympathise with him that no matter how hard he worked during his year, most of his achievements would be simply recorded for posterity as being executed by 'the Lord Mayor of London'. He agreed that it was true that the actual Lord Mayor's name is rarely cited. Then playing his ace, Peter mentioned the fact there are just two occasions when a Lord Mayor's name appears on a document. Those are when he grants Letters Patent and Freedom certificates. And moving quickly on, Peter told Alderman Sir Anthony Jolliffe how particularly honoured the Engineers would be if he were able to present their Grant of Livery.

Sir Anthony smiled and said that if he had not been a chartered accountant he would have been an engineer. However, as much as he would love to do this for Peter, there was absolutely no space in the mayoral diary. Undeterred, Peter gently suggested the diary might be sent for just to check whether there was the tiniest chink in which to slot the event. When the diary arrived it revealed a pencilled entry for a Ward luncheon on 1 November. Sir Anthony commented, 'I can lunch with the Ward any time', and proceeded to replace that entry with the words 'Engineers' Presentation of Letters Patent'.

Raymond Cousins, in the Junior Warden's lecture of 1999, takes up the story:

> Armed with this knowledge Sir Peter then went to see the City Chamberlain requesting that a Grant of Livery should be made within this mayoralty to which the Chamberlain answered, 'Quite impossible. The Lord Mayor has not got a free date in his diary before the end of his mayoralty and in any case we could not complete the formalities in that time.'

'Well,' says Sir Peter, 'I understand that the Lord Mayor does particularly wish to present this Grant and I wonder if you would mind checking his diary for November 1' The City Chamberlain immediately rang the Diary Secretary at the Mansion House and was most surprised to be told that the Lord Mayor was due to present a Grant of Livery to the Engineers' Company on that day. 'My goodness,' he said, 'I suppose we will have to get on with it then!'

In fact everyone concerned had to 'get on with it' and at a cracking pace. No one had heard of a livery company being formed so quickly before and, with subsequent changes in the rules, this record is unlikely to be broken.

On 5 July 1983 a petition to the Rt Hon The Lord Mayor and Court of Aldermen of the City of London was submitted for the granting of Letters Patent for the creation of a Livery Company of the City of London. Seven days later the Grant of Livery for the 94th Livery Company was approved. At the same time as events moved forward on the legal front, practical steps were being taken to ensure everything would be in place for the presentation of Letters Patent to the Founder Master of the Worshipful Company of Engineers. One thing everyone is convinced of is that this could never have taken place so quickly without Peter's help. 'He knew his way round the City,' one founder member put it succinctly, 'and he drove the company in the early days.'

A coat of arms was needed. Again it was Peter's intervention that ensured Sir Colin Cole, the Garter King of Arms, accepted an invitation to dine with the Engineers one evening. After some discussion and a few sketches on the back of envelopes, the Worshipful Company of Engineers' coat of arms began to take shape. The representation of the Iron Bridge as the base of their coat of arms was without doubt Peter's inspiration. This famous Shropshire bridge, the first in the world to be constructed from cast iron, has become recognised as a symbol of the Industrial Revolution. Its presence in the Engineers' coat of arms also signified strength and endurance. In the centre of the coat of arms is a shield which rests on the Iron Bridge and within the shield stands Tower Bridge, indicating the close ties between engineering and the City of London. The two supporters are seen wearing the Lord Mayor's badge of office recognising that the Founder Master was a past Lord Mayor of London. The archivist of the Worshipful Company of Clothworkers, David Wickham, suggested the motto 'Certare Ingeno' ('To use one's skills to the best of one's abilities') which comes from book two of Lucretius' *De Rerum Natura*.

It was not just a coat of arms that was needed. There were the gowns, ordinances of the company, badges for the officers, and an illuminated Grant of Livery all needed by the 1st November if events were to go ahead. Design was only the half of it. Everything had to be made to the highest standard in time. Peter knew that the Engineers would benefit from royal support so Prince Philip was invited to become the first honorary liveryman and graciously accepted.

Demonstrating yet again his skill at making connections, Peter foresaw the mutual benefits of links with the Royal Engineers. The livery company wanted to have a close association with one of Her Majesty's services and the Royal Engineers wanted a presence in the City. A perfect match. It was arranged that the Chief Royal Engineer (an honorary position which The Queen confers on a retired General) would also become an honorary liveryman whilst he held the position. In return the Master of the Worshipful Company of Engineers would become an *ex officio* member of the Royal Engineers. As a useful by-product of their association, the livery company has been able to call on the services of the regimental band for one event every year.

In the summer of 1986, the Institution of Royal Engineers invited Peter to become an honorary member because, 'The Corps has been particularly appreciative of the way in which the relationship between the Worshipful Company of Engineers and the Corps was so firmly established during your tenure as Master; a relationship which continues to flourish, I may say. In recognition of this and your contribution to the profession as a whole we hope you will be able to accept this invitation.' Peter was appreciative of the honour conferred on him.

As Raymond Cousins noted, 'All this had been completed in just over four months which was quite unique in this century and probably at any time in the history of the City. It is also believed to be unique that the sponsoring alderman for the company was the Founder Master.' He of course was Alderman Sir Peter Gadsden.

Those were not the only firsts for this new livery company. Not long after its formation the company was aware that it required a ceremonial mace so professional institutions were approached for donations. Sir Ronald Ellis, former head of Defence Sales and a director of Wilkinson Sword, put forward the novel suggestion (possibly recalling the wonderful sword that they had made for Lord Mayor Sir Peter Gadsden a few years before). He asked if the Worshipful Company of Engineers would like to have a ceremonial sword instead of a mace, in which case Wilkinson Sword would be pleased to present them with it.

The beautiful sword, with a scabbard bearing motifs of a rocket, an oilrig, Concorde, a spade and rule, a gear and pinion and Tower Bridge was presented to the company at a dinner in the Tower of London in 1984. The first time it was carried in procession was in October that year when the Lord Mayor, Lady Donaldson, consented to it being carried in front of her at a banquet in the Mansion House. Some people were surprised that the Lord Mayor should agree to a sword being paraded in the Lord Mayor's own house. Indeed some subsequent Lord Mayors did not accept that the Engineers' sword constituted their mace and permission to carry the sword was withdrawn for a while. However, Lord Mayor Sir Francis McWilliams, an engineer and member of the Worshipful Company of Engineers thought differently. His mayoralty coincided with the 10th anniversary of the foundation of this livery company and he was happy

77. Presentation of the Letters Patent to the Founder Master of the Worshipful Company of Engineers (Alderman Sir Peter Gadsden) by the Lord Mayor, Sir Anthony Jolliffe.

to grant permission for the company to carry the sword in front of the Lord Mayor in perpetuity.

The Worshipful Company of Engineers have other links with Peter's beloved county of Shropshire that go beyond the depiction of the Iron Bridge in their coat of arms. When the new company required regalia, presentation silver and items for their own collection, Peter turned to Alan Henn in Much Wenlock. Alan had several silver workshops and craftsmen able to execute designs he developed. The results were beautiful and unusual because Alan was convinced this new livery company required contemporary silver, not copies of old designs. All of this seemed a far cry from the days when Alan and Peter knew each other as schoolboys and Peter bought his first motorbike from Alan.

78.   The Worshipful Company of Engineers have close links with Ironbridge and with the museums in the Gorge. As Founder Master, Peter unveiled a plaque on the world-famous bridge to commemorate the links. Also in the picture is Lady Labouchere, a descendant of Abraham Darby III, the bridge builder.

Another piece of silver which was given to the Worshipful Company of Engineers also had a Shropshire origin. Lady Labouchere, a direct descendant of Abraham Darby III who built the world's first cast iron bridge, presented the company with a piece of antique silver. A silver tankard inscribed with the initials of Abraham Darby III and hallmarked 1771 (believed to have been a 21st birthday present) was presented to the company at a luncheon during their first official visit to the Ironbridge Gorge Museum Trust in 1984.

Links between the Worshipful Company of Engineers and the Ironbridge Gorge Museum Trust have been of benefit to both parties. The liverymen have paid regular visits to the museum and have been delighted to play their part in assisting the museum. On their side the museum has valued contacts with the City of London which have brought them much needed City money and support.

A silver replica of the Iron Bridge was designed by Alan Henn from engravings and made in his workshop. It was a special present to Sir Francis McWilliams, the first of the Engineers' liverymen since its formation to become Lord Mayor in 1992. Only five silver replicas of the bridge were ever made. One is owned by the Engineers' Company, one was presented to the museum by the trustees of the Development Trust, and one was given to Sir Peter Gadsden.

In 2004 the Engineers' Company was granted a Royal Charter of Incorporation which was presented by the Duke of Kent at a ceremony held in the Merchant Taylors' Hall. The Duke of Kent also presented Peter with a certificate in recognition of his outstanding services to the Company as the founder master.

Peter has always taken a particular interest in Bermuda because it was Belinda's birthplace. He and Belinda had hoped to be able to visit the island during his mayoralty but that was not to be. However, the idea for a visit was born at the 1985 Lord Mayor's Show. On that occasion Peter met the Governor, Viscount Dunrossil, and the Premier, the Honourable John Swan. Following this meeting the Premier of Bermuda invited Peter to visit the island in his role as chairman of the Royal Commonwealth Society and to give a lecture. Peter was pleased to accept and at the end of May 1986 he and Belinda spent a most enjoyable week staying at Government House as guests of the Governor and Lady Dunrossil.

In fact Peter gave several lectures during his visit including one to the Bermuda Chamber of Commerce and another to the Hamilton Rotary Club

79. The Bermuda Society owes its existence to Peter. He has visited the island where Belinda was born several times and is seen talking to the curator outside the Maritime Museum after giving a lecture in May 1987.

about 'The City of London'. Arising from his conversations with various people, Peter became convinced that Bermuda would benefit from more representation in the United Kingdom. He suggested the formation of a Britain-Bermuda Society in London to develop, amongst other things, friendship, good relations and mutual understanding between the peoples of Bermuda and the United Kingdom. Bermuda and the UK, he argued, would both profit from a closer liaison particularly in areas like finance, commerce and economics. As he explained, 'This British Dependent Territory [as it was then known—Bermuda is now a British Overseas Territory] is a first-class off-shore jurisdiction which is totally self-governing and can claim to be the third oldest democracy in the world.'

Peter formed the Britain-Bermuda Society with its first inaugural meeting held in Guildhall in November 1986. Sir Peter Gadsden was elected as the founder chairman and Sir David Gibbons as vice-chairman. Because Peter was extremely busy with his business, civic and charitable work, he was aware that he would not be able to devote as much time as was needed to the setting-up and running of the society so he approached Suzanne Stubbins, who had previously been his personal assistant and secretary prior to the birth of her daughter, to undertake the work.

A year after it began, the Britain-Bermuda Society became a private limited company and four years later changed its name to the Bermuda Society. Peter is a strong believer in the need for new blood in any organisation and, after three years as chairman, he stood down. Shortly before he retired from the chair, Peter enjoyed being an honoured guest at the ceremony to twin Lyme Regis with St George's, Bermuda. He and Belinda visited Bermuda with a party from Lyme Regis in 2004.

The Bermuda Society continues to flourish with membership open to people resident in the UK or Bermuda who have business or social links with the island. The society holds six lectures a year as well as an AGM and a luncheon, usually held in Guildhall, but the undoubted highlight of its year is the annual dinner in London. The Bermuda Society's aims of fostering closer links between the UK and Britain, promoting Bermuda as a good place to do business as well as giving Bermuda a face in the City, have been largely realised. Their success owes much to Peter's vision and energy at the outset and his ability to put the right people in the right place in order to make things work.

To most onlookers, Peter's mayoral year had been an exceptionally busy one but the ones that followed during the 1980s and 1990s proved no different. As an alderman, in 1984 Peter was elected governor of The Honourable The Irish Society. This ancient society was originally constituted in 1610 by James I to associate the City of London with the colonization of Ulster by English and Scottish Protestants. Amusingly Peter's new post added to the forms of address he encountered on his travels. He said when he travelled to Ireland he was always referred to as 'Governor', when he went to Shropshire they called him 'Colonel' and in the City he was addressed as 'Alderman'.

Naturally as a rector's son, Peter had a special interest in the City's annual dinner for the sons of clergy. He attended the first dinner when he was Lord Mayor but has been in *locum tenens* on several occasions when a Lord Mayor has been unable to attend. Peter served as a governor of the Corporation of the Sons of the Clergy (a charity which helps the dependants of the clergy) and he was a member of the Court of Assistants from 1978–83.

In 1987 Peter received honorary membership of the London Metal Exchange when it took over the running of the exchange and its rooms from the Metal Market and Exchange Company Limited. Amongst the other posts he has held, Peter has been a member of the Publicity Club from 1983 until 2001 and throughout that time has served as the club's president. This was a natural interest for a person who has been much occupied with marketing. Alderman Sir Roger Cork took over from Peter as president in 2001 but died suddenly in 2002. The club asked Peter to return and resume the position of president until a new appointment was made.

Chapter 17

Australia

Australians all let us rejoice
For we are young and free
We've golden soil and wealth for toil
Our home is girt by sea.
Our land abounds in nature's gifts
Of beauty rich and rare
In history's page let every stage
Advance Australia Fair.

(The Australian National Anthem, 'Advance Australia Fair')

Peter has a long, much cherished friendship with Australia. 'I feel just as at home in Australia as I do walking down the street in London,' he told one Australian newspaper. 'I am in my element. It's my environment, I have never felt out of place in Australia.' Even today Peter says, 'It's a wonderful country. I love it and would like to live there only I'm too old now!' At one point in his business career when he was spending such a large amount of time down under, Peter discussed with his family the possibility of them all moving out to Australia, but this came at a time when his civic life was taking off so the family decided to remain in England.

One of Peter's ancestors, who might well have had aspirations to become a Clothworker because he was a London silk dyer, went to Australia in 1833. Like Peter, he too had seen the inside of the Old Bailey but unlike Peter, Richard Gadsden arrived in Sydney aboard a convict ship after being sentenced to transportation for stealing a leg of lamb. Recent research has uncovered Drurys who were transported to Australia as well as Gadsdens. Matthew Drury was transported for stealing a shirt from a drowned man, George Drury for taking £42 from a Gainsborough farmer and Elizabeth Drury for obtaining goods by false pretences. However there is no evidence that these Drurys were ancestors of Peter's mother May Drury.

Richard Gadsden was followed down under in 1879 by 20-year-old Jabez Gadsden, a bootmaker from Britain who travelled to Melbourne of his own free will seeking work. He began by stitching calico and hessian bags which he sold to farmers and grocers for the bulk transport of goods like flour, salt and meat. The business, which had begun as a partnership, thrived when Jabez took over as sole proprietor. He was a most astute businessman who could turn all manner of situations to his advantage. Although many firms went to the wall during the First World War, Jabez Gadsden's enterprise boomed. His calico bag production was adapted for transporting oats for horses used in the war, then as the war ended, he swopped to the production of flags to be waved during victory parades. The man's entrepreneurial skills were truly amazing. The calico business moved on to make stockinet to wrap meat in Queensland. At the same time the firm's ability to print on calico was adapted to tinplate printing. This enabled them to print on toys such as drums, buckets and money-boxes.

When Peter's father arrived in Melbourne, unknown to him his distant relative Jabez was experimenting with the production of tin cans that would hold various goods, ranging from tobacco and shoe polish to custard powder. Once again Jabez Gadsden's keen eye and brain identified another emerging market and the firm was soon making cans to hold car paint and oil for the new motor industry. And so it continued. Although Jabez died in 1936, his sons Stanley and Norman inherited their father's business acumen and developed the company further.

Their tinplate production led them to make crown seals for beer bottles in the 1930s, tinplate cans for Schweppes and Coca Cola in the 1960s and then easy-opening drinks cans in the 1970s. Also in the 1970s the firm became involved in the production of cartons for the dairy industry, branded as Pure-Pak packaging. By that time the firm's calico and hessian work had ceased but not before a successful sortie into the manufacture of Slumber King mattresses in the 1930s. The legacy of Jabez Gadsden is impressive.

Today the firm of J Gadsden Australia Limited continues to be one of the biggest names in packaging but no longer led by members of the Gadsden family. In 1986, after 107 years and three generations of Gadsdens, the majority shareholding in the company was acquired by SAB Investments Pty Ltd and Ronald and Bruce Gadsden retired from the board.

Peter was unaware of either his famous or his infamous ancestors when he first travelled down under in 1957. He arrived late in the evening at his hotel only to find the best the proprietor could do was to fix up somewhere for him to sleep in the lounge. The next day he received all sorts of messages which made no sense to him. Then Mr Norman Gadsden, the newly appointed chairman of J Gadsden Australia Ltd, appeared in the lounge, fresh from a night's sleep in a bed. On another occasion Peter checked in at Lennons Hotel, Brisbane, and was given a luxurious suite. Later in the morning he was telephoned at Murphyores and asked if he wouldn't mind moving out because he had been given the suite reserved for Mr Norman Gadsden. There were several more instances where there was confusion between Peter and the Australian Gadsdens, who would have been far happier if Peter had had a different surname.

Peter also got very peculiar looks from a Sydney hotel receptionist when he asked for the bill at the end of his stay on one occasion. According to her records Peter had only just checked in! Eventually the various muddles led to branches of the Gadsden family being reunited. What struck many observers at the time was the similarity in their looks. People seeing Norman's son, Lindsay Gadsden, and Peter and his brother David standing together said it was clear they must all be brothers or cousins.

Peter has always thought a love of Australia must be 'in his blood'. Thirteen years' ministry in the state of Victoria gave the Reverend Basil Gadsden a lifelong love for the country and Peter grew up with a knowledge of both the sights and sounds of Australia even before he had been there. This was because he had often watched the sets of lantern slides of Australia his father used when he gave lectures. Peter also recalls that his father, having spent many years in the bush, was able to imitate all the bird noises and he could entertain an audience for an evening with Australian bird songs. In fact Basil Gadsden was such a good mimic he even performed on the radio.

Quite unexpectedly, links with Australia were reinforced for Peter at Wrekin College. The Reverend Guy Pentreath, the headmaster who played such an influential role in Peter's schooldays, came to Wrekin from St Peter's College, Adelaide, where he had been principal. He too had a great fondness for the country and entertained the boys with stories of his time there and of his wartime exploits returning to England from Australia on a freighter. The story gained more credence with the boys when Pentreath was asked to give a talk on the wireless entitled 'The family on the freighter'.

Despite Peter's growing fascination with the country, he never got the opportunity to visit it until he was 27. Then, as an employee of Fergusson Wild, he undertook a long business trip to Canada, USA, Australia and the Far East which kept him from home for almost three months. Thereafter Peter generally travelled to Australia on business annually. His business connections kept growing, particularly when his principal employer became the Australian mining company New South Wales Mining/Murphyores and later Associated Minerals Consolidated, another Australian company for whom he was a consultant for 20 years.

During one of his early visits down under, Peter took the opportunity to visit Buchan and see the place where his father had been a minister. Returning to his car feeling very moved by the experience of standing in his father's church, Peter was confronted by the local constable. Apparently Peter's car was parked the wrong way. He very quickly discovered you must park your car in the direction that you are travelling. Peter apologised and began explaining about his father, but that did not impress the policeman who gave him a thorough ticking-off.

On another visit when Peter was in Queensland, he was asked if he would be going to the Melbourne Cup held on the first Tuesday in November. He hadn't planned to go but changed his mind when one of the girls in the offices said she had had a dream that a horse called Vanderhum had won the race. Peter laughed and flew to Melbourne to join Bruce Gadsden's party. At the racecourse he decided that for a bit of fun he would back Vanderhum. The odds were so very good he was sure he must be throwing his money away. However, shortly before the race began there was a torrential downpour. This apparently gave rise to conditions that favoured the New Zealand horse and the odds suddenly shortened. When Vanderhum romped home first, no one was more surprised than Peter.

It has not been unknown for Peter to have the odd flutter despite being brought up in a household where gambling was considered the devil's pastime. He put some money on a horse owned by an American 'Gadsden' on the tote at Goodwood then wandered off and forgot about it. It was only later by chance that he learned the horse he had backed had come in first. After much tipping-out of pockets, Peter vaguely recalled he had thrown the ticket away. A friend said, 'Don't worry. Write and explain you have lost it. You'll get your winnings.' This he did but never held out any hope. Months later, when he had completely forgotten about the incident, a nice little cheque came through the post because the ticket had not been claimed.

Peter has always prized his close links with Australia. 'Because I was interested in promoting friendship between our countries,' he said, 'I joined the Britain-Australian Society in London and the Cook Society, being a past chairman of both. Now I am a vice-president of the Britain-Australia Society and the Robert Menzies Memorial Trust.' Interest in the Robert Menzies Memorial Trust was perhaps natural because Sir Robert Menzies had been an honorary member of the Clothworkers' Company and Peter was present at the launch of the trust at Clothworkers' Hall in June 1979, which offers scholarships for postgraduate studies.

For Peter involvement with an organisation always means more than being a name on a mailing list. He frequently serves on the committee and often takes his turn as chairman or vice-president.

So strong is Peter's affinity with Australia he says that 'when it came to designing supporters for my coat of arms, it was decided to have a koala bear as one of them, and he holds a geological hammer because of my interest in mining'. That was not received quite as well in all quarters as Peter thought it might be. When he met the Lord Mayor of Perth during the Lord Mayor of London's state visit to the province in 1980, Peter was told: 'I'm delighted you have a koala holding a pick on your coat of arms. It shows your Australian connections. But I'd rather you had a crayfish or something because a koala is not indigenous to Western Australia.' You can't please everyone!

It was natural that Australia should feature prominently on Peter's itinerary for the mayoral tour in August 1980. The tour was judged a great success not only because it reinforced many personal friendships but also because it was five years since a Lord Mayor of London had set foot in Australia.

The visit started in Perth where the civic party was met by the Lord Mayor and Lady Mayoress of Perth and many dinners, luncheons and receptions followed. At one Melbourne dinner, the host checked with Belinda whether Peter liked a cigar after his dinner. 'Yes,' she assured him. 'He does enjoy a cigar after a *good* dinner.' After the meal, which came at the end of a long day's travelling, Peter was feeling a little jaded so when his host offered a cigar, he politely declined. The host took his refusal as an expression of good manners and so offered again. After Peter declined a second time, his host demanded to know what was wrong with the dinner!

80. Peter as Lord Mayor makes friends with some locals during a visit to Buchan, Victoria, where his father was curate (see page 6).

Peter has many treasured memories of this trip and those linked to his past are particularly cherished. It was his special request to pay a return visit to St Mary's, Buchan, where his father had served as curate between 1918 and 1920. This was accomplished with a small civic party, comprising the Lord Mayor and the Lady Mayoress accompanied by the Common Cryer and Serjeant-at-Arms. (It was on the trip to Buchan that the Australian minister, Peter Nixon, rescued a child from drowning.)

Reading the lesson at morning service in the very church where his father had ministered 60 years earlier was a very moving experience for Peter. At the conclusion of the service Peter planted a tree to commemorate his visit. (Eight years later, during the Britain-Australia bicentennial celebrations, Peter went back to add a plaque below the tree to commemorate his father.) After the tree planting in 1980, a barbeque luncheon followed and the Lord Mayor was amazed and delighted to meet some people who actually remembered his father's ministry in Buchan 60 years earlier.

Peter's dealings with Australia increased further when the mayoral year was over. Business travel continued to take him down under and he maintained an active involvement in the Anglo-Australian societies in London. Early in 1984 when the Foreign and Commonwealth Office received an invitation from the Australian Government to participate in their bicentennial celebrations scheduled for 1988, Peter was the obvious choice to plan and co-ordinate Britain's participation.

In March 1984 he was approached by the parliamentary Under-Secretary of State about his willingness to be chairman of the Britain-Australia Bicentennial Committee (BABC). Although this was clearly going to be a very taxing five-year job involving fund-raising as well as planning and co-ordinating events, Peter had no hesitation in accepting it. He loves a challenge.

The Queen graciously agreed to be patron-in-chief of the BABC and the Duke of Kent president. Peter appointed Ann Beeching secretary and Maureen Betts secretary of fund-raising. Around 30 vice-presidents were appointed from the great and the good and Peter formed an active committee of about 30 people. There were frequent meetings of the committee and these were held in Guildhall whilst the BABC office was established at the Royal Commonwealth Society in Northumberland Avenue.

Writing some years later, Peter explained:

In 1984 the Britain-Australia Bicentennial Committee was formed to encourage and co-ordinate a programme of events and projects to celebrate the 1788–1988 bicentenary of the first European settlement in Australia and to strengthen the close links between the United Kingdom and Australia.

The Committee established the Britain-Australia Bicentennial Trust, a company limited by guarantee and a registered charity. The Committee was involved in a programme of over 200 events in the United Kingdom and Australia and, in addition to the £1 million made available by the British Government as their contribution towards the celebrations, has raised almost £2 million in donations, sponsorship and gifts in kind.

Events included Britain's gift of the sail training ship *Young Endeavour*, the Bicentenary Banquet in Guildhall City of London, the Bicentennial Ball in London, the British Museum (Natural History) exhibition 'First impressions: the British discovery of Australia', the Bicentennial Service in Westminster Abbey and a Gala Concert at the Theatre Royal, Drury Lane.

The bicentennial celebrations increased awareness and understanding of Australia's rich and varied heritage and provided an opportunity for Australians not only to appreciate their past, but also to meet the challenge of the future.

Peter achieved this by gathering a strong and dedicated team together who would focus on developing and reinforcing links between Britain and

Australia rather than simply looking backwards at history. 'The themes for the celebrations are Living Together and Celebration of a Nation,' he wrote in the foreword to the programme.

The Bicentennial Committee also set out to assist groups from Australia who wanted to visit Britain. Amongst these were the Pembroke Girls' Choir who arrived from South Australia to sing Evensong at some of Britain's great cathedrals like Winchester and Canterbury, and at Westminster Abbey. Musicians, sports teams and artists also came to perform. But the Australian High Commissioner remembers with delight one particular team who came to Britain in the bicentennial year. 'Thanks to the enormous co-operation we received from the then Secretary of the MCC, Colonel John Stephenson, we had the privilege and enjoyment of watching an Australian aboriginal cricket team play one of their matches on the hallowed turf of Lord's. Bob Hawke thought that was simply marvellous,' Doug McClelland recalls.

From the outset Peter wanted young people to play a significant role in the celebrations. This linked in well with those Anglo-Australian societies in London he knew at first-hand. A Schools Linking Scheme was set up along with an educational trust so young people from all over the UK could get involved.

Peter threw himself into the planning with energy and vision. Not only did he initiate schemes in Britain but he also travelled to Australia regularly to liaise with interested parties there and to publicise the UK's plans for the celebrations. During one visit he was shown round the kitchens of the Mount Isa Mines in Queensland. Keen to show an interest and make conversation, Peter asked the chap chopping up fruit if he was enjoying himself. 'Yeh,' came the reply. 'It's for the big barbie tonight. Making a fruit salad's good. Cleans under yer nails!'

Whilst he was there, Peter was interviewed for the Australian Broadcasting Corporation by Anthony Howes. In a conversation following the interview, Anthony remembers Peter saying, 'I feel there should be more high-profile events in the UK featuring the talents of young Australians, especially in the Arts and, to date, there is very little being suggested to me.'

A seed was sown in Anthony Howes' mind. It came to fruition in the Midnite Youth Theatre Company, 65 of Perth's most talented young performers, who included a 23-piece orchestra. Peter took great personal interest in the enterprise from its inception, even making a special return trip to Perth to be present at the theatre company's founding. This was

81. The Australian Prime Minister, Bob Hawke, receives a copy of the Britain-Australia bicentennial list of events from Peter, the chairman of the Britain-Australia Bicentennial Committee.

more than a token interest and the theatre company were enormously grateful to Peter for setting in motion the official wheels in Australia and in Britain that enabled them to tour the UK. They did this most successfully in January 1988 with their performance of *Midnite*, a classic Australian children's story. For the artists the highlight of the tour was a Command Performance in the presence of HRH Prince Edward in London. Anthony Howes believes that the Midnite Theatre Company is 'a lasting tribute to the generosity of spirit and breadth of vision of this very extraordinary man'. Peter is vice-patron of the Midnite Youth Theatre Company and in 1997 received the Christ Church Midnite Award.

Peter's phenomenal energy meant that at the same time as he was assisting the Midnite Theatre Company he was pursuing numerous other contacts. As soon as the new Australian High Commissioner to the United Kingdom was appointed in August 1986, Peter wasted no time in phoning him at home in Sydney to introduce himself and let His Excellency know what stage the planning had reached. Douglas McClelland remembers that first phone call:

> I immediately knew that the British government had appointed the right person for the job. One could hear the enthusiasm in his voice, a sort of anxious plea for early action, the type of nervous feeling a footballer has as he awaits the sound of the referee's whistle to get the game under way. He told me how the members of his committee were spending hour after hour, night after night, in the development of plans for the celebrating of the bicentennial in every nook and cranny of Britain. They were determined to ensure its success and were keen for me to know in detail what they had planned. I recall I was so impressed that the next day, when I flew to Canberra to attend the parliamentary sitting, I told the Prime Minister of the phone call. He was very pleased indeed.

Doug McClelland offers a useful insight into the huge amount of work that BABC entailed and the fact that Belinda was also involved:

> Peter and Belinda had contacts far and wide throughout Britain and they opened many a door for us. They and their committee worked closely with the Britain-Australia Society, the Cook Society (of which Peter was most supportive) and the Australian Women in London group. Expatriate Australians, British citizens who had had relatives migrate to Australia, businessmen, academics and sporting people who had formed a close association with their counterparts in Australia flocked to join the bicentennial crusade. In next to no time we had countless thousands of people throughout the land activating themselves and joining our celebrations.

In order to make the bicentennial celebrations meaningful for everyone in Britain, Peter had the foresight to involve all parts of the United Kingdom. 'National and regional committees throughout Britain were established,' Doug McClelland remembers. 'Liaison officers were appointed to co-ordinate the various activities being undertaken in the various counties and special sub-committees for agriculture, arts, education, maritime activities and a host of others were set up. They all performed magnificently.'

The result was a wide range of events: a pro-celebrity cricket match took place in Edinburgh; the Australia Ballet performed at the London Royal Opera House; the Flint and Australian Male Voice Choirs sang together in concert in Flint; there was an exhibition of 'Yolngu, Aboriginal Cultures in Australia' in Brighton, and a microlite flew from London to Darwin to mention only a fraction of the 200 'official' events. Such was the interest generated that small groups grasped the opportunity to foster links with the other country, like the UK bell-ringers who toured Australia.

Thanks to excellent organisation behind the scenes, everyone's hard work came together at the right time and the British celebrations of the bicentenary were officially launched on 13 May 1987 with a spectacular water pageant in Portsmouth, the Solent and the Isle of Wight. An enormous amount of planning had gone into the re-enactment of the sailing of the First Fleet to Botany Bay on the same day in 1787. Full-sized replica boats were sent on their 21,000 km voyage by The Queen, who fired a starting gun. At the end of this glorious pageant, a letter came from Buckingham Palace thanking Sir Peter for his role in the planning and noting that 'the day was a most imaginative combination of events'.

Doug McClelland recalled the gruelling schedule of public appearances he and his wife put in alongside Peter and Belinda. From the day the First Fleet re-enactment set out until December 1988,

> we spent probably two or three hours of each day, morning, noon or night attending an event of one kind or another to honour the first settlement of Australia by Captain Arthur Phillip and his first fleeters…With our spouses, Peter and I went to all parts of Britain, undertaking speaking engagements and attending functions that had been well planned by the local communities. We visited Bath, Belfast, Birmingham, Chester, Ipswich, Shropshire, Liverpool, Manchester, Newcastle, Portsmouth, Southampton—to name some of the places. You name the spot, we went there… For eighteen months this hectic life continued—day after day, night after night. But not for one moment did Peter or Belinda flinch. They never tired, they forever retained that enthusiasm that I discerned in Peter's voice when he first rang me in August 1986.

Peter was in the habit of travelling to Australia once every year but in the bicentennial year he flew out four times. On one of those visits Tony Harvey from the British Museum (Natural History), who also served on the BABC committee, accompanied him. Tony recalls one amusing 'close shave' they had. The group flew to Longreach to present a picture to the Stockmans' Hall of Fame. After the event they were to fly back that same evening in order to be present when The Queen opened Expo 88 the next morning. Before they began their three-and-a-half hour flight to Longreach, Peter had watched the picture being safely stowed aboard and said to Tony, 'Don't let me forget it.' Knowing what his memory was like Tony replied, 'Don't rely on me!'

Part way through the evening's reception, Peter leaned over to ask Tony where the picture had been put. To their horror both men realised the picture was still on the plane that was standing at the airport ready to take them back. At least it should have been. To compound the problem, for

82.   Peter with The Queen and Prince Phillip when they attended the launch of the First Fleet in the Solent in May 1987. Peter can be seen standing in the middle row on the steps with the Australian High Commissioner Douglas McClelland.

some unknown reason the pilot had returned to Brisbane after depositing his VIP passengers. Fortunately he arrived back at Longreach, with the picture, in time for Peter to make a presentation to his hosts at 1 o'clock in the morning at the airport.

Expo 88 was hailed as a great success with 13 million people attending. Peter accompanied the Prime Minister, Margaret Thatcher, around the British Pavilion where she inaugurated the special British day celebrations in the exhibition's amphitheatre on 5 August. In the evening the party attended a Last Night of the Proms concert complete with 'Rule Britannia' and 'Jerusalem'. There were many notable visitors to the British exhibit including The Queen, the Prince and Princess of Nepal, the Prime Minister of Fiji, a Maori Queen and government ministers from many countries. The popularity of the British Pavilion was such that only those of the Australasian states and Japan attracted more visitors.

83. At the Guildhall Banquet for the Britain-Australia bicentennial celebrations, Lord Shackleton sat on Peter's right and the Prime Minister, Mrs Thatcher, on his left.

For Peter one of the highlights of the Britain-Australia bicentennial celebrations was the presentation of the UK's birthday present to Australia.
When he had first been appointed as chairman of the committee 'a Government gift' to Australia was mentioned but nothing had been decided and
there was uncertainty about how it would be funded. Whilst an official
piece of silver could have been given and would undoubtedly have been
well received, Peter thought something relevant to young people was
more appropriate. Under the guidance of his chairman of the Schooner
Committee, Arthur Weller, Britain's birthday present became the *Young
Endeavour*, a specially designed sail training ship built at Lowestoft. The
finished boat sailed to Australia with a carefully chosen crew of young
people from both nations. To symbolise the joint venture the ship was
crewed by a British Master, an Australian First Officer, four watch officers
and 24 young men and women chosen from both countries.

Under Peter's chairmanship the Britain-Australia Bicentennial Committee raised the necessary money: £1 million came from the private sector
and an equal amount from the government and from the Schooner Trust,
set up by the committee to ensure the long-term future of this venture.

The success of the Britain-Australia bicentennial celebrations took everyone by surprise; it exceeded people's expectations. So delighted was the
Australian government by the British involvement that Sir Peter Gadsden
received the award of Companion, Order of Australia (AC). The award
was made in recognition of his services to Australian-British relations,
with special reference to his role as chairman of the BABC.

Peter's interest and affection for Australia continues unabated. The
numerous personal friends he and Belinda have made over the years are
visited when they holiday down under and many have enjoyed Gadsden
hospitality on visits to the UK.

Peter's membership of the Cook Society has given an official dimension
to his connections with Australia. The society was founded in 1969 by
Sir Alec Douglas-Home and Sir Robert Menzies and aims to 'promote
Anglo-Australian relations at a high level'. It has counterparts in all
Australian States with which it is in constant touch. Membership of the
Cook Society in the UK is limited to a hundred and 'the membership
represents a wide range of national interests including senior business
men and women, politicians, civil servants, academics and those from
the professions. Every year the society holds a series of informal private
luncheons at which a nucleus of British members entertain visiting

84. To honour Peter's successful leadership of the Britain-Australia Bicentennial Committee, he received the award of Companion, Order of Australia. The Governor-General, the Right Honourable Sir Ninian Stephen, invested Peter with the insignia on 6 January 1988. Lady Stephen is seen in the centre of the picture.

AUSTRALIAN HIGH COMMISSION

AUSTRALIA HOUSE
STRAND
LONDON WC2B 4LA
01 438 8220

THE HIGH COMMISSIONER

December 14, 1988

Dear Peter,

Now that the Australian Bicentennial celebrations in the
United Kingdom are coming to an end, I am dropping you these
few short lines to thank you and Belinda for going to such
efforts to ensure the success of the Bicentenary in all
parts of your country.

The Britain-Australia Bicentennial Committee could not have
had a more devoted or dedicated person as Chairman. Both
you and Belinda have been magnificent and my country, Australia,
is indebted to you.

For our part, Lorna and I are delighted that we have had
the opportunity to represent Australia in Great Britain
in 1988. It has given us a marvellous opportunity to meet
many people and make new friends, and top of that list are
you and Belinda.

We thank you, not only for your friendship, but for your
devotion to the task of improving the bonds of friendship
between our two countries.

You are now entitled to a well-deserved rest.

Warmest personal regards,

Yours sincerely,

(Douglas McClelland)

Sir Peter Gadsden, GBE, AC
Chairman
The Britain-Australia Bicentennial Committee
606 Gilbert House
Barbican
LONDON   EC2Y 8BD

85. Letter of thanks from Douglas McClelland, the Australian High Commissioner.

members from Australia and other invited guests. Points of interest to both countries are freely discussed.' The chairman holds office for one year only and Peter took the chair in 1999. Every 18 months a party of British 'Cooks' visit Australia followed 18 months later by a visit of the Australian 'Cooks' to the UK.

The close ties Peter fostered between Australia and Britain continue to the present day, as does another link he started. The annual service and address at St Mary-Le-Bow Church, Cheapside, to commemorate the memory of Admiral Arthur Phillip was instigated by Peter. The first service took place on 23 January 1992 when a memorial bust to the founder of Australia was unveiled and dedicated by the Bishop of London. On that occasion an address about the life and times of Admiral Phillip was given by a Mrs Maurine Goldston-Morris OAM, president of the Arthur Phillip Society. This tradition has continued and an annual service is held around Australia Day. The first 11 addresses have now been published. It is usually attended by the Lord Mayor, aldermen for the Wards of Cordwainer and Bread Street, a sheriff of the City of London, the Australian High Commissioner and the Agents General of the States of Australia. The congregation comprises members of the Cook Society in the UK, the Order of Australia, the Britain-Australia Society and the Australian and New Zealand Chamber of Commerce. Following the service there is a luncheon at Grocers' Hall. This popular annual City event was the brainchild of Peter Gadsden.

The Australian High Commissioner summed up Australia's debt to Peter, and to Belinda, when he said: 'Peter and his wife Belinda never stopped working to ensure the bicentennial's success in Britain, and Australia is eternally grateful to them. They are wonderful people. I can't emphasise how fortunate Australia was to have them at the helm.'

Chapter 18

A Shropshire Lad

Then here's to all friends round the Wrekin!
Let honour be paid to the toast;
There's no other shire
Could ever inspire
A sentiment prouder than Shropshire can boast,
Then here's to all friends round the Wrekin.

(Traditional Shropshire toast)

Peter has always relished his long association with the county of Shropshire although he concedes 'I cannot claim to be a Shropshire-born lad, but perhaps I can say I am a Shropshire-bred one since most of my childhood was spent in the county.' Even when they were living at the Barbican, the family often spent weekends with various friends in the county and loved it. As one of Peter's daughters put it, 'His heart is in Shropshire. He is himself there.'

It comes as no surprise to learn that for much of his 40 years in the City, Peter was a member of the Shropshire Society in London. The fact that he took out a life-membership of the society at the outset shows that deep down this much-travelled man knew where his roots were.

The Shropshire Society in London was one of dozens of county societies set up in Victorian times; indeed this particular county society may go back further because references have been found to them meeting as early as 1750. Today very few such county societies remain but the proud Salopians keep going. When their society was formalised at the end of the nineteenth century they pledged,

to foster patriotism, to spread sociability and cheerfulness, to renew old associations, to preserve records of interesting and historical events, to enable its members to make new friends with the Salopian spirit, feelings and memories,

257

and to provide a timely and enjoyable rendezvous for young people from the County who feel lonely in London. Also to give any Salopian who hits a bad time a helping hand financially by assistance from the Benevolent Fund, all prompted by love for the dear old County of Shropshire.

Members of this society were so proud when for the first time one of their number became Lord Mayor of London. Peter was more than delighted to invite the Shropshire Society to a reception at the Mansion House in the February of his mayoralty. The year after he proved an extremely popular speaker at their AGM because he offered a behind-the-scenes account of his year in office.

In 1986 Peter was invited to become president of the Shropshire Society in London, which he accepted graciously. Michael Jenks remembers what an extremely good president he was on account of his amazing connections. 'He was also a reliable supporter, who never talked down to anyone. During his presidency committee meetings took place at Guildhall which was a great privilege for the members.'

Naturally the Shropshire Society in London's annual reunion takes place in the home county and is held at the time of the annual Shrewsbury Flower Show. In 1992 this all came together beautifully because Peter served as president of the Shropshire Horticultural Society that year. It is a tradition that members of the Shropshire Society join the president and chairman of the Horticultural Society for tea at the annual Flower Show in Shrewsbury.

In his message to the people of Shrewsbury and further afield in 1992, Peter as the president wrote in the programme:

Earth puts on her dress of glee,
Flowers and grasses hide her;
We go forth in charity
Brothers all, beside her.

(15th century carol)

It is appropriate that I should be writing this message during the Roman celebration of 'Floralia' or the Festival of Flora, the goddess of flowers. Flowers remind us of the importance of preserving the environment and the need to maintain the quality of life.

Shropshire is one of the most beautiful counties in England and Shrewsbury the 'Town of Flowers'. So it is right that the Shrewsbury Flower Show should be acclaimed throughout the county and country.

86.   Peter has been a regular visitor to the annual Shrewsbury Flower Show and served as president in 1992.

We owe a debt of gratitude to *everyone* who has been involved with this Flower Show—committee members and other volunteer helpers, permanent staff, gardeners and exhibitors. We thank them for their hard work and dedication. It is also important to acknowledge the great contribution made by the society each year through gifts and sponsorship.

Although not a Shropshire 'born' lad, I am proud to be a Shropshire 'bred' lad who spent his childhood at Astley Abbotts, Bridgnorth, and I am honoured and delighted to be President of the Shropshire Horticultural Society.

I wish the 1992 Show every success and I hope you enjoy your visit which is a time for colour, beauty, pageantry, good humour, relaxation, fellowship and fun.

Although today it seems so natural that Peter should have his principal residence in Shropshire, it was never a forgone conclusion that this City gentleman would make the county his home. In fact it was his mayoral visit to Shropshire in 1980 that really clinched things for Peter.

He was interested to learn that a feudal bond existed between the City of London and the county of Shropshire, but what surprised him most was that the connection had been virtually on the Rectory's doorstep and he had been totally unaware of it.

Up the road from Astley Abbotts is the tiny village of Eardington just outside Bridgnorth. Dating from the reign of King John, and first recorded in documents from 1211 called the Shropshire Serjentries is a ceremony called the Quit Rent. The medieval document states the City of London is the tenant and occupier of a piece of wasteland, called 'The Moors, in the County of Salop'. In recognition of this, and another piece of land the Corporation of the City of London holds elsewhere in England, an annual Quit Rents ceremony is held in the Royal Courts of Justice when payment is made. The rents are token payments because long ago the services rendered by the original tenants were commuted by the Sovereign, so the tenants are now 'quit and free'.

In today's ceremony, the Queen's Remembrancer presides and the Comptroller and Solicitor from the City present a token payment in the form of a blunt billhook and a sharp hatchet. Peter explained this further when he lunched with Shropshire County Council and presented them with replicas of these items during his official visit in May 1980. 'The City Comptroller and Solicitor demonstrate the qualities of two "knives"—one very sharp and one very blunt—or, as the Hundred Roll of Shropshire said in 1254, "one must be capable of cutting a hazel rod and the other should bend in green cheese".'

The day after this civic luncheon, Peter visited Moor Ridding Farmhouse in Eardington which is built on the piece of wasteland called 'The Moors'. Rural Shropshire had never seen anything like it; no Lord Mayor had ever visited the county in recognition of the City's feudal links. Peter arrived in his full mayoral regalia accompanied by the Queen's Remembrancer, one of the sheriffs of London, the secondary and under-sheriff and the Serjeant-at-Arms. At the farmhouse Peter unveiled a commemorative plaque fixed to the wall on a piece of oak that had once formed part of the roof of Guildhall, to mark the land for which the City pays a Quit Rent.

When Peter was president of the Shropshire Society in London in 1986, he used his famed skill at making connections to arrange for society members to attend the ancient ceremony at the Law Courts in the Strand that year. Two of the knives offered in payment on that occasion were given to the Shropshire Society in London by the Queen's Remembrancer and the society arranged for them to go on permanent loan to Rowley's House Museum in Shrewsbury.

Following Peter's official visit to Shropshire he became convinced that this was really where he wanted to live and from then on he and Belinda began looking for a suitable house in the county. They decided to search for a property that could be more than a two-up two-down weekend cottage because they considered this might well become their principal residence once they left the Barbican.

Friends kept their eyes open and forwarded details of likely properties Peter and Belinda could inspect at weekends. The discovery of Cheriton Cottage, however, came unexpectedly when Peter was visiting the dentist in London. Amongst the magazines he flicked through in the waiting-room was a slightly out-of-date copy of *Country Life*. One advertisement featured a cottage at Middleton Scriven in Shropshire. Peter knew his friend Barry Jenkinson from Wrekin College had a Middleton Scriven phone number so he reasoned it must be close to where Barry and Joy lived and probably not far from where they had grown up. He phoned Barry and asked if he could investigate whether the cottage was still for sale and whether it might suit them. The answer came back, 'We are sure you will like the cottage but it needs a lot of money spending on it to bring it up to an acceptable standard.' How right they were! Peter and Belinda were delighted by Cheriton Cottage (as it was then called) as soon as they saw it. The location and views were breathtaking and it was clear the house and garden had great potential if given some loving restoration.

87.   Cheriton Cottage, Belinda and Peter's home in Shropshire.

What the garden required was construction more than restoration because it was a piece of field from Old Castle Farm that had been tacked on to the property. Leylandii were the only things growing and glass littered the ground from a greenhouse that had long since collapsed. Over the next six years the garden took shape and Peter relished the chance to grow his own vegetables. He found himself putting into practice all the things he had learned from his father in the Rectory garden only a few miles up the road. In much the same way as Peter's mother had lavished her attention on the flower garden, Belinda used her talent to create a beautiful cottage garden from part of the former field.

In 1999 Cheriton, as they decided the house would be called, became Peter and Belinda's main residence. The Barbican flat, which had been the family's home for 30 years, was sold.

Having a Shropshire base has enabled Peter to assist many county organisations. Being commissioned into the King's Shropshire Light Infantry as a National Service Officer in 1948 gave Peter an interest in military matters. This was reinforced when as an alderman of the City of London in 1971 he became an honorary member of the Court of the Honourable Artillery Company. During the mayoralty in May 1980, Peter was able to include Shrewsbury Castle, home of the Regimental Museum and headquarters of the KSLI (part of the Light Infantry) in his official visit to Shropshire.

In 1988 he was invited to become Honorary Colonel of the 5th (Shropshire and Herefordshire) Battalion The Light Infantry (Volunteers)—5LI. The battalion remembers his period as Honorary Colonel with affection and gratitude because, as Major Jeremy York recalls, Peter took 'a keen interest in the TA battalion's training, welfare and achievements, regularly visiting the battalion summer camps as far afield as Belgium, Inverness and Dorset'.

There are some chuckles over the time Peter visited the battalion in Germany as the Honorary Colonel. He was invited by the GOC General Sir Charles Guthrie (now Lord Guthrie). Peter said:

> I thought it would be appropriate to wear my best trousers to speak to the recruits, but I had never tried the trousers on beforehand. When I did, to my horror they were much too small. I couldn't get into them. Since I was staying with General Sir Charles Guthrie who was commanding the Northern Army Group, I reported the fact to the General's ADC. He said he would try and get a replacement pair. Unfortunately he couldn't get any. 'They have all been sent to the Gulf' was the official reason. So I had to wear the only pair I'd got, which were combat kit.

When I was collected in the staff car, I was reminded by the Adjutant that it was not combat kit. I was 'improperly dressed'. So I explained the situation. Then on arrival at the barracks I was reminded by the Commanding Officer this time that I was 'improperly dressed'. I again explained and I had to carry out my duties in combat trousers rather than the official 'trousers lightweight'. It was kindly suggested that I had started a new tradition.

Peter's five-year tenure (1988–93) as Honorary Colonel of the 5LI covered a period when some difficult debates over the future of the battalion were going on.

Major-General Anthony Makepeace-Warne in his history of the Light Infantry, *Exceedingly Lucky*, recounts what happened when the government launched its 'Options for Change' initative.

There was an almost audible gasp of astonishment across the Regiment: delight at the saving of the two northern battalions was coupled with disbelief at the proposal for the 5 LI which was unwelcome and, of all possible outcomes, the least expected. Indeed, the Regimental Council was caught flat-footed, having never even considered such a possibility at any of their meetings. Apart from being very damaging regimentally, the proposal would effectively eradicate the TA presence in Shropshire and Herefordshire, leaving only two battalions of infantry in the whole West Midlands area.

An immediate, and very vociferous, campaign to preserve the 5 LI was mounted with the Honorary Colonel, Sir Peter Gadsden, playing a crucially influential part.... There followed a veritable explosion of spontaneous activity at grass-roots level, with friends of the Regiment raising petitions in the towns and villages of Shropshire and Herefordshire, encouraged by a large advertisement by a well-wisher in the *Shropshire Star* newspaper telling those who wished to 'Keep 5 Alive' to lobby their MP and others of influence.

Sir Peter Gadsden wrote personally to a very large number of influential people and organisations, asking them to put their views to their MPs and without exception, the Lord Lieutenant, deputy Lord Lieutenants, mayors and chairmen of town and district councils expressed their support.

In December 1991 the Secretary of State announced the future structure of the TA. Every TA infantry battalion was to be reduced to three rifle companies. The Light Infantry would retain all four TA battalions but one of the three rifle companies in 5 LI would be found in The Worcestershire and Sherwood Foresters Regiment (29th/45th) ... Although this was not an ideal solution, it was infinitely better than any of the proposals which had emerged during the previous months. The Regiment owes a very considerable debt of gratitude to a great many individuals for their help and support throughout the 'options' process.

88. The Honorary Colonel of the 5th (Shropshire and Herefordshire) Battalion The Light Infantry (Volunteers).

89. Peter took an active interest in the life of the 5th (Shropshire and Herefordshire) Battalion The Light Infantry (Volunteers) when he was Honorary Colonel visiting them on exercise on several occasions as seen here during camp in 1992. Peter is seated sixth from the right on the front row.

Peter was certainly one of the key players and gained considerable satisfaction from his successful participation in the 'Save the 5LI' campaign.

Shortly before the end of his five-year tenure of office as Honorary Colonel, Peter found himself holding a slightly different title. This was because in November 1992 the 5LI and 4WFR (The 4th Battalion The Worcestershire and Sherwood Foresters Regiment) merged, so for the final six months, Peter was Joint Honorary Colonel with Colonel Thomas Dunne (Lord Lieutenant of Hereford and Worcestershire) who succeeded him in June 1993.

Peter's departure was marked by a presentation from the battalion at camp followed by a dining-out in the evening. As a mark of gratitude for Peter's enthusiastic support for the 5LI, he was granted the honorary rank of colonel. Peter showed his personal appreciation to the battalion by presenting them with a bugle to mark his tenure as Honorary Colonel.

Before Peter's honorary army role came to an end a new challenge presented itself. On 25 August 1992 the IRA bombed the Shropshire Regimental Museum at Shrewsbury Castle with a blast and two incendiaries. This caused a huge amount of damage and was a chilling reminder that the threat of terrorism is never far away. It was estimated that around £500,000 (including insurance received) would be needed to restore the museum's collections of the KSLI, the Shropshire Yeomanry and the Shropshire Royal Horse Artillery as well as materials relating to the county lieutenancy and to establish a capital sum to meet the costs of a curator. Peter immediately took on the role of chairman of the Museum Appeal. Major Jeremy York, the Regimental County Secretary, remembers everyone's delight when, under Peter's chairmanship, the necessary money was raised in seven years. 'Without his dynamic leadership, unbounded enthusiasm and invaluable contacts countrywide, the Appeal simply would not have achieved its ambitious targets. With the successful termination of the Museum Appeal Sir Peter immediately agreed to be chairman of the Shropshire Regimental Museum Friends' Committee. As a result, the Friends' scheme has got off to a flying start.'

Peter continues to be actively involved in the Regimental Museum both as a trustee and with Friends' activities. The Museum is extremely grateful, describing 'his loyalty, boundless enthusiasm and warmth of character as really second-to-none'.

Peter's links with another museum go back a long way. He thinks they probably date back to 1943 when he used to pass through Ironbridge on his way to school at Wrekin College. The great dark skeleton of the bridge that spanned the Gorge fascinated him. Later when he met Belinda, Peter wanted her to see Shropshire and borrowed his father's car in order to take her to see the amazing spectacle of the world's first cast iron bridge. In the 1950s the whole area around Ironbridge and Coalbrookdale was very run-down and Belinda recalls being distinctly unimpressed by the sight that Peter was so proud of. However, it wasn't long before she too came to understand the great significance of Ironbridge and indeed of the whole area.

Early in the 1970s they returned as a family so the girls could see the recently created museum at Coalbrookdale. Then it was a little hut with a few exhibits displayed in sand and some very enthusiastic supporters who had a vision of what the museum might one day be. Excavations were also beginning on Abraham Darby's furnace close by. Today this impressive exhibit is housed under a purpose-built cover; the little hut has long since gone, giving way to a large museum complex of 80 acres.

When Peter was Lord Mayor in 1980, he included a tour of the Iron-bridge Gorge Museum in his official visit to the county. On that occasion he managed to see three of the museum sites: the Museum of Iron at Coal-brookdale, the Coalport China Works Museum and the Blists Hill Open Air Museum. What he saw impressed him greatly. Equally impressed were those officials and guides who showed the mayoral party around the museum sites because they could see the Lord Mayor of London had a genuine interest in their work.

This led the museum to ask Peter if he would consider involving himself further in their work. The post that they hoped he might consider was that of president of the Ironbridge Gorge Museum Development Trust, the body responsible for raising capital to enable the museum to develop further. Peter graciously accepted the post and threw himself into the work wholeheartedly.

A City of London Ironbridge Committee was formed under the chairman-ship of Lord Layton with leading City figures like Stanley Heather, 'Bunny' Morgan, J Reid, A Shaw and RNM Ward as well as Peter. As Peter had iden-tified at the outset, the skills and trades which the Blists Hill Museum brings together and demonstrates to visitors are exactly those the City livery companies symbolise and protect. Peter could see the wonderful opportunity that existed for a partnership between the museum and the City which would be of mutual benefit.

He initiated an annual invitation to the masters, prime wardens and upper bailiff of the City livery companies, their clerks and spouses, to spend a weekend at the museum. On the first occasion about 25 attended this livery weekend. It was so popular that it is now part of the City diary with over 200 liverymen and their spouses attending. As happened on the first occasion, Peter and Belinda continue to escort their guests around the museum's many sites. It is an occasion they never miss.

Knowing the mining and engineering associations Ironbridge has, Peter also arranged for the Worshipful Company of Engineers to visit in 1984 and thus began a long and fruitful connection between the livery company and the museum. Peter has always been keen to promote the Ironbridge Gorge museums in the City of London and he also arranged for members of the Institute of Directors City of London branch to visit in 1994.

'A great facilitator and enabler' Peter has been called and he certainly enjoys making connections everybody profits from. One example of this occurred soon after he became president of the Ironbridge Gorge Museum Development Trust. He knew the museum had been offered a late nineteenth-century doctor's house complete with surgery. Here was wonderful opportunity for the museum to add another property to their Victorian town at Blists Hill. What was needed was the funding to dismantle and re-erect the building. Wearing his other hat as chairman of PPP (Private Patients' Plan), Peter could see that sponsorship of the Victorian doctor's surgery would be excellent publicity for the company and the members of the PPP Board were in full agreement.

In September 1985 Peter attended the laying of the foundation stone and the burial of a time capsule. In October the following year he arrived for the official opening of a fully fitted Victorian doctor's surgery. The event drew plenty of media attention because the actor Peter Davison, who had appeared as the vet in *All Creatures Great and Small*, then as a doctor in *A Very Peculiar Practice* and as Dr Who, was invited. Peter Davison arrived suitably attired as a Victorian doctor. Local schoolchildren, dressed in period costume, eagerly queued up to be 'seen' by the doctor. Peter Gadsden entered into the fun by appearing at the surgery door suitably swathed in bandages alongside 'Doctor' Davison. The Ironbridge Gorge Museum were delighted by the success of the doctor's surgery, describing it as 'an exhibit of outstanding interest and excellence'. Evidently others agreed because 9,000 visitors arrived the first weekend it opened. The following year the Prince of Wales paid a visit to the museum and was escorted by Peter, who took great pride in showing him the completed doctor's surgery.

Amongst the many organisations Peter has supported in Shropshire has been the Upper Severn Navigation Trust. Although not specifically a part of the Ironbridge Gorge Museum Trust, the Upper Severn Navigation Trust does have close links. It was formed in 1978 to acquire a Severn trow (the name given to a particular kind of barge which travelled the River Severn between Ironbridge and Bristol carrying cargoes like coal and china) and to restore it to working order. In 1992 Peter first lent his support to this worthy project and some years later was delighted to see the fully restored *Spry*.

So many Shropshire organisations have profited from Peter's support that there is not enough space to mention them all. The League of Friends at the Robert Jones and Agnes Hunt Orthopaedic Hospital benefited from the visit of the Lord Mayor in 1980. On that occasion he presented them

90.   A time capsule was buried beneath the Victorian doctor's surgery at Blists Hill on 22 September 1985. As chairman of PPP (Private Patients' Plan) and President of the Development Trust of the museum Peter was able to successfully bring the two together.

with a cheque from a trust fund administered by the Court of Aldermen. Appropriately enough this had been set up by a former Lord Mayor of London, Sir William Coxen, who had been interested in orthopaedic treatment for young people. Peter has supported the Shropshire and Mid-Wales Hospice by serving as vice-president from 1989–98 and he continues to be a patron. He is also a patron of the Development Trust at Harper Adams University College.

The Telford and Wrekin Community Trust was formed in 1992 and not long after approached Peter to assist them with the launch of their Community Chest 2000 Appeal which set out to raise money to support local voluntary organisations. Pam Bradburn has fond memories of Peter's reply when she asked him if he would consider being chairman of that appeal. 'He said, "I'd be delighted and honoured, my dear." He was so supportive and understanding. And he always does what he says he'll do and his attention to detail was paramount. He was also generous with his goodwill and encouragement. We were very proud and honoured to have someone of his calibre to be our guiding light.'

In 1990 Peter was Master of the Worshipful Company of Clothworkers and Alan Henn, his silversmith friend from Much Wenlock, was Master of the Worshipful Company of Clockmakers. The two men thought this was an ideal opportunity to arrange 'A Shropshire Dinner in London' for their many Shropshire friends who had never had the chance to go to a London livery dinner. So in July 120 of their guests dined in Salters' Hall.

For the occasion Alan composed an amusing ditty called 'Henn and Gad, the Masterful Duo' which they could perform. Peter, with his schoolboy aptitude for amateur dramatics, is always willing to indulge in a piece of fun. However, their many commitments meant they never had time for a proper rehearsal so they had to rely on meeting in the cloakroom beforehand to run through their performance!

Fortunately a copy of the *magnum opus* survives to give a flavour of that enjoyable evening.

> **Alan:** *Master Clothworker, you're gregarious, hale and hearty,*
> *Pray welcome these good people to our party.*
> **Peter:** *Master Clockmaker, I accede to your suggestion,*
> *First a sip of wine to aid digestion.*
> **Alan:** *Prithee sir, advance the task in hand*
> *Lest I begin the ceremony and be damned.*

Peter: *Calm yourself Clockmaker, we have ample time to spare,*
I will perform your wish with much delicacy and care.
Noble Lords and gracious Ladies all
I welcome you to London and this Hall.
Enjoy our hospitality and good cheer and
And the warmth of our affection…

Alan: *Hear, hear!*
Gadzoks, methinks I have interrupted you
And now I am standing wondering what to do.
I know I will tell them of your Company's birthdate
For you were chartered in 1528.
Your history started somewhat earlier though
As the learned ones amongst you surely know.
Your hall which was destroyed in '41

91.   Peter at the Shropshire Dinner with his former Wrekin College housemaster, Major Thornburn and Mrs Thornburn. At Wrekin (see page 37) Major Thornburn was known as 'Thrush' on account of his singing and in the KSLI, where he was OC D Coy 4/KSLI, as 'Ned'.

92. The Henn and Gad ditty being performed at the Shropshire Dinner at the Salters' Hall. Lady Boyne sits on Peter's right, with Lady Forester sitting on Alan Henn's left.

> Is now rebuilt and fair to look upon.
> You are forsooth much more grand than I.
> **Peter:** Come now good Clockmaker do not cry,
> You have an illustrious past like mine,
> You are Master Clockmaker number 359.
> Your collection is the envy of us all
> And can be seen in the Clock Room in Guildhall.
> And though in line I am ahead of ye,
> Alphabetically speaking, ye are ahead of me.
> **Together:** We are not poets as you can tell,
> But now together we bid you well.
> We are most grateful for your presence
> Indeed we think it is the essence
> Of good fellowship, it stand the test,
> We raise our glasses to you our guests.

Two other Shropshire charities Peter has been pleased to support include the Ludlow Museum Development Trust, which came to fruition in 2003 when The Queen opened a wonderful new library, museum and archive centre in the town, and the Shrewsbury Abbey Heritage Project.

Chapter 19

Retirement?

Shadow and Sun
So too our lives are made:
Yet think how great the Sun
How small the Shade.

(Verse from a sundial at Dudmaston, Shropshire)

Retirement and Sir Peter Gadsden just don't go together. Anyone glancing at his diary can see that. And it is not just the current year's diary either, the following year already has a large number of appointments booked.

In 1999 Peter turned 70 and had served the Ward of Farringdon Without as an alderman for 30 years but was obliged to retire from his aldermanic duties by reason of age. The Court of Aldermen accepted the resignation of its senior member at their meeting in September. In their resolution the aldermen recorded that,

> Sir Peter has always taken a very keen interest in the work of this Court and, in 1996, became its senior member. His brethren have always appreciated his warm humour and they have been extremely grateful for his good advice and guidance which has contributed significantly towards the quality of their discussions. On taking their leave of Sir Peter, his brethren desire to assure him of their warm affection and high regard and unite in extending to him, and to Lady Gadsden their very best wishes for their future health and happiness.

The Committee of the Court of Clothworkers also came together to observe this and to register their pride in a most distinguished City career which spanned 30 years' service to the Corporation.

Peter continues to visit the City at least twice a month. As before his time is given to various activities, some business, some civic, some charitable and some social. One social event Peter derives great pleasure from is his

93.   Peter and Belinda with the Governor of Queensland, Major-General Peter Arnison and Mrs Arnison at the Mansion House in 2003.

membership of The City Pickwick Club. This august body was founded in 1909 and dines four times a year at the George and Vulture in George Yard in the City.

When Peter was first elected to membership in 1961 members were still attending in morning suits although that changed soon after. Like all members Peter was given a sobriquet from Dickens' *Pickwick Papers*. His was Brother Tadger, although no one is sure of the reason that name was given him. When Peter was elected president in 1999, in accordance with tradition he became Mr Samuel Pickwick and in the opinion of Cedric Charles Dickens, grandson of the novelist, 'Peter is a very perfect Samuel Pickwick'. The sobriquet Brother Tadger then passed to one of his sons-in-law, three of whom have City connections and are members of the Pickwick Club.

94. Peter (aka Mr Pickwick) along with Belinda attended a dinner at The City Pickwick Club and is seen here with the recorder of London, His Honour Judge Michael Hyam (aka Job Trotter) and Mrs Hyam.

As well as enjoying the conviviality, Peter, who was elected a member of The City Pickwick Club in 1961, has worked as president to take the club from strength to strength. At one time there was a real danger that the club was in decline but under Peter's leadership it has become one of the most successful private dining clubs in London and has a six-year waiting list. Whiffin, the Town Crier of Eatanswill, explains that now the membership is a

> Roll call of Lord Mayors both as Pickwick and members. Former Lord Mayor Sir Murray Fox stepped down as Mr Pickwick; former Lord Mayor Sir Peter Gadsden steps in... But 'umble persons also admitted: Sheriffs, Judges, Common Councilmen, odd sprinkling of City strays. Fine body of men, sir! All members take an appropriate name after Pickwickian characters. Membership initially limited to 30 but increased to 50 in 1911 and to 60 in 1913, now 83.

It is true today that the membership list of The City Pickwick Club reads like a page from *Who's Who* with 5 past Lord Mayors, 3 judges, 19 aldermen or members of Common Council. Membership is open to those with City connections or with an academic interest in Dickens.

Records of the early meetings of the club were never properly kept, but when Peter became Mr Pickwick, he put everything on a proper footing. Records are now made and kept in the Guildhall Library. Some of Peter's innovations include instituting a Ladies' Night, inviting the Lord Mayor to visit the Club (whether or not he is a member) and making a donation to the Lord Mayor's Charity. Augustus Snodgrass believes Peter's best ideas were the ones designed to make the club's evenings jollier. That not only meant changing the format, but opening the bar at six and leaving it open for the whole evening. Definitely a popular move!

95. 'Australia is in my blood,' Peter says. Not only has he travelled extensively on business there, he has also enjoyed many holidays there with Belinda.

It is amusing to note that many members of The City Pickwick Club are convinced that as Peter gets older, he looks more and more like the Mr Pickwick who appears on the President's badge: 'a splendid example of manhood, a real Christian gentleman', in the opinion of the secretary Augustus Snodgrass.

Although he officially retired in 1999, Peter has continued to assist many charities. He still continues as a non-executive director of William Jacks plc, a post he has held since 1984, and a director of PPP healthcare foundation and the Australian company, Albox. Despite Shropshire being his principal residence, Peter Gadsden remains a much respected, well-

96. Three eminent Old Wrekinians meet at a Guildhall dinner. From left to right: Field Marshall The Lord Inge, Alderman Sir Peter Gadsden and Sir Brian Shaw.

known face in Guildhall and around the City. He attends several dinners and luncheons there every month.

In June 2001 Peter arrived at Wrekin College as guest of honour to give a short speech and present the prizes. The event took an unfortunate turn when he had a heart attack during the ceremony and had to be rushed to the Princess Royal Hospital. He was immensely fortunate that amongst the parents were some with medical training who immediately came to his aid and resuscitated him. He was upset that he had not finished his speech. A couple of months later Peter successfully underwent a triple bypass operation in a London hospital.

The episode was not only a great shock to Peter, but to everyone else, because he is always so fit and well. The late Sir Peter Studd once commented: 'Peter Gadsden is never ill, never feels the cold, never gets sunburnt and used to walk six miles a day round the City.' John Brookes, a former business colleague also marvelled at Peter's resilience. 'I recall taking him on the barge to North Stradbroke Island [in Australia] to inspect the mineral sand mining operation there. It was winter and what made it stick in my mind is how the locals, including myself, were all rugged up against the cold while Peter was in short sleeves enjoying the sunshine!'

Peter made a full recovery from his heart surgery thanks to the surgeon, anaesthetist, cardiologist and Belinda's solicitous attention. A letter she wrote to a friend three months later gives an insight into her care: 'Peter has recovered well from his heart by-pass op and we are going for long walks almost every day which is doing us both a lot of good. We are also being careful with our diet and have both lost quite a lot of weight.' Three and a half weeks of late autumn sunshine at their apartment in Spain also aided Peter's convalescence.

This was the second trauma to hit the family because in the 1980s their younger daughter, Elizabeth, was struck down by viral encephalitis and spent several months in St Bartholomew's Hospital. Again thanks to first-class nursing and her mother and father's loving attention, she too made a full recovery. Celebrations for Elizabeth's 21st birthday had to be postponed on account of her illness, but a party was held at Selsdon Park Hotel to celebrate her 30th birthday. Peter was at Wrekin College with Basil Sanderson, the proprietor of the Selsdon Park Hotel, Sanderstead. Basil and his wife Shelagh have been close friends of Peter and Belinda and generously entertained them at their hotel on many occasions.

Now that he has 'nearly' retired, Peter says family life occupies much of his and Belinda's time and interest. They adore going to stay with their four daughters and watching their seventeen grandchildren, of whom they are immensely proud, grow up.

The final words about Sir Peter Gadsden come from someone who has known him well as a business colleague and friend. They not only give an interesting insight into the man but also sum up what so many people have felt and said. John Allen wrote, 'Peter has always shown an interest in my career and in me as a person and I feel that he has been my mentor throughout my life. I hold him in the highest regard and esteem. He has always had time for others and his family have always been most important to him. Although he rubbed shoulders with the highest in the land both nationally and internationally he always found time for me.' What greater compliment could anyone wish for?

When I was a babe and wept and slept,
Time crept:
When I was a boy and laughed and talked,
Time walked:
Then, when the years saw me a man,
Time ran:
But as I older grew,
Time flew:
Soon, as I journey on
I'll find time gone.

(The Reverend Pentreath's last sermon at Wrekin College quoted this verse from Chester Cathedral.)

Index

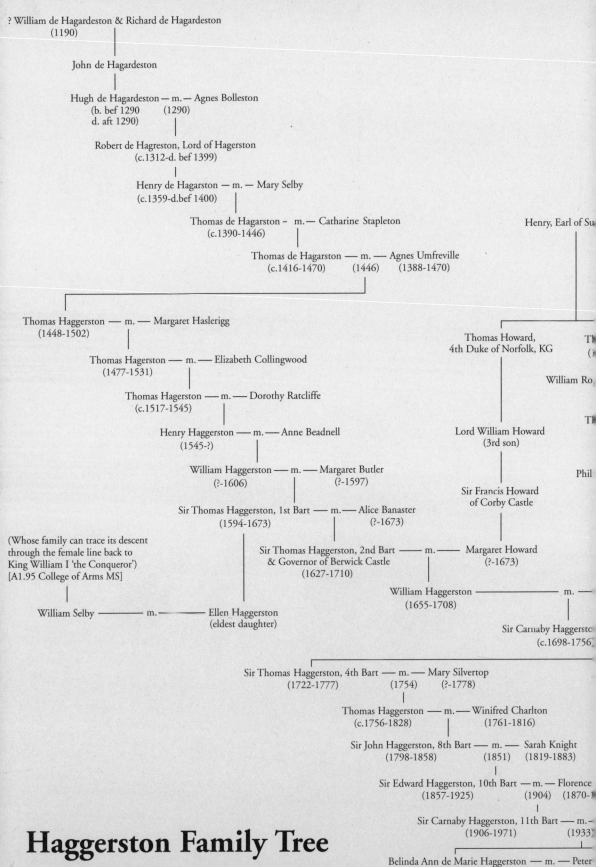

? William de Hagardeston & Richard de Hagardeston
(1190)

John de Hagardeston

Hugh de Hagardeston — m.— Agnes Bolleston
(b. bef 1290   (1290)
d. aft 1290)

Robert de Hagreston, Lord of Hagerston
(c.1312-d. bef 1399)

Henry de Hagarston — m. — Mary Selby
(c.1359-d.bef 1400)

Thomas de Hagarston - m.— Catharine Stapleton
(c.1390-1446)

Thomas de Hagarston — m. — Agnes Umfreville
(c.1416-1470)   (1446)   (1388-1470)

Henry, Earl of Su

Thomas Haggerston — m. — Margaret Haslerigg
(1448-1502)

Thomas Hagerston — m. — Elizabeth Collingwood
(1477-1531)

Thomas Hagerston — m. — Dorothy Ratcliffe
(c.1517-1545)

Henry Haggerston — m. — Anne Beadnell
(1545-?)

William Haggerston — m. — Margaret Butler
(?-1606)   (?-1597)

Sir Thomas Haggerston, 1st Bart — m.— Alice Banaster
(1594-1673)   (?-1673)

Sir Thomas Haggerston, 2nd Bart — m.— Margaret Howard
& Governor of Berwick Castle   (?-1673)
(1627-1710)

Thomas Howard,
4th Duke of Norfolk, KG

William Ro

Lord William Howard
(3rd son)

Phil

Sir Francis Howard
of Corby Castle

(Whose family can trace its descent
through the female line back to
King William I 'the Conqueror')
[A1.95 College of Arms MS]

William Selby ———— m.——— Ellen Haggerston
(eldest daughter)

William Haggerston ——————————— m. —
(1655-1708)

Sir Carnaby Haggerst
(c.1698-1756)

Sir Thomas Haggerston, 4th Bart — m. — Mary Silvertop
(1722-1777)   (1754)   (?-1778)

Thomas Haggerston — m.— Winifred Charlton
(c.1756-1828)   (1761-1816)

Sir John Haggerston, 8th Bart — m. — Sarah Knight
(1798-1858)   (1851)   (1819-1883)

Sir Edward Haggerston, 10th Bart —m.— Florence
(1857-1925)   (1904)   (1870-

Sir Carnaby Haggerston, 11th Bart — m.–
(1906-1971)   (1933)

Belinda Ann de Marie Haggerston — m. — Peter
(1933-)   (1955)

Haggerston Family Tree

Compiled with the help of the College of Arms and
The Lord Mowbray, Seagrave and Stourton